Yvy DeLuca

Tainted Beauty

The Memoir of an Authentic Creation

Limited Special Edition. No. 6 of 25 Paperbacks

Yvy DeLuca describes herself as a delicious Yvycake made up of an assortment of ingredients designed to stimulate the mind, as well as satisfy a hunger for self-expression. As a proud Indian transgender woman, Yvy uses written and video blogs to talk about trans issues by using #LetsTalkAboutTrans and uses her social media to spread awareness and support for the LGBTQ community. Yvy grew up in Blackburn and currently resides in Salford, Greater Manchester, with her husband and their two cats, Pirlo and Nyssa.

To my loving husband, Jack. It's disgusting how much I love you.

Yvy DeLuca

TAINTED BEAUTY

THE MEMOIR OF AN
AUTHENTIC CREATION

AUSTIN MACAULEY PUBLISHERS™

LONDON • CAMBRIDGE • NEW YORK • SHARJAH

A CIP catalogue record for this title is available from the British Library.

ISBN 9781528914819 (Paperback)
ISBN 9781528961011 (ePub e-book)

www.austinmacauley.com

First Published (2019)
Austin Macauley Publishers Ltd
25 Canada Square
Canary Wharf
London
E14 5LQ

Chapter One

London, 2008

I came out of the cubicle of the ladies' room and took one last look in the mirror before I went back into the restaurant. I'd never been to a restaurant at a Hilton hotel before, let alone the Kensington Hilton. Being a young girl from Blackburn, I don't see extravagance of this level at all. I mean, my version of extravagance is splashing out on a pair of heels from Faith for sixty quid, which I hardly get the chance to do since I'm always skint! Yet here I was, on a date with a man I had only met a few hours ago.

It was close to midnight and the date was pretty much done. I knew exactly where I wanted this night to go. I wanted to sleep with him so badly. Don't get me wrong, I'm not the type that goes around sleeping with random men I hardly know, even though there's nothing really wrong with doing that either. However, when an opportunity knocks, I can't help but open up…to new adventures.

I stood in front of the mirror, admiring the reflection before me. My caramel skin was shimmering under the soft light, my long black hair fell all the way down to my lower back and my white lace maxi dress left just enough to the imagination. I felt confident and beautiful the way every woman should feel. Nobody could tell me otherwise. I reapplied my lipstick and headed out to the restaurant.

As I made my way past the crowded bar, I saw my date already waiting for me by the lifts. His name was John. He looked so handsome standing there in his black Armani suit. I wasn't sure how old John was, but he must have been in his early forties. That didn't bother me though. If I was right about his age, he looked damn good for forty, and he clearly didn't care that I was only twenty-three. Besides, we were both consenting adults. That's all that matters.

John stood taller than me at just over six foot. He was broad with a physique that didn't require hours of gym time to look stocky. I could tell that he had a naturally big build which filled that suit he was wearing deliciously. He had short brown hair, Alaskan blue eyes and a soft tan that he recently acquired from his travels to the south of France. As soon as he saw me emerge from the crowd, his face lit up and he flashed me a gorgeous smile. He'd been such a gentleman throughout the evening, treating me like a real lady. I was his treat for the evening, and he was mine.

I stood in front of him, gazing at his face, taking in those slow seconds that only seem to occur when one becomes infatuated with another. John's eyes were warm and inviting as he tilted his head gently to the left. He leaned in, landing a tender kiss on my cheek.

'I can't resist that adorable dimple, Yvy,' he said with a grin.

My smile grew from shyness, making the dimple on my left cheek even more prominent. I let out a soft laugh and gave him a kiss on his cheek.

'I hate that you can make me feel shy,' I said jokingly.

'Funny, I quite enjoy it!'

'I would never have guessed!'

'You ready to get out of here?' John asked.

'Yeah, sure. You going to tell me how much that meal cost you then?'

'Nope!'

He held my hand and led me to the lift. I had no idea what floor we were on in the hotel, but from the magnificent view from the windows of the restaurant, we were definitely high up. The lift doors opened and we soon found ourselves making our way down to the hotel lobby. At first, there were a few people in the lift with us, but that didn't last long and John and I were soon alone. As the other people in the lift left and the doors sealed shut, my heart began to beat faster. I felt my skin tingle with anticipation, that uncontrollable feeling of excitement when delving into the unknown. All I wanted in that moment was to be ravished by this decadently irresistible man.

We stood side by side; close enough to touch but keeping our hands to ourselves. I could see from the blurred reflection of the lift door that John was smiling.

'So, still feeling shy?'

I knew he was trying to push my buttons. I knew he was fanning the flames. I loved every second. I fought the urge to look at him and kept looking at his blurred reflection.

'No,' I said. 'I'm feeling very…'

He turned to face me, intrigued. I kept facing forward, watching his image moving in the lift door. I could feel his eyes on me, making my skin melt. He ran his hand down my shoulder, his fingers slowly making their way down my arm and into my hand. I turned to John, his hands coming up to my chin and slowly tilting my head up. My eyes locked on to his, my heart began to pound in my chest. He pulled me close to him. His cologne filled my head with the sweet scent of masculinity. His warm lips pressed against mine and I couldn't hold in my uncontrollable urges anymore. I wanted John so badly. I wanted to feel him inside me.

When he released his lips from mine, I stared into his eyes, his beautiful blue eyes, and instantly I knew that I was ready. Without thinking, I threw myself forward towards him and kissed him ferociously, the way I'd wanted to this whole evening but kept myself from doing so. He was completely caught off guard by my advance but soon took full advantage and grabbed my hips and pulled me close enough to feel his body against mine. I could barely catch my breath as his kisses ripped through me.

We were pressed into the corner of the lift, our hands all over each other. I released my lips from his and took in a gulp of air as he ravaged my neck with his firm embrace. His kisses made me feel so good. I could barely speak. I tried so hard to control myself but I couldn't help but give in to passion. My heart was pounding against my chest and trying to breathe normally seemed impossible, but I didn't care. The lift continued down to the lobby. The thought of it stopping on one of the floors and those gold doors opening made it so dangerous, so sexy. I looked up at what floor we were passing, 10, 9, 8, 7 and knew that we had to stop.

I pulled away from John's hold, gently caressed his face and neatened his ruffled hair. John trailed the straps on my white cotton maxi dress back on my shoulders. He straightened his tie with a subtle smile on his face and before we knew it, DING! The lift doors parted and we were in the lobby of the ground floor. It was almost midnight, so the lobby wasn't too busy. I glanced around and could see the staff busying themselves with work. The front desk staff were staring at computer screens and sorting check-in for the small group of visitors. Cleaners were hovering around the reception and rearranging flowers. Neatly dressed porters were wheeling Louis Vuitton bags on shiny gold trolleys. Still, I felt like all eyes were on me. They must know what we were up to just moments ago.

What if they had cameras in that lift? Shit!

I can just imagine a sweaty security guy watching us going at it whilst taking care of his tumescent member.

Ahh fuck it, who cares!

We reached the front doors and the cool breeze blew my hair off my shoulders, exposing my smooth skin. The air felt so crisp as

I took it in with a slow inhale. I could tell John liked seeing my long, dark hair flowing behind me in a frantic dance, as he instantly put his arm around my waist to pull me closer. He attempted to mask his gesture as a way of shielding me from the cold, but to be honest, I warmed up plenty during our time in the lift. I didn't even notice that I wasn't wearing my jacket in the cold outdoors. A line of black cabs were parked up outside the hotel and we jumped into the one parked in front. The cab pulled away from the hotel and off Holland Park Avenue, and we soon found ourselves on the busy London streets. I had no idea where we were going, but he said his place was close by. I felt an element of fear inside me, which I liked. I liked feeling a sense of danger that anything could happen tonight and putting my faith in a man I barely knew to treat me right. He'd been so respectful throughout the evening, and he only advanced on me when I allowed him to which tells me this guy was on the level. Still, you just never know when a person can turn on you.

Stop! Stop thinking like this! Just go with it. You'll be fine.

As I watched the London lights float past, my mind became pleasantly hazy. I was unsure if that was due to John or the vodkas I had earlier; nonetheless, I felt elated. I looked over at John, the street lamps blazing through the cab window and racing across his face. I smiled and shuffled over to him, resting my head on his shoulder. His kiss on my forehead made my nerves prickle.

Before I knew it, we were at John's flat. It was huge. The flat, that is. It was so spacious and decorated with an elegantly classic yet masculine taste. It almost seemed a bit forced. From the black, crocodile-skin tub chair in the corner, to the gold-plated candelabras sitting on the large white marble fireplace, it was as if he was trying to exude a rich, bachelor lifestyle. I wasn't really impressed by his wealth, but the lifestyle of the rich definitely intrigued me.

Looking around the immaculate flat, I wondered if this was how John really lived. My heels clicked along the wood flooring as I made my way toward the bay window, taking in my surroundings. The floors were a dark, rustic wood. The kind that would suit a quaint cottage in the country instead of the cosmopolitan style that John was aiming for. The colour scheme was mostly beige, with gold finishes on most of the lamps and ornaments. The fireplace was grand and impressive. The white marble was so polished I could almost see my reflection clearly. The candelabras were magnificent, so detailed with Parisian elegance that they could easily be sitting on a dining table in the Palace of Versailles. Another thing that didn't quite fit in with his contemporary decor. Standing by the bay window, the night view of London was beautiful. A blanket of black, illuminated by points of light. The moon reflected on the delicate ripples of the Thames.

'Wow,' I said. 'This place is beautiful'

John popped open a bottle of champagne. I turned to see him in his open-plan kitchen that was off the living room. Fitted with white cabinets and appliances, my first thought was *that must be a bitch to keep clean!*

'How long have you lived here, John?'

'I've been here about a year now,' he poured the champagne into two flutes and handed me one. 'But I don't see much of it.'

'Why is that?'

'My work takes me all over, so it's not often I get to stay long.'

'Ahh, the hard life of Public Relations; must be a killer travelling the world!'

The smile on John's face let me know he understood my sarcasm.

'Well, it has its perks, but sometimes I find what I'm looking for at home.'

I felt his eyes burning into me as he took a sip from his champagne flute. I sipped my drink and walked back towards the bay window, confidently.

'So where are you off to next?' a sincere question, but I could tell that he knew I didn't really care, and it was just small talk.

John placed his glass gently on his granite worktop and leaned against the side. His eyes were piercing, looking straight into mine. I felt calm and confident. John watched my body move in my flowing white dress, admiring every curve. The dress hugged my waist and sat on my hips, driving him crazy. He walked up behind me and pulled my hair off my neck, running his fingers gently down my shoulders. I wanted him to feel my breasts but instead he moved his hands down my arms and buried his lips softly into my neck. I took a deep breath in and felt my skin tingle from his touch; his cologne filling my head again with that sweet scent. I was in a position to be much more forward than I was in the lift. I didn't have to worry about the doors suddenly opening and being greeted by a crowd of wide-eyed hotel guests. We were completely alone. I turned to him, locked his gaze and began to remove his suit jacket. His smile said it all. He knew I was ready for him, and judging from how he was growing, he was ready for me.

He lifted me up and carried me to the bedroom. As he put me down on his bed, his crisp white sheets feeling cool against my skin,

John began loosening his tie. The key to seduction is to tease, and John knew he was teasing me. Watching his fingers work through the silk knot made me want to rip the shirt buttons right off. John's eyes travelled down my body. I knew my breasts were pushed up a little as I held my body up by my elbows. Seeing me laying there in my white dress was driving him crazy. Like a boy on his birthday who couldn't wait to unwrap his present.

I unzipped the side of my dress, letting the straps fall off my shoulders. I stood up and let the dress slide off my body, unveiling my lavender lace lingerie. His eyes examined the contours of my body with excitement. He embraced me hungrily and we both fell onto the soft king size mattress. I couldn't help but laugh at his uncoordinated actions as we collapsed on the bed. Thankfully, he laughed too and tried to regain his composure after nearly falling off the side in the attempt to not crush me on impact. He regained his focus, kissing my breasts and working his way to my stomach. He began to pull at my panties and I felt the lace moving down my thighs, gently crossing over my knees.

His hands sunk into the covers as he made his way up my warm body. He stared into my eyes, giving me the sweetest smile. I sensed his sincerity from the way he handled me so gently. He kissed me softly and pressed his body on mine, moving me into position. I craved him so much, I couldn't wait any longer. He kissed me again, holding me firmly by the wrists.

This is it.

My breath was shallow as he moved in and entered me. A rush of adrenaline flowed inside me as I wrapped my body tightly around him. I wrapped my arms around his broad back, pulling him in deeper. His motion became harder and the bed began to shake with every thrust. I was so close, I wanted to last longer but his body felt so good. I bit into his shoulder, held on even tighter and—

I opened my eyes and felt the sharp sting of the fluorescent lights above as they strained to focus. My eyelids were heavy and struggled to stay open. As my vision regained some focus, I saw that I was in a hospital ward. To my right was an empty, neatly made bed and across from me were two more. The sunlight poured into the room, and on my left was an open door that led to the hospital corridor. As the haze cleared and my eyes adjusted to the bright afternoon light, the reality dawned on me.

I was dreaming. It was just a dream. DAMNIT!

I felt an uncomfortable tightness around my waist, so tight it was as though whatever was wrapped around me had broken the skin.

I lifted up the hospital sheet and found layers of hospital gauze secured tightly to my pelvis. I leaned back from exhaustion and stared at the ceiling. The sting of the lights returned, but I no longer cared. My mind became clear and the reality of what I had just gone through hit me like a ton of bricks.

I did it! I can finally be me.

It's funny, when I think about dreams and reality, it can be easy to mix the two and get lost in what you believe to be true and what isn't. Being the woman that I am, I learned a long time ago how to live in dreams and yet be completely aware of reality. You're probably wondering what I'm jabbering on about, but stay with me because I'm about to explain it to you.

My head jolted forward at the sound of the rattling vibration of my phone. I looked over to find it sitting on the side table at the end of my bed. I could barely move due to all the bandages, so I buzzed for a nurse. It didn't take long before she came in the ward with a smile on her face. She was more than willing to bring me my phone and a much needed glass of water to sooth the sore throat I suddenly realised I had after trying to speak to her.

I flipped open my Motorola Pebl and the screen lit up with a new incoming message. It was from John. A smile grew on my face as I read his message, telling me that he had a wonderful time with me the other night. I was so giddy, like a high school girl, and wanted to respond to his message straight away. My thumb went to push "reply" when I stopped myself. I paused for a moment, thinking about John. About meeting him for the first time, a chance encounter I wasn't anticipating. Then I thought about my situation now, having just woken up from having gender reassignment surgery.

I began to realise that for a brief moment, I lived in a dream wrapped in reality. Only 48 hours ago, I was on my way to Charing Cross hospital to complete the last step of my transition. To complete something that I had waited twenty-four years to achieve. For over two decades, I lived in a reality that wasn't mine, and I was finally going to be able to live in the world, authentically, as myself. John was an unexpected encounter, and if I had my way, it would have ended up the way it did in my dream. However, the reality was very different. Meeting John, I knew that we could never end the evening the way I would have liked but that didn't mean I couldn't

13

enjoy an evening with him. It didn't mean I couldn't live the dream of a perfect date and bring it to an end before reality came in. He didn't know why I was in London, nor did he need to. He was simply a kind man, who crossed paths with yours truly. We've all had those moments in life when you live a dream for a brief moment before returning to reality.

Lying in a hospital bed at Charing Cross, I felt so many emotions. It's hard to put into words what I was feeling, but if I had to, I would have to say I was feeling an overwhelming sensation of pleasure, an orgasm of happiness. John may have been a dream encounter, but it didn't compare to the dream I had waited my whole life to come true. I am a woman, I always have been. It was a long road getting there, but on September 16 2008, I made my dream come true.

Let's Talk About Trans...

Before we continue with what you'll soon come to see as one of the greatest real-life stories you've read in a good long while, I'd like to clear a few things up first.

This is not going to be a how-to guide on being transgender. In fact, I'd want this to be as far from that as possible. If you want to learn about what transgender means in all its clinical terms, there are plenty of texts on the subject. Opening up your life to somebody is never an easy thing to do, and the transgender community treat their lives as sacred. To understand what being transgender really means, you need to look past the clinical aspects. You need to stop thinking it's only about what we have between our legs and understand that it runs deeper than that.

Transgender awareness is so important, and with awareness comes visibility. Many trans people are happy to open up their lives to others but some prefer not to. It has nothing to do with being ashamed but the need to live a life without fear of discrimination. I understand that need completely, but in order to move forward to eradicate discrimination, we need to show society that we aren't afraid to be seen. I'm not afraid. Want to know more? Read on...

Chapter Two

When you go through life, the road to self-discovery can be both scary and thrilling at the same time. The thrill of new experiences, of making choices that take you down roads you never thought you would go down, eventually leading to that final destination and to the person you want to be. It's an interesting journey…or so I've heard. I never made such a journey, because I'm one of many, many people in the world who knew exactly who she was before the world could catch up. My identity was as clear as glass and I didn't need to go on a journey of self-discovery. Instead, my journey was about understanding what my true identity meant to me. It's a crazy feeling being able to see yourself so clearly but not have that image reflected back at you every time you walk past a mirror. Taking that second glimpse at yourself, knowing that something just isn't right. As the days, weeks and years roll by, that reflection becomes a ghost that you just want to leave behind so you can flourish and be the person you really are.

As I sat alone in my living room, staring down at old photos spread across my solid wood coffee table, I tried to recall my earliest memories of childhood. Recalling the earliest defining moment that set me on the journey that I subsequently embarked upon. The journey of transition. Looking down at the glossy photos, I barely remembered them being taken, mostly because I was either too young or they were taken before 84 when I wasn't even born yet. My eyes travelled from photo to photo, examining every detail. Photos of my older brother, Fareed, dressed in his balaclava and dirty, white trainers when he was just a boy. A photo of me and my big sister, Feroza. I was about three or four, which would have made Feroza around nine, as she's five years older than I am and the eldest of the three of us. The photo was of us standing in the living room at the old house where we grew up in Blackburn. Feroza was wearing a white dress with blue polka dots. The dress stopped just above her ashy knees. I was right by her side, her arms wrapped around me. I wore a white singlet with royal blue shorts. The blue woollen jumper that went over the singlet was stylishly set on my head, with the sleeves falling down each side of my happy face. The perfect wig for a fabulous child like me. I picked the photo up and smiled.

I was born a female, trapped in the body that presented as male. I was born transgender. This wasn't a choice I made, or something I had any control or say over, this was simply how I was brought into the world. It's a basic privilege for a vast majority of people to be born into the body they were meant to be born into. For transgender individuals like myself, we must endure a process to reach that point in our lives where we can also receive that very privilege most people take for granted.

Looking through all the pictures, I found it hard to believe that it was me as I sifted through childhood memories. I could barely remember living those moments, but I remembered how I felt at that age. It's awful to be a part of this world, and yet be so disconnected from it. To watch your friends and family experience the joys and heartbreaks that life throws, and not be a part of it because you feel as though the world isn't ready to accept you. It's difficult to be yourself when you're expected to act and sound a certain way. You can't be who you truly are under someone else's rules, regardless of who is dictating these rules. Being a part of this world means existing as your truest self. Self-discovery is a wonderful journey to embark upon, but self-acceptance is the bravest thing a person could ever do. Learning to accept who you are and building your true self is one of the scariest but most rewarding experiences one could ever go through.

It's very easy to label a person into a particular category, especially when you don't understand who they are or why they chose to live the life they live.

It's been ten years since I completed my journey of transition, which is a long time, but when I think about it, my life didn't start a decade ago. I've been here for thirty-four years, and the first two decades of my life needed to happen so that I could become the person I am today. For years, I denied anything about my life before my transition. I couldn't bear the thought of existing before that time, let alone looking at old photos, because I felt like it was a completely different person living that part of my life. It took years to realise that I shouldn't try to erase those memories because it was those defining moments that built me up.

I spread the pile of photos further and came across one that was in a small, grey cardboard frame. It was a photo of me and Feroza from when we were at Griffin Park Primary School. We're going back so many years that it's hard to believe that the person in the photo was really me. In some ways, it wasn't me. I looked at the child in the shoddy grey photo frame, the adorable young kid sitting in front of their sister and smiling. The dimpled cheek, the short black hair and the drab grey V-neck school sweater. Perfectly content. I had no idea what laid before me, but then again who does? When you're so young, you don't think about what the world can throw at you until you come face to face with reality and stop living in a dream.

When I was a child, I always knew my true identity, even when I didn't know how to articulate what my identity was. In my mind, I was me. Nothing else mattered. I never thought of myself as male or female. Gender was never an issue for me when I was a child because it was an aspect of myself that I never needed to address. I was just being me. When you're so young, being true to who you are is such an easy thing to do, because you don't know any better. Nobody remembers every detail of what they got up to as a child, but you always remember that sense of freedom. It's the purest form of self that is completely undiluted. I can remember that feeling as if it were yesterday. I was free of inhibitions and never felt restrained from expressing myself any way I wanted to.

I picked up a photo of me and my beautiful mum, Zohra. I had the biggest smile on my face with my jumper wig secured perfectly on my head. Mum looked so happy to see me enjoying myself. I was holding a colourful plush elephant and posing for the camera. I remembered how much I loved that stupid elephant because it changed colours when it got wet. Every time I took a bath, that elephant was always there. Whenever Mum dressed me in a pair of pants and a jumper or a t-shirt, I was compelled to take off the pants and put the jumper on my head. I preferred to wear her long nightgowns and was most comfortable dressing that way. I never felt as though I was in the wrong body or that something was wrong with me, because at that age the world had not reached me yet. I wasn't aware of the rules of society because I was too busy having fun in my own little world. Living on Hancock Street, I was embraced by my siblings and never felt like an outcast. Fareed and Feroza always made time to play games with me, and Mum never tried to stop me from expressing myself and let me flourish as a child.

We weren't a well-off family, but our house was a home. Our terraced house on Hancock Street wasn't anything to look at, but it

18

was our home so I never noticed. We were just another working-class Indian family in the '80s, living the best way we could. My family consisted of me, Fareed and Feroza. Being the youngest, I spent the least amount of time at Hancock Street before we moved, but the memories I have of living there with Mum and Dad were happy ones.

It didn't take fancy toys or pristine home decor to make our house a home. My family always made me feel as though I belonged there and that I was a part of something really special, the way only families can do. Feroza had the best toys that I wanted to play with. I was particularly fond of her Jem and the Holograms doll that I would love to play with when she wasn't. Every time my parents bought me a toy for boys, like a Thomas the Tank Engine or a remote control truck, Fareed was always taking them to play with. Fortunately, I had no interest in those things, when I had long jumper wigs and Mum's nightgowns to play with! I look back on those days as some of the happiest and truest days of my life. I never felt ashamed or unhappy being who I was and was blissfully unaware of anyone's opinions or judgements of me. For most children, that feeling of complete freedom is always taken for granted, as you're completely unaware that with every passing day, the world is creeping closer. That sense of freedom starts to shrink more and more as the clouds begin to roll in and you start to become more aware of the world you live in.

My earliest memory of becoming more aware of the world around me was on my fourth birthday. My parents had planned a big birthday party for me and invited all my closest family. Aunts, uncles and many cousins were going to show up to celebrate my big day. *Four years old!* Mum went all out to prepare for the party. Delicious homemade food, birthday banners and balloons and she even spelt my name with tinsel above the fireplace. I was so excited! Before the party, she dressed me in a pair of blue denim pants with an elasticised waist and a Fred Flintstone patch sewn on the pant leg, a white singlet and my favourite blue and white jumper. Soon after she dressed me, I took off the pants and turned the jumper inside out on my head. Just like I always did. I was perfectly content in my own little world, but as the guests began to arrive, Mum took me to one side and put my pants back on. After that, she took the jumper off my head and turned the garment the right way around. She placed my arms through the sleeves again and put the jumper back on me the way she originally did.

At that moment, I felt as though I had done something wrong. Although it didn't feel like Mum was punishing me or being cruel to me, I still didn't understand why I had to take the jumper off my head and wear it properly. She was in no way being malicious, as Mum always let me be me as a child, but I was still confused in that moment. I can't recall ever putting a jumper on my head in front of my family again. Something changed inside that made me more aware that my behaviour was questionable.

Throughout my childhood, I never grasped the concept of gender. I never defined myself by my physical self so it never mattered to me if I liked playing with "My Little Pony" dolls or my sister's toys. When I first started at Griffin Park, I made friends with a girl called Amanda. I was never interested in having male friends and was always drawn to hanging out with the girls. Amanda soon became my best friend and we were inseparable in school. Mum told me that we would always play in the playground together and be silly in class, causing mischief. Even if the teachers tried to sit us apart in an attempt to stop us from disrupting the class, it would only make us laugh louder. Amanda was the first friend I had and she never treated me like I was different. Being so young, we both gravitated towards each other's personality and spirit. That's the beauty of being a child, you really don't give a fuck about anything else but being happy. I never realised it at the time, but the reason I loved being around Amanda was because I was able to invite her into my little bubble without having to burst it and let reality change things.

When my family moved from Hancock Street, I left Griffin Park and had to change schools. I never saw Amanda again after we moved, which devastated me. I remember being so upset but not really expressing it to anyone. We moved from the terraced house on Hancock Street and across town to a semi-detached house near Corporation Park. It didn't take long before I made new friends in the neighbourhood, and having Fareed and Feroza made it less isolating as I always had someone to hang out with. I met a girl who lived down the street. Her name was Kirsty. She had beautiful red hair and freckles on her cheeks. Her Mother, Dotty, was an absolute diamond. She was very eccentric, especially with her fashion. You couldn't miss Dotty walking down the street. She wore bright colours that always clashed and pale pink lipstick that really washed her pale complexion out against her short, mousy brown hair. With that said, the moment Dotty opened her mouth, the most charming personality sprung forth and you couldn't help but love her.

Kirsty's dad didn't come out of the house much, except to do the odd spot of shopping. It was a while before I understood that his arthritis hindered him from going out as frequently as he'd probably would have liked. Kirsty was a year older than I was, but we became fast friends the moment our family moved into the neighbourhood.

At first, we would meet outside my house, riding bikes or going to the park with our mum's watching closely. But it didn't take long before I was going round to her house and hanging out in her back garden. Kirsty's back garden was much bigger and nicer than ours. Ours was a concrete square, filled with Mum's plant pots and garden tools. It was just about big enough to fit a car inside, but there wasn't room for much else. Kirsty's backyard was a lot more spacious, and had a grassy area that we would lay a blanket on and eat cut-up apples and pears that Dotty prepared for us. Toward the back of the garden, stood a tall stone building belonging to her neighbour next door. The wall that was facing Kirsty's backyard was covered in climbing plants that sprouted leaves and flowers all year round. At the top of the wall was a large, round glass window. I wondered what was in that building, as it was so tall that it looked more like a barn than a house.

Kirsty and I loved playing "mums and dads" at her house. We didn't have any other people participating in the game, so we had to make up imaginary children. Kirsty played the mum, which secretly made me feel sad. I always wanted to play the mum, but I wasn't sure why I didn't like being the dad. I soon changed it and said that I could be one of the children instead, which made me more comfortable.

As more children moved into the neighbourhood, I began to build a small group of girlfriends that I liked to hang out with. Back in those days, we would play in each other's backyards and always make sure we were home before the amber street lamps came on at dusk. It was a simple way of living because I had no reason to question my gender in any way when I was with my friends. I was free to be completely uninhibited and not worry about my actions.

Starting at St James's Primary School was so exciting. I remember the huge black chalkboards, the carpet area in the corner of the room where we all sat, legs folded, as the teacher read a story and passed out small, white cartons of milk. The black tar playground that had markings for hopscotch and snakes and ladders on the floor. It was a brand new experience for me and I was so keen to see what it would be like.

On my first day, Mum took me to St James' and dropped me off in the playground with all the other children. I was not at all nervous about meeting new people. I saw a flurry of children running about, screaming, laughing, playing. Then, a teacher blew her whistle and everyone stood still. I watched as they began to form a line, ready to lead the way back into the classrooms. I decided to follow suit and get in line with everybody else.

As I lined up, I stood behind a boy whose name has since escaped me. He was beautiful. His smile was so wide it went from ear to ear. His skin had a Mediterranean tan and he had brown eyes that swirled in speckles of green. The cells in my body began to tingle whenever I was around him; my fingertips were electric. I could feel myself being drawn to his presence and I couldn't take my eyes off him for a second.

I didn't know it at the time, but he was my very first crush. Being so young and clueless, I had no idea what those feelings meant, so acting on them never entered my mind. I just knew that I liked him. He always made me smile, even though I never spoke to him. We weren't in the same class together, so I only saw him during playtime. I watched as he played about with a football or on the slide and swings with the rest of the boys. I was busy playing in the gardens and looking up every now and then to get a glance of him and smiling. As I had no real concept of male and female, I never thought that how I felt towards the boy in the playground would be considered wrong by some. I never defined myself with what was between my legs. To me, it was no different to another part of my body, it was just a part of me. I never thought at that age that it would be the very thing society would use to define me as a person on a basic level.

I always loved making art in school. I enjoyed all the subjects I did, but art was my favourite. I loved being able to take a blank sheet of paper and transform it into anything I wanted. I would lose myself and let my hands take over, freeing my mind to make something truly wonderful with paints and brushes. When the bell rang for playtime, I was eager to run out into the playground and have some fun, but if I was making art, I was never in rush to leave what I was doing. My favourite thing to draw were pictures of myself in strange and exciting places. I could escape to a different place simply by putting pencil to paper and drawing castles, islands and underwater caves. I drew myself the way I saw myself in my head. I wouldn't need to draw a jumper on my head as I was free to let the pencil glide across the page and create long locks of hair. Through my drawings, I was free to be me to the fullest. I never felt the need to hold back and I could express myself, it was an escapism of self-expression that required no words when I didn't know any other way to do so.

There was a moment in my childhood when reality rushed in and broke that escapism, leaving me feeling vulnerable and confused. In Year 1, I was in class one day during Art period. Everyone was asked to make a picture using dried pasta, glitter and that dreaded PVA glue all of you born in the '80s know all too well! I was always happy making pictures so Art class was my favourite time of the school week. We had a teacher's helper who assisted and took care of us. She was an elderly Asian woman whom everyone in class liked, including myself.

During the lesson, the bell rang for afternoon break and all of my classmates raced to the door to go and play outside. I was too engrossed in my art and didn't go out to play. The teacher of the class left the room for some reason, leaving me and a couple of other kids in the class alone with the teacher's helper. She came over and tussled my hair as she looked at my picture and asked me what I was making. I remember telling her that it was a picture of myself. She turned to me with a confused look and picked my picture up from the desk, letting bits of glitter and pasta fall off. She said to me, 'This isn't a picture of you, this looks like a little girl!'

I could feel my cheeks flush a little as I told her that it *was* a picture of me. The other children in the room came over and had a look at my creation and said they liked it, but the helper continued to question what I had made. She pulled the chair out from under me and made me stand side by side with my art piece. My cheeks began to flush again as she asked the other children if the picture looked like me.

What happened next would be something that to this day I will never forget. The children began to laugh amongst themselves and didn't really take any further interest in what the helper was saying, so she turned to me and kneeled down, her eyes level with mine. For some reason, I felt like she was about to give me a telling off for something I'd done wrong.

Instead, she told me, 'This is a little girl, you're not a little girl, are you?'

I stared at her, not knowing what to say. *What are you saying? I don't understand what you're asking.*

Then, she took her hand and gently patted me on my crotch and said, 'See? You're a little boy.'

23

I flinched uncontrollably and stood back for a second. Not fully realising what she did and filled with confusion, I ran out to the playground without looking back.

That was the moment. That was the first time my identity was judged by what was between my legs. It was one of the strangest moments of my life because that was the moment I began to feel confused about my identity. I was so confused because I didn't know why I was being judged by the body I was born in instead of who I was on the inside. Every day after that, the world I created began to get smaller and smaller, and the world around me became more real. I started to pay attention to the remarks and opinions of my classmates, and I didn't like what I heard. The truest moments of my life were the moments before that incident with the helper in school. Before that, I never related to my gender because it was never an issue to me. I just wanted to be me, whoever that may be. Gender was never a part of being me, it had nothing to do with being a boy or a girl.

Children at a very young age go through life with an open mind and an open sense of self, not caring what anyone else says or thinks. But we all have that moment when we wake up from what we think life is about and see the truth of the world. It's scary and confusing, but the world doesn't stop to let you process what's happening. Instead, the world continues to rush in like a thunderstorm and you have learn how to take cover. Sometimes, taking care of yourself means questioning yourself and your identity. That's what I did. I began to question my identity but didn't find any answers. I questioned the very foundation of my identity and what it meant to be me. I found myself stood out in the rain with nothing to shelter me.

Looking back at the photos of days gone by, they captured some really happy moments. But the memories that I remember clearly are the ones that weren't captured on a glossy piece of paper. Sifting my fingers through each photo, I felt a million miles away from the smiling child looking at the camera. When you're a child, it's easy to find yourself in a situation where you don't have any answers to questions you're afraid to ask and give up. The answers I was looking for didn't magically come to me overnight. For years I tried to understand what being me meant and how to exist in the world. It took a while, but I would eventually find the answers I was looking for. As children, being who you are comes easily. You know what makes you happy and the world is your playground. Nothing holds you back or makes you feel anything else other than yourself.

That sense of freedom begins to change as the years go by and you find yourself battling against the world.

When being exactly who you are is all you know, it's hard to understand why the people around you respond in ways that say what you're doing and how you're acting is not the way you should be. When that happens you reach a point where you begin to question who you are, and become confused about how to function in the world.

That happened to me the moment Mum put that jumper back on me at my fourth birthday party. I know now that she didn't take the jumper off my head because she was embarrassed or ashamed of me, as she always let me be myself as a child, but it still confused me. It was meant to be a day full of happiness and celebration, yet it felt like the birthday my family wanted to celebrate wasn't mine. It felt like nobody knew the real me and only knew the person they saw on the outside. They only saw the clothes I was dressed in that matched the body I was born into. They only saw the name my family gave me at birth. They only saw the boy they called Saleem.

By the time I was six years old, I found myself developing the real me inside and having to portray someone else on the outside. The real me only came to the surface when I was alone. I put long sleeve tops on my head and danced around my bedroom, flipping through my sister's magazines and daydreaming about the girl I wished to be when I grew up. As soon as I was with my friends and family, I concealed the real me and pretended to be the boy the world thought I was. It almost felt like a dual personality, yet I was fully aware of both people. It was never as though I became one person and the other disappeared, I always knew who I was but I became so confused about why people didn't understand me that I began to act like someone else. I thought it would be better that way. I thought that it would help me fit in.

As the years went on, I didn't just become aware of the world and how it was reacting to me, I began to understand what it was saying. I would hear people calling me "gay boy" in the playground by the time I was in Year 5, but I was protected. I kept myself hidden away from the world and Saleem was the one who faced it. I speak of him in third person because it feels as though he had his own life, his own struggles and was my best friend throughout those hard years. I remember being alone a lot in primary school. I made some friends and I had fun at times, but I knew I wasn't being myself. As a result, I always felt out of place. Saleem was gentle and kind; he always had a smile on his face, but it was difficult for him to fit in.

At that age, sexuality was not something I ever thought about because I didn't have any sexual attractions to anybody. So when the children in class called me "gay boy" I didn't quite understand what it meant. I just knew it must be something bad. Saleem was my protection from the pain; he was the one who faced the harsh words and the loneliness. But I experienced everything he did, because we were one and the same. Everything he felt, I felt. Everything he said, I heard. It's difficult to describe what I went through as a child, because it doesn't feel like I was the one who really went through it. I experienced it through someone else's eyes. Although I was becoming more knowledgeable of people's opinion of me, I was able to fool them all. They thought they knew me, but they had no idea. My classmates, my neighbours, even my family. None of them had a clue. Everyone thought I was just this feminine little boy who would probably grow up to be gay.

There was a moment during break time at school that I remember so clearly. I was about six years old, and I hung out with a couple of girls I'd made friends with and we'd pretend to be a certain kind of animal around the playground. I would always be a bird of some sort. I'd wear my dark blue coat and zip it up all the way to my neck. It had a huge collar that stood up so my face would sink in to my nose and my eyes peered over. I'd sit quietly for a moment amidst all the screaming children around me. Everything fell away and I wouldn't register the boys playing football. I wouldn't hear the girls chatting nonsense and laughing out loud. I could let the world fall away around me and stay perfectly still, listening to my own breathing inside my big collar. At first, I'd breathe heavily, like a flame struggling for air within an enclosed glass. But as the front of my collar warmed with every exhale, my breaths got more shallow, more controlled.

That's when Saleem, or Sal I was mostly referred to, would be the one who got the chance to hide inside, and I was able to rise to the surface. My arms came out of my sleeves and I opened my eyes. The light stung them a little, as I always forgot how long I'd kept them closed. I put my hands into my sleeves ever so slightly and began to flap them as hard as I could. My legs began to run and I'd feel as though I was soaring, flapping my feathered wings across the sky. Nothing could touch me; I was free.

Looking back, I bet I looked ridiculous running around the playground, wafting my coat sleeves up and down like a lunatic, but it gave me a shimmery purpose in a world I felt no connection to. I felt like I was flying high enough that nothing and no one could reach me. I could come to the surface of the body I was born into and look out at the world feeling hopeful. My legs got so tired and I'd head to the small patches of grass on the edges of the playground and fall to my knees, rolling uncontrollably as my hands remained tucked inside my coat. I'd laugh hysterically and my friends would catch up with me and join in the laughter. Such fun! They never realised it, but my friends were laughing with me, not Sal. It felt wonderful, but it was short-lived. The school bell would ring and it was time to go back inside and for Sal to resurface. I'd play in the playground with the girls and try to stick with the people I felt the most comfortable with, but inside I knew that I wasn't being myself.

As each day passed, I was becoming more and more petrified of what might happen to me if I tried to be who I really was. Having the knowledge that the people around you are judging you for being who you are is a heart-breaking feeling, especially when you haven't yet figured out what being you really means. It's confusing to be judged when you're still developing the very thing people are already judging. I couldn't get my head around it. I tried so many times to push it to the back of my mind, but there were moments in my childhood that forced me to experience these judgements without warning.

One morning, as I was playing in the playground, I put my arms into my blue coat and began wafting my sleeves frantically around the yard preparing to take flight. The school had two playgrounds, joined by a set of steep concrete steps that linked the main playground down to the gravel playground below. The gravel playground was usually reserved for the boys who played football, and it also had a ditch that they would play in. The top playground was where the majority of the children played as it was surrounded by green grass where I and the girls would practice our handstands and make daisy chains when the flowers were in bloom.

As I was using all my strength to build momentum and prepare to feel the weight lift from under my feet, I found myself stopping as I peered down the concrete steps that led to the gravel playground. My eyes focused as I saw a group of boys pointing at me and laughing. My cheeks flushed as I started to put my arms back into my sleeves. I managed to get one arm in when I felt a presence behind me. When I turned around, a group of boys forced their hands against my back, causing me to lose my balance. Standing at the top of the concrete steps, my legs gave in and I began to fall. One arm was still trapped in my coat as the other felt every crash of the concrete slabs it made contact with. I fell for what felt like a lifetime, until I finally reached the bottom of the steps and my head collided with the dirty grey gravel stones. My eyes faded to black.

I came to in the school hallway, lying on the ground with a teacher hovering just outside my focus. She told me not to move and that she'd called for a special doctor to come take a look at me. I felt a rush of adrenaline course through me that willed my body off the floor. I didn't feel any pain whatsoever. I ran to the toilet and stood by the sink, ready to vomit. Nothing came out, but I felt sick to my stomach. My head hung above the sink and I could feel my cheeks getting heavy. Then, a small crimson droplet appeared near the plughole. It slowly swirled into a long stem as it circled toward the drain. I looked up at the cracked mirror above the sink and gazed at Sal's reflection. As my eyes focused, I saw the blood that streamed down his face and set across his cheeks. His right eye was bloodshot and gravel stones were embedded in his forehead where fresh blood continued to leak down and drop off his chin, leaving stains all over his white school polo t-shirt. I began to cry uncontrollably and the teacher came rushing in after me, telling me that one of my relatives had come to take me to the hospital.

I always knew who I wanted to be, but I didn't understand how I could be that person without being laughed at and ridiculed, even punished. The one thing I learnt from those early years is what felt like a dual personality was actually my defence mechanism. I was unsure of how to exist as myself and thought that the person I was showing the world was a completely different person. But it wasn't. I was Sal, just as he was me. We existed as one, but we were able to be completely aware of each other. The primary school years went on and Sal spent most of his energy trying to blend in and not draw attention to himself. He began to shy away from letting people in, and I was hiding in plain sight. The days where I would fly across the sky at playtime and do handstands against the school walls became fewer and fewer, and Sal put on a brave face every time the children at school tried to hurt him.

The embarrassment of lining up every morning for school assembly was the worst by Year 6. We would line up, single file, with girls at the front of the line and boys at the back. Every day, without fail, the school kids lined up in the morning for school assembly after our teacher finished checking us off the register. The boys never wanted to stand next to the girls, and the girls always snubbed the boys' childish remarks and thought they were beneath them.

I went to line up for assembly one morning when I noticed that every boy who stood in front of me began going to the back of the line. As each boy did so, I found myself inching closer and closer to the girls until I was directly behind my friend, Farheen.

At first, I smiled, because I was standing with my friend, but that soon waned when I noticed the boys sniggering for some reason. I felt one of them plant their hands on my shoulders and say, 'You stay here, Saleem; you're half and half, aren't you?'

My heart sank. I could feel the blood rushing to my cheeks as I used every ounce of strength not to well up. A lump began to form in my throat. I felt the touch of Farheen's hand link into mine. That hand was my only comfort in that moment. She could see the pain in my eyes, just for a second, as both Sal and myself.

Now nearly thirty years later, it feels like Sal was a completely different life that I have no association with. A distant memory from a past life that I once lived. I kept that part of my life locked away and completely ignored any reference or idea of him. But when I think about it, Sal is now the one who is hidden away, and I am finally strong enough to protect and shield him from the pain and heartbreak of the world. Without him, I wouldn't be the strong woman I am today. He taught me so much and I was able to grow and evolve whilst he dealt with a world I was not ready to face. That's why when I look back at my childhood, I view it as a totally different person because it wasn't I who survived it. I merely viewed through the eyes of another who gave me the opportunity to grow until I was ready to take the wheel.

Chapter Three

Pleckgate High School, Blackburn, 1996

What did I learn from my high school days? That's a tough one! I guess for many of us high school is such a tough period in childhood that we sometimes feels like we won't make it through. Being that my primary school years were riddled with an unconscious insecurity that plagued my existence, I truly believed that high school would be different. It was unknown territory and I thought I would get the chance to start anew.

During the summer holidays after I had left primary school, I felt very grown up. I finished small school and I knew that the next step for me was grown-up school. It was a big deal! High school was when I began to pay attention to a little thing called sexuality, the way it worked, what it meant and what a bitch it could actually be to a youngster. Sexuality was never a topic I ever consciously addressed before high school, even when I was being judged by others for what they assumed was my sexuality. Instead, I was going through life completely oblivious of what the majority of the people around me were saying. All I knew was that they just didn't like me…for whatever reason that may be.

The summer of 95 came to an end, and it was time for me embark on a new journey. *High school.* I thought I was so prepared for high school. Turns out, not so much!

I walked into that school with my burgundy backpack, my navy blue school blazer and my signature '90s curtain hairstyle that I had to sleep on without moving so that it would stay straight. Pleckgate High was situated at the bottom of Pleckgate Road. It was a long, downward road that made your footsteps grow heavier as the pavement descended. The school itself was on a hill with wide concrete steps that climbed up to the entrance.

On my first day, I stood at the bottom of those steps, knowing that each one led to the unknown. I walked into the school assembly hall and saw rows and rows of grey plastic chairs and a stage at the far front. I felt so nervous, gazing across the sea of new faces and navy blue blazers with the school crest stitched on. As the new students began filling the seats, I quickly sat down towards the back and saw a few familiar faces from primary school and gave them a little wave. They called me over and I felt relieved to know somebody and not feel so naked, sitting in a room full of strangers by myself. During the summer after primary school, being at home and hanging out with Kirsty every other day for six weeks became my sanctuary. I was no longer fearful of being taunted or teased for reasons I didn't understand. Sharing a bedroom with my brother, I learned to hide the feminine side of myself as much as I could. I preferred it when nobody was paying attention to me. When no one pays attention, you become invisible. I liked feeling invisible. I liked being in my bedroom with one of my long sleeve tops on my head and wearing a dress from Mum's wardrobe. Sometimes, when I was alone in the house, I even dared to put on a pair of Mum's heels. I'd sneak into the living room and through to the kitchen. The kitchen floor was tiled and the moment I stepped on it, the heels began to click. My heart raced as I took those steps on the kitchen floor, listening to the beautiful echo of those heels. Being invisible gave me the strength to break out of the prison I was living in, albeit just for a moment.

I wasn't stupid though, I knew that my ability to feel invisible wouldn't work in high school. It was an exciting chapter to embark on, but I was petrified of anybody really noticing me. I was still locked away and having to present as Sal, but this time I couldn't be a child, I had to live in a teenage world. A teenage world that came with a whole new set of rules and a whole new set of dangers.

High school is such an important time for all of us because we're all going through that stage in life where we are developing into ourselves and learning more about *the birds and the bees.* I was no different except for one thing…I was developing a sexuality that made me feel like a gay boy and a straight girl simultaneously. On the inside, I was a blossoming girl who was gasping to experience the world and my sexuality, but on the outside, I presented as a sexually confused boy who didn't know how to act or who to talk to about how he was feeling. It was such a mind fuck. Trying to relate to anybody in school was no easy task, and it turned out that there was no place for a queer acting Indian lad who loved to hang out with girls rather than play football like I *should* be doing. I thought that the friends I had in primary school would be friends with me still, but that soon changed when they started their own little cliques that didn't include me.

31

My first year at Pleckgate, I started to become aware of the concept of sexuality from the childish banter between the boys and slowly came to realise that I had nothing in common with their beliefs. I had no intention of talking about "smashing a bird" or "giving her one" at all! I found myself nowhere near those conversations! I'd listen to the girls in school talk about boys, including my old friends from primary school and sit just within earshot of them and close my eyes.

I'd imagine chatting amongst them about a fit lad from year nine that I liked. He was tall and broad and had skin like cream. He had the cutest smile and his hair bunched up across his face every time he played football as the sweat saturated his forehead. I never knew what his name was but I always saw him at morning break at the year nine playground with his football buddies, kicking the ball around. But as soon as the school bell rang and my eyes opened, I found myself sitting in front of the art building, alone.

The constant taunts from school made me question my sexuality and learn what being attracted to boys meant. I always felt like one of the girls, but my physical form begged to differ. My sexuality was absolutely clear to me. I was attracted to boys. But what did that mean for Sal? As the taunts and name-calling became more and more frequent, I began to learn the meaning of the words. Being called "puff" and *khusra* on a daily basis started wearing me down.

On the inside I was attracted to boys, on the outside I was gay. That was my label. That was the box I was forced to live in by others. Inside, I never felt like a gay boy, because I wasn't. I was a girl, but I had no idea how I could be the girl I was when everyone else saw me as a boy. I was torn, feeling lost, and I had no one to talk to. I could never tell my family who I really was, I was too scared of how they might react.

What would they think? What would they say?

I was so petrified of what my family would say.

Would they disown me? Kick me out?

I had no idea what to do or where to turn. The fucked up thing about high school is that it has the cruel ability of forcing you to deal with other people's opinion of you in one of the harshest ways. It bursts any bubble you may have and invades you before you have the chance to protect yourself. Like a pack of lions, bullies search out the weak and attack until there's nothing left. Whether it be with words, violence or both, they attack hard. I learnt that the moment I stepped into high school and lived it until I left.

By the time I reached my second year, I knew the only choice for me was to wait until I was strong and confident enough to be the real me. At that age, I had no idea what transgender was or that it even existed. Blackburn in the late '90s was hardly a haven for the LGBTQ community and that's putting it nicely. As my sexuality began to develop, so did my understanding of the terms "gay" and "straight". Straight boys like girls, and straight girls like boys. Gay boys like boys and gay girls like girls. Imagine my confusion being a straight girl who likes boys, yet having to live life as a closeted gay boy and being tormented at school as a result of that persona. It was so difficult to come to terms with it all. But I had no choice but to put up with it and hope that things would get better and the path to my true self will get clearer in time.

When you're on a search for your own identity, it can be a rough journey. But when you already know who you really are and you're certain of your identity but you cannot express it, it feels even harder. That's precisely what I discovered when I was in a hostile environment where being yourself in any way came at a price, unless you fit in with everyone else.

I'm sure you're probably thinking, *Why not try and fit in, if it would have made life easier?*

Well, I did try. But it never worked, in fact, it made things even worse. I had absolutely no interest in being athletic or playing sports of any kind, so it was even worse being laughed at every time I was forced to join in the games in P.E. I hated pretending to have the faintest interest in football stickers like the rest of the boys. I hated trying to change my demeanour in front of people, only to look ridiculous and still have everyone laugh at me. I only did it because I wanted to blend in, to become invisible, but the more I tried to fit in, the more I stood out. The kids at school knew exactly what I was trying to do and used it to exploit me even more.

The day I finally gave up on trying to fit in was the day I was a victim of a hit and run. It was getting close to the end of my second year, and I was on my way to school, walking the 20 minutes it took to walk down the long sloping road. It was a two-way street so I paused before crossing over. I was wearing my blue bomber jacket and my burgundy backpack on both shoulders. As I crossed the road, a blue Nissan came out of nowhere. I was in the middle of the road and almost to the other side when the car sped towards me. The horn blasted and my bones jumped out of my skin as my head made a sharp turn to the left. I saw the car coming towards me but I was completely frozen on the spot. My reflexes failed me and the car screeched as it collided into me, sending my body flying across the hood and hurtling towards the pavement curb.

I don't know how long I was unconscious. When I came to, I saw footsteps going past me and over me. I heard the giggles of schoolchildren, probably people I knew. The haze began to dissipate and I attempted and pull myself off the ground. I looked up and saw a group of boys looking back at me and laughing. I couldn't quite make out who they were, but they apparently knew me and had a laugh at my expense. The car that hit me was long gone. My right arm was twisted in the strap of my backpack and I found it difficult to stand.

I looked up and saw a woman in a red car stopping traffic in front of me. She got out of the car and helped me up. She asked me if I was okay, to which I couldn't answer. I couldn't string a sentence together. I was trying so hard not to burst into tears.

Be strong, don't cry.

I told her I was fine and I made my way back home. I rushed through the front door and ran upstairs. Mum was already at work but I knew Feroza was home. I went into her bedroom and I burst into tears, hard tears. She told me to take off my ripped school pants and she saw that my left thigh was covered in blood. She took care of me and I stayed home from school for the rest of the week. I never found out who it was that hit me, but I'll never forget hearing the laughter of the people who left me on the ground instead of helping me.

From that point on, I never tried to fit in with the people at school. I knew that would cost me dearly, but a part of me didn't care. I learnt that people are always going to find something to hate on, regardless of how hard you try to fit in. High school gave me no insight into my own gender or sexuality, but more of the moronic and immature views of people who felt the need to belittle people like myself to mask the fact that they were completely clueless when it came to their own identity. As a result, high school taught me nothing.

During my high school lows, I found that my understanding of gender and sexuality came from outside of those walls and in the real world. For me, high school was a place of inexperience and torment from both the students and the teachers. I lay in bed every morning, praying that Mum would forget that I was there and leave me under the covers. But every morning, she came into our room and woke me up for school. At first, she made sure that I got up, got dressed and went to that place. As the years went by, she could see that it was destroying me. She had no idea of the extent of what it was doing to me, but a mum like mine always knows when her child was in pain.

After a while, she let me stay home and I eventually went back to school with an absence note. When I returned to school, my tutor got the class to applaud as I walked in, which I absolutely hated and died from embarrassment. I discreetly handed him my absence note and he occasionally addressed the class with his booming baritone.

'What's the reason this time, Saleem?' he said as he unfolded the note and read it out loud to the class.

It's not easy to learn anything when you feel as though everything and everyone is against you.

You're probably thinking, *Yeeeesh, Yvy! This is a cheerful tale you're telling!*

Hey! That's life! Or that's what they say anyway. I suppose we've all got our tales to tell and for the vast majority of us, it doesn't always start out good. For a teenager, you never think about life lessons or what you're supposed to learn from your experiences. In the end, those years can be a real son of a bitch. We act out our frustrations and insecurities in different ways, some rebel, some become angry, others become bullies and then there are some, like myself, who just want to be left alone. Being a teenager is hard enough without having to be that quiet one who is constantly harassed by the bullies.

Outside of school, I had to find ways to escape from the pain I was feeling. Since I was little, one of my all-time favourite things to do was to visit my aunty, one of my mum's sisters, who lived in Sheffield. She had two children, a son and a daughter, who were older than I was whom I loved going to see. My aunty's daughter, and her eldest child, was by far the main reason why I visited Sheffield. I used to love being around her because she always treated me well. We both had the same love of art, shared the same taste in music and I loved spending days out with each other. I always felt like myself, at a time when I was becoming more aware of people's opinion of me.

In the early years, she took me to visit her college and university friends, and as I got older, we spent more time, just the two of us hanging out. Being so far away from Blackburn, I could feel all the stress floating off me. I frequently visited my cousin over the years and be myself in a completely different place with someone who loved my company. I didn't have to explain my actions or apologise for my behaviour. Even though I never discussed how I was feeling,

I enjoyed the same inhibitions I hadn't felt since putting jumpers on my head when I was three. As I grew older and started high school, my subconscious escapism began to dissipate. I no longer had the ability to escape the questions that swirled around in my head every day. Questions that I longed to be answered but was too afraid to ask. Soon enough, those trips to Sheffield didn't give me that escapism I so longed for until the time came when I just stopped going.

I had a big family on both my mum and dad's sides, but I hardly saw them. I saw more of my mum's family because most of them lived in Blackburn. The rest were scattered across the country. One of my Aunties lived quite close us, with her five daughters and one son. I didn't have much to do with them, except with my cousin Hamed, who frequently came round to our house to see me or Fareed. I sometimes had sleepovers at his house and we spent the evenings playing video games or making fighter planes with Lego blocks, back when Lego was just a kids' toy and not a trendy status for adults.

One night, Hamed told me he wanted to show me something he found in one of his sister's rooms. He looked so mischievous that I was intrigued by what it was he wanted to show me. We snuck upstairs quietly, so as not to alert his sisters or my Aunt who were downstairs and crept into his sister's bedroom. I stood in the middle of the room, nervous, wondering what it was Hamed was rummaging for inside one of the dresser drawers. He finally found what he was looking for and pulled out a glossy magazine. I remember it being some type of lifestyle magazine, telling human-interest stories and giving tips on the perfect hair and makeup. Hamed flipped through the pages frantically, making them clap with every turn, until he came to what he was searching for.

He lay the magazine on the bed and looked at the full page spread with a gleeful smile. As I looked at the magazine, it showed pictures of women. They stood naked, side by side, showcasing their breasts and genitalia. Each woman had a different shape. Some curvy, some very thin, but every woman on the page stood proud in their womanhood. I could tell that my cousin had a rush of adolescent horniness as he stared at these women, but my intrigue was very different. I stared at these women, and I was totally spellbound by their beauty. It was the first time I had ever seen the form of a woman in this way, and I was in awe. I wanted to be just like them. I wanted to be one of those women. For years, that feeling stuck with me, but I didn't have an understanding of what it meant to feel that way. I tried to mask that feeling by conforming to how society wanted me to behave, but I couldn't ignore the questions in my head.

What does a person do if they are born in the body of a boy but whose gender is a girl and attracted to boys but must keep this a secret from fear of persecution? Looking at those women, it dawned on me that I would never be as beautiful as the women on those pages. I would never wake up in the body I yearned for and blossom into the girl I knew I was. I wouldn't have any of that. A tear welled in my eye and I disguised it with a sneeze. Hamed and I heard the creak of the bottom step of the stairs and quickly got out of the bedroom. After seeing those women, I convinced myself that I had to try and find a way to survive with all the confusion. I had to keep searching for answers, and until I found the answers I was looking for, I kept what I was feeling to myself.

Chapter Four

Blackburn, Lancashire, 1997

Even though I had both my parents around during my early years, I never had much of a relationship with my father. In fact, my relationship with him barely had a pulse. I remember him mostly for his tendency to be uninterested in anything I did, and his brutal, unfair behaviour towards my older brother. I remember the copious amount of cigarettes he smoked, clouding the living room with the foul aroma of Gold Benson & Hedges. He was never a major influence in my life, and I can't in all honesty say that he contributed to my personal views about life. He was just the man I called *Dad.* That's pretty much it. My parents decided to split when I was thirteen.

After he moved out, Mum thought I might have been distressed and began spoiling me, treating me sweetly and buying me little treats. I eventually asked why she felt the need to do such things, of which she told me that she was doing so because she felt I might be upset or distraught over my father's departure. I smiled at her and told her not to worry. *I was fine!*

It was true, I was fine. It didn't faze me in the slightest when my father left. I never felt his presence when he was living with us, so it made no difference when he left. As the stale smell of tobacco in the living room began to air out, so did the rising tension that was building in the months coming up to his leaving. I never hated my father. It wasn't as though I harboured any resentment towards him. I just felt nothing. I had no feelings for my father whatsoever. Because of that, it was easy to let him go and move on. I didn't need him in my life because I couldn't recall a time when he ever was there in any real way.

I remember seeing him doting over my younger cousins and I would think to myself, *Why isn't he like that with his own children?* As the years went by I came to accept that he wasn't ever going to be the kind of father I really wanted him to be, and I was okay with that. I never held it against him or tried to change him. I didn't want to delude myself into thinking that one day he would turn to his children and treat us like we were the most important treasures in his life. I knew that was never going to happen.

I continued to use every ounce of energy I could to survive every day I had to attend high school in the hopes that it would begin to improve. I kept to myself at first but slowly tried to make an effort to blend in. It began with an attempt to make friends with a bunch of boys in my tutor group. I didn't have anything in common with them, but I knew that if I didn't find a clique to hang out with and become an outcast, the school was going to eat me alive. There were four of them in the group, all from different backgrounds, but they seemed pretty cool. It started with sitting at their table during morning register and grew into hanging out with them at break, that is when they weren't playing football. We became acquaintances, but I was always made to feel like an outsider looking in. Even in classes, they refused to sit with me. During every English class, I walked in and found a seat near the front. The tables were set up to fit four students, but any table I chose to sit at, nobody dared join me.

'Don't sit next to the khusra!'

Instead, they'd try to fit five or six people to one table. It hurt watching how the people I considered friends would pick and choose when to acknowledge my existence. The thought of why I was being treated that way plagued me.

What exactly did they think would happen if they sat next to me in class?

They assumed I was gay, but even if I did come out in high school, what difference did it make to them? I'm sure you've also had those same thoughts, you know, the whole "why the fuck am I even bothering?" thoughts that drain the life out of you. It's exhausting. I grew tired of trying to make friends with people that didn't care and decided to break away from it all.

That moment happened one day at lunch when I started my third school year. We used a small green plastic token that bought you a school dinner. To say the school dinners were nutritious for a growing child would be a lie, but with that said, the school cafeteria did a garlic bread with chips and beans to die for! We lined up for lunch in the school hall by sitting on the grey seats, moving up one as each person at the front of the line got their lunch. I hated waiting on those grey seats. I always had someone behind me kicking through the hole in the back, leaving muddy shoe prints on my crisp blazer. I had my green token in my hand and moved up a seat as the

39

line started moving, eventually leading to the queue against the wall that led up to the cafeteria station. By the time I reached the food, I chose to have some chips and beans with a garlic bread. For dessert, a chocolate sponge with mint custard. *My favourite!* I dropped my token in the clear white box and the dinner lady signalled me to move on.

The dinner tables in the assembly hall were filling up fast. Everywhere I turned, different cliques occupied different tables. The girls with the movie star hair and napkins for skirts. The Asian boys who thought they looked tough with their signature short back-and-sides haircut and Rockports. The skinny football students that got rowdy purely for attention.

Where should I sit?

Beyond the cliques, I saw an opening at a table that had couple of my tutor friends and decided to go over.

'Hey!' I said, looking straight at the couple of boys who knew me. 'Is it okay if I sit here?'

The whole table turned to look at me, their piercing eyes cutting through me like shattered glass. Before I could ask again, one of them put their scruffy bag on the vacant chair. *A clear rejection.* I turned myself around with my dinner tray and spotted another vacant seat, thankfully with nobody near it. As I approached to sit down, my tray suddenly launched out of my hands and into the air. Somebody had purposefully flipped my tray. My lunch landed on me in a hot splat and I let of out a girlish scream. Hearing my scream, the boys burst into a fit of laughter, encouraging the rest of the students to follow suit. It was my own personal Carrie moment with baked beans and garlic butter as a substitute for pig's blood. *They're all gonna laugh at you!*

Following that moment, I decided to walk the long road back home every day for lunch so that I didn't need to be around such people if I could help it. My mind completely checked out that day at school. I had no interest in friends, no interest in education, no interests at all other than surviving high school without going crazy. As I barely spent my breaks and lunches at school, I rarely had the opportunity to explore my sexuality there. I never wanted to make a connection with anybody at school. I felt safer being alone. If I was alone, nobody could touch me. I wanted so badly to disappear so nobody would acknowledge I was even there, and at the same time, I wanted so badly to reach out and make a connection with someone. The more I tried to achieve this, the more I failed and suffered the hurtful consequences.

Developing a thick skin does wonders for when you have to face situations in life when people around you try to bring you down. Developing a thick skin was my defence mechanism in high school. On the outside, I couldn't care less what people said. On the inside, every criticism felt like a bullet laceration. Every morning, I went to school with my poker face and I never let anybody see how I was really feeling.

Because of this, I found it difficult to build relationships with anyone, especially romantic ones. I had no doubt that I was attracted to boys, but I had no clue what to do about it. I listened to all the boys and girls talk about pursuing each other and stealing kisses behind the maths building. Everyone seemed to know how to make a connection. I had no clue. By the age of fourteen, I felt like I was the only closeted homosexual in school that got laughed at on a daily basis. *Who the hell would want to date me?* At that age, sexuality grows stronger and stronger and you learn more about what it all means…in the biblical sense. I knew what procreation was, as I think we can all safely say we learnt at that age from those laughable and cringe-worthy science videos every pupil in school inevitably watches. All the sexually inexperienced boys go on and on about their sexual escapades when it was more than likely that they had no clue what it even felt like. The girls were even worse, wearing pounds of make-up, trying their best to imitate Posh Spice in the vain hope that it would bag them a boyfriend who respected them for who they really were. *Fuck off!*

High school became a playground of sexual innuendoes, secret rendezvous and classmate gossip about whose hooking up with who…and I wanted to be a part of it. I wanted to have a conversation with the girls about boys and sneak kisses with a cute one between classes. I wanted to be objectified by a guy who thought that I was the hottest thing he'd ever seen. I wanted to have the boys talk about me and try to chat me up at break time. I wanted to be part of the sexual chemistry that was invading everyone at school. But I never could.

I was going through the same stage as everyone else, but I had no way of acting on it. I felt like just one of the girls in school, but it only came across as the gay boy whom no one wanted to associate with. So what to do? I had to keep it all to myself. I knew that I was developing and the more I did, the more I felt like a girl. When I was alone in my room, I daydreamed of someday turning into a girl. I laid on my bed, closed my eyes and saw it happen so clearly. I imagined being in my living room, surrounded by my family.

Everyone was there, Mum, Dad, Fareed, Feroza and all my aunts, uncles and cousins. I sat on the carpet, playing on my brother's Mega Drive, at a time before wireless controllers when I had to sit on the floor in front of the television to play games. As I sat playing Sonic, a sudden glowing light began to surround me. Delicate flecks of shimmering gold. My family gasped as they saw the light build into a glowing mist above me. As the energy grew stronger, my body lifted from the floor and I was bathed in the light, feeling the energy flow through me like water. Everyone shielded their eyes as the light intensified from gold to brilliant white. A fantastic explosion shook the room. When the light faded and I reached the floor again, there I was, a beautiful girl. I was me, and everyone embraced me.

I knew that I couldn't be the girl I wanted to be, so the only way I could have any kind of sexual encounters was as a gay male. For me, exploring my sexuality in a physical way was an uncomfortable thought. I didn't know where to begin as I had no idea where to start. It seemed so easy for other people to act on their sexual instincts because everyone could be open about their sexuality. But not me. I had to keep my true self hidden because I had no clue how to express myself the way I really wanted to. I didn't know any other gay people in school, so all I could do was live vicariously through all the girls who were able to express themselves freely without judgment. When I started primary school, I was friends with a really nice boy named Matthew that I instantly became close friends with. We played in the playground together, sat in class together and I always remembered having the best times hanging out with him. It was such a lovely friendship to have as we both felt comfortable enough to be ourselves without the worry of being ridiculed.

Our friendship grew stronger and we became best friends. I frequently went round to his house on the weekends and we started a nature journal, going through people's backyards and finding different wildlife. I was the artist and he was the data gatherer which made our journals look great! It soon turned into an environmentalist journal and we learnt more about how to look after the planet and everything on it. We had such a great time whenever we were together. Some of my best memories of childhood were when we hung out. I was gutted when he and his family moved to Wilpshire and Matthew had to change schools. I think I was around eight or nine years old when he left. I felt so alone when he disappeared. I never found another friend like him and as primary school came to an end and I entered high school, it became apparent that I never would.

A few years later, I bumped into him in Blackburn Town Centre one day and I was so surprised to see him. He had changed a lot. He still had his short brown hair, but he had lost weight and was even cuter than he was in school. We didn't get a chance to say much to each other but swapped mobile numbers. I didn't text him right away as I wasn't sure if he really wanted to hear from me. I swallowed my reluctance and put my phone to some good use besides playing that ancient version of "Snake" and sent him a text.

'Hi Matt, it was great to see you.'
'Hi! It was good seeing you too.'

Phew! I was so happy he actually responded. There was something about Matthew that I connected with. I wasn't sure what it was about him in school, but we were so alike that we gravitated toward each other. Being that it was years later and I had learnt more about my feelings, I couldn't help but wonder if he also felt the same way.

There was only one way to find out.

'So how have you been, it's been so long!'
'I've been okay. I miss hanging out with you.'
'Me too. I've gone through so much.'
'Like what?'
'Oh, just having a tough time at school.'
'So am I. I'm gay.'

My heart began to pound in my ears when my green phone screen lit up with his message. I couldn't believe it! I was overjoyed! I found someone else who was going through what I was going through.

'I'm gay too.'

I waited for Matthew to respond. I was so nervous, but I didn't know why.

Finally, my phone lit up.

'Do you want to meet up sometime?'
'Definitely! When?'
'I can meet you in town tomoz. 7 pm?'

My nerves were beginning to take over. *He wants to meet up with me. In the evening. Just us two!* I had no idea what to do or how to feel. *Is this a date? Is that what's happening?* So many questions were swirling around in my head. I decided to meet him and find out where this might lead to. Mum would never let me go out at night by myself, so finding a way to get out of the house was difficult. *I guess I'll just have to lie to her and I tell her I was invited for tea at Kirsty's.* I felt bad for lying, but at the same time, I was so desperate to meet up with my best friend from all those years ago.

The next night, I made my way into town and saw Matthew waiting for me outside the old Apollo Cinema on King William Street, opposite the Town Hall. The Apollo was housed in an ecclesiastical style building that stood beautifully in the heart of Blackburn Town Centre.

I approached Matthew and gave him a hug, then we started walking around the town square. I can't for the life of me remember a single thing we spoke about. All I recall was the feeling I had. I felt like all the other boys and girls at school. I felt like I was making a connection with someone. And that someone was making a connection with me. It was my first taste of romance, or my understanding of what romance was. I felt my nerves tingling as we walked around together, talking, laughing, catching up. Before we knew it, an hour had passed and all we did was walk around the same town square over and over. We walked down the side of the Town Hall and saw a small archway with some stone steps. It was dark outside and I could barely see what was in the archway. For all I knew, some homeless man was sleeping in there and we were about to trample over him. We decided to go in and see what was in there. It felt like old times, searching in gardens and alleyways for things we hadn't discovered before. As we stood in the archway, we were positioned very close to each other. I could feel his breath on my cheek.

As he moved in a little closer, I felt butterflies fluttering in my stomach. He leaned in and whispered in my ear. 'Can I kiss you?' he said softly.

My heart was pounding. I was frozen on the spot when his eyes locked with mine. Of course I wanted him to kiss me but for some reason, I couldn't say the words. He linked his fingers with mine and pulled me closer. Soon enough, he didn't need to hear me say it. We both knew what we wanted to happen. I closed my eyes and felt his warm lips press against mine.

My first kiss.

It's strange to think that after that night we never saw each other again. We barely texted each other afterwards and the strangest part is that we both didn't feel bad about it. In fact, it was incredible. I never understood at the time why I felt that way but now that time has passed, it all makes sense to me. I was going through a stage in my life where I needed to understand more about making a connection with someone in a physical way and so was my friend from primary school. He too was going through the same stage as I was. Attracted to boys and scared to make a connection. We were both feeling alone, not knowing how to make a connection because we were both frightened by what reaction we would receive. The moment we saw each other again that night, we both knew that we could give each other what we needed, craved even. A connection. We both needed to feel that sense of romance, that hairs-standing-on-the-back-of-your-neck moment we'd heard so much about but never thought we would ever experience. That's exactly what we gave each other that night, and it was beautiful. It had nothing to do with sex, it was about intimacy.

I thought that I was ready for sex at that age, but after that moment in the archway, I realised that I had experienced true romance which made me so much more excited than the idea of sex. I learnt a valuable lesson about myself that night. I learnt that I was capable of creating a beautiful connection with another human being, feeling acceptance and overwhelming joy. That meant so much more to me than trying to impress someone with a physical act that I wasn't ready to do. That was what Matthew gave me that night, and I gave him the same thing. I know now that we came together for that very reason.

After that moment, the idea of life as my truest self didn't seem so far away. I had a shimmer of hope that one day I would be able to embrace life as the person I felt that I was inside. Though I didn't know how I was going to achieve this, the idea of it seemed that little bit closer to my grasp. I subconsciously became more confident in myself at school and began to speak up in class. I tried not to shy away from experiencing high school life. I knew this would be good for me, as well as Sal, but I also knew that I would pay a high price.

The bullying became worse as my time at Pleckgate moved towards its abrupt end. It didn't matter how much I tried, I couldn't escape it. It began to creep further and further outside the high school walls and into the real world. If I bumped into students in town when I was shopping, or when I was hanging out near my house with Kirsty, my whole body tensed up if I saw someone from school. My eyes were fixed on them, my skin sweating, knowing that as soon as they spotted me I was done for. Fareed and Feroza helped me as much as they could when they witnessed it. Fareed and I always had fights and feuds, but when it came to anybody saying something hurtful about me, he and his mates would corner them when I wasn't around and scare the living shit out of them. At first I thought it would help, but it only made it worse. In school, the same students tormented me, knowing that I was soft and I didn't have my big brother to protect me. I was even chased with scissors across the school field and had pieces of my hair cut off.

Feroza and I were once shopping together when a group of young lads decided to shout 'khusra' from across the way. My cheeks flushed, and I begged the ground to crack open and swallow me whole. *Please don't embarrass me in front of my sister.*

They laughed and pointed as they chanted in unison, 'Khusra! Khusra! Khusra!'

Feroza realised that they were directing their chant at me and asked me if I knew them. I told her to leave it as all I wanted was to get home. I hated feeling so weak and pathetic around these bullies, but I never wanted my sister to see it. She never judged Sal in any way, as he was her baby brother, but inside I felt I was being weak because the real me wasn't strong enough to come to the surface and take control.

Feroza, however, did take control of the situation and marched right over to the boys who were calling me out. Now, one thing you need to know about my big sister is that she didn't take shit from anybody. I always admired that about her. I admired her ability to take on anything that came her way. She was fearless when faced with a situation when she or someone she cared about was being attacked. I wanted so much to be just like her. Standing in the town square, my feet were frozen to the pavement as I watched Feroza storm over. I was so scared of what was about to unfold.

What if they hurt her? What if she gets upset too?

When she reached the boys, I saw that she was looking all three of them dead in their eyes.

'What the fuck did you just say?' Feroza was angry as hell.

'I wasn't talking to you, right!' one of the boys said, acting cocky.

'Well, you can fucking say it to me since you're such a big man! Go on then? Fucking say it!'

The boys weren't sure how to respond, letting out an awkward laugh. Feroza backhanded the one she was talking to and he went flying towards the pavement, tripping clumsily on one of his friends. I tried so hard not to laugh, but that smile on my face couldn't be contained.

'If I ever find out you've said anything about my brother, I'll fucking do worse. Got it?'

Feroza turned around and walked back to me with a face like thunder. As I looked behind her, they boys looked shamed. Wounded even. They walked off quietly, not saying a word to me anymore.

Having a subconscious confidence in high school had nothing to do with the influences and experiences around me but more from an internal truth that was dying to come out. It got to a point where I felt like I was suffocating in the body of Sal. I was so tired of watching him go through life with such sadness, while I stayed dormant, afraid to come to his aid. All I wanted was to get away from it all. I wanted to escape and try and find a moment of peace. I wanted to find a fragment in life that I could slip into and hibernate until I was ready to burst forth like a force of nature. I wanted to be understood for who I really was and not be ridiculed by what society thought I was.

Chapter Five

I was raised in a Muslim community. From my own experience, each Muslim that follows the ways of Islam interprets the religion in their own way. In some cases, it brings tolerance, respect and happiness. For others, it brings judgement, ignorance and tribulation.

I grew up in an Islamic culture that left little room for diversity. Don't get me wrong, I have nothing against the Islamic religion, or any religion for that matter. However, I cannot deny that growing up surrounded by people who believed that being anything but straight and cisgender was a sin made life extremely difficult. I like to think that I am a very open-minded person, but I found it hard as a child to understand why even members of my own family would judge how I was because my choices in life didn't agree with their religious beliefs. I am proud to be Indian, there's no denying that. I've always loved and accepted who I am and being Indian is a big part of that. When I was a child, Mum never sent me to mosque. Feroza and Fareed both went to mosque for a brief period, but they were taken out after Feroza came home one day and told my dad that the moulvi who was teaching had hit her as a way of punishment. Dad went into a furious rage and raced over to the mosque to confront the teacher in front of all of his peers. He screamed at him, demanding that the moulvi explain how he had the audacity to strike his daughter. The mosque subsequently sent a group of moulvis to the house, admitting that what happened was wrong and should not have taken place. Their hollow apology fell on deaf ears and Fareed and Feroza never stepped into a mosque again. I was very young when all this went down, so when I grew up, Mum took it upon herself to teach me how to read and learn the ways of Islam.

Every day, she'd get out the textbooks and teach me how to read the Quran. I was okay at it, but nowhere near as good as my sister. She could open the Quran and just start reading it, but then again, she had quite a head start on me. I could never read it like she could, even when I really tried! Mum never forced Islamic teachings on me, but she knew it was something I should learn so I made sure I applied myself. Although I really tried my best, learning the Quran just didn't sink in. As I grew older and started high school, I noticed that a lot of the comments made about me came from Muslim children. I noticed that a lot of the taunts and cruel names came from the fact that the way I was didn't sit well with their religious beliefs. I was a *khusra*. A gay boy. That word was said to me so many times that towards the end of my high school days I was pretty much called *Khusra* instead of Saleem by the students. It was humiliating. At that age, I never understood why it was such a problem to them, especially when I too was Asian. I didn't understand why I couldn't just be accepted by fellow brown-skinned brothers and sisters.

I didn't grow up in a very religious household. Mum was born in Tanzania but was of Indian heritage. She moved to the UK when she was in her early teens and grew up to be very westernised. Although she was brought up as a Muslim, she never forced her children to do the same. Instead, she taught all three of us what being a Muslim meant and gave us the choice to follow the religion. She gave us the opportunity to choose what we wanted to believe in. My father was born in India and he also came to the UK in his early teens. He too was Muslim but never came across as overtly religious. I never felt compelled to follow religion at home or felt the need to subscribe my life to the Quran.

I was given the tools to learn about Islam by my parents, but I had no interest in pursuing a life of religion. It's a shame that my experiences of growing up in a Muslim community were so negative, as I came to know many Muslims overs the years who are absolutely amazing people. They follow the religion to bring a sense of enlightenment and happiness to their lives, which I think is a great thing. I have the upmost respect for anyone who follows a religion to make their own life better and to treat others with kindness and respect. That's what religion *should* do.

However, I've also come to know people who used religion as a way to judge others. I was always told as a child growing up that the way I acted was wrong, but when I finally came out as gay, I was told by a lot of people that I was condemned to Hell for being who I was. That really got me down. I was upset at the thought of a higher power judging me for being who I was. Being gay in a Muslim community was not acceptable. Out of every single Muslim person I had ever encountered growing up, I was apparently the only one who was gay. Something tells me that wasn't exactly true! But

I soon came to realise by the time I left high school that people in my community were using religion as an excuse to judge others. It's much easier to condemn someone's actions when a whole community is doing so. To stand out can cost you dearly. Some people are happy to live a lie in the name of religion. Regardless of what the religion may be. It's heart breaking to think of the many people who force themselves to live a life they don't want to lead, just so they can fit in and please others who pass judgement and punishment on people they have no tolerance for. It's pure ignorance.

I didn't want to be one of those people. I couldn't live a lie because of a religious ideal that dictated who I should be. Of course, I'm aware that not all Muslims are like this but a lot of them are. As a result, a lot of Muslims battling with LGBTQ issues are afraid to come out and brave society as themselves. Honest, loving and respectful Muslims who want nothing but happiness for themselves and others are forced in to marriage, forced into domesticity, forced to live a life that brings them nothing but inner turmoil. And for what? To please people who use religion as a way of control and judgement.

In my opinion, religion is not evil. Religion doesn't cause suffering. People cause suffering. I've never met a single Muslim whose religious ideals match another Muslim's ideals exactly, because every person interprets a religion in their own way. You see it all the time, on television, in newspapers and social media. How many times have we seen one Christian person read a line from the Bible and have a completely different view on its meaning compared to another Christian? That's exactly what it's like in the Muslim community. Many Muslims have embraced the fact that we are all put on this Earth by Allah and that in His great wisdom we have the right to be who we were born to be and we should respect one another. It's those Muslims that follow the way of Islam for their own spiritual and emotional enlightenment. Not to spread hate and judgement on society. It's hard enough to find your way in society, without worrying that the faith that you've been brought up to believe in wholeheartedly is the very thing that is going to condemn you, for no other reason than the fact that you have the courage to be yourself.

Growing up, I just couldn't stand the contradictions. So many Muslim people in my community told me on a daily basis that who I was went against the ways of Islam. From family relatives, to high schoolers and eventually college classmates and work colleagues as

I got older. I was so tired of hearing the endless comments. Mum gave me the opportunity during my teenage years to make my own choice as to whether I chose to follow Islam, and by the time I got to the end of my high school years, I knew that it wasn't for me. In my heart, I knew that I didn't want to live my life under any kind of rules. I had to let my life take its course, knowing that my mum brought me up right and I would make the right decisions for me and respect the decisions of others. Some people have tried to interpret my views as being negative towards the Islamic religion or Muslim traditions as a whole, but that would be completely wrong. I've always believed that whatever religion you choose to follow is your choice. Your beliefs should aid you in being happy and respectful to others, always remembering that every human being has the right to be themselves. I respect anybody's decision to follow religion and ask that they respect that fact that I chose not to.

I may not have thought of myself as Muslim, but I embraced being Indian. Indian culture is fabulous! The beauty, the art, the cuisine, it all captivates me. When I was a child, I watched Bollywood movies with Mum and was swept away by the dramatics of the story and the beauty of India. I never had a clue what they were saying as I didn't speak Hindi, but somehow I was able to follow the storyline so clearly without the need for subtitles. The leading ladies in Bollywood movies were what I loved most. Women like Madhuri Dixit and Juhi Chawla, who were the most beautiful women I had ever seen on screen. I admired them so much as a child and even had a poster of Juhi on my wardrobe, which acted as both a secret shrine to her beauty and a decoy to keep up my vain attempt at convincing people of my apparent heterosexuality. I'd watch the leading ladies dance and sing in beautiful gowns and flawless makeup and wish that I could do the same. It was a completely different world, another escapism I loved to journey to with every push of the tape into the VHS player.

Bollywood movies of the '80s and '90s had a flare for dramatics and spontaneous musical numbers, but that was what made it that much more fun to watch growing up. Going to the Bollywood video shop just off Whalley Range in Blackburn to rent movies was a regular occurrence, one that I thoroughly enjoyed doing with Mum when I was a child. I'd push the heavy silver door open and hear the bell jingle as we walked in. The store itself was a tiny cube that could just about fit three or four customers. The counter was raised and below it were glass cabinets that housed shisha pipes and cigarette boxes that I thought were for trinkets. The walls behind the counter were covered with posters of old Bollywood movies that I didn't know, but from looking at them, it was clear that they came out in the '60s and '70s. Opposite the counter, the video wall held empty VHS boxes of Bollywood rentals, sat on metal shelves that lined the wall from floor to ceiling.

'As-Salaam-Alaikum,' Mum would say to the shop owner, as we entered.

The owner returned the greeting with "Wa-AlaikumSalaam". As they engaged in conversation, I wandered to the video wall to look at the titles. I never grasped speaking Urdu fluently, given that my immediate family always spoke English and I never went to mosque, so I never knew what any of the titles said. I didn't care though, because with any Bollywood movie, you can always tell what it's about just by watching.

When I was around eight or nine years old, my favourite Bollywood movie was *Mr. India*. It's a fantastic tale of a man who uses a device to make himself invisible in order to fight the evil crime lord, Mogambo. *It's amazing, trust me!* I was obsessed with the leading lady, Seema, played by the exquisite Sridevi. She was so beautiful and I was instantly drawn to her from the moment I saw her on screen. I sat intently, watching the story of *Mr. India* unfold, not understanding a single word they said but knowing exactly what was going on. Seema had an elegance and beauty that needed no words.

Seeing *Mr India* for the first time, one particular musical number caused my heart to explode with delight. I watched as Seema landed a kiss on her invisible admirer, her lips pressing onto his, and then, the flute began to whistle. My eyes were fixed on the television screen, I knew that a song was about to burst forth! Seema was in a beautiful garden at night, surrounded by water fountains and stone gazebos. The moonlight was shining down on her as she ran into the garden and flipped her hair back, her eyes filled with desire. She wore a breath-taking blue saree, chic yet simple, that danced with every move of her curves. As the flute whistled a second time, Mr India materialised for the audience as Seema yearned for him to approach. He walked towards Seema from behind, unbeknownst to her and landed a loving kiss on her neck. And as quickly as he materialised, he was gone. Then, the music kicked in. With every blasting note, Seema began to move her body, dancing into a seductive frenzy for her lover. As the music came to a romantic pause, Mr. India said those magical words that puts a smile on her face. *I love you.*

I was in awe. I fell in love with a song of which the only lyrics I understood were "I love you". Regardless, I learnt every word to the song. I watched Sridevi, examining every move she made as she danced under the moonlight and was mesmerised.

What I would give to be able to do that!

Mum bought me the soundtrack to Mr India on cassette and I secretly practiced my moves in my room. During my early adolescent years, I was no longer freely expressing myself like I did when I was much younger. I was too scared of being ridiculed or possibly punished for revealing my true self, but I could watch a Bollywood movie and lose myself in the beauty of it all and for a few hours, escape to a different place. A place where I felt like the beautiful Indian girl inside.

Just like Sridevi.

One day, I snuck into my mum's room while she and the rest of the family were downstairs. Her door always made a racket when you turned the doorknob, as it always stuck and you had to push it with force, making a loud noise. As I went to use the bathroom, I noticed that her door was ajar, which gave me the golden opportunity to grab something from her wardrobe. *A scarf maybe, or even a dress!* I leant over the bannister to check if the coast was clear. I could hear Mum and Feroza downstairs, talking. Dad was at work and Fareed was out with his mates. I pushed her door open and it swung gently and quietly. My mouth was dry as I slowly stepped forward into her bedroom. A voice in my head was telling me not to do it, but I wasn't listening at all!

I stepped in, and the curtains were closed. I couldn't see very well, but I knew the layout so I knew where I was going. Mum's wardrobe was in the far corner, next to the window. The double bed dominated the room so I had to walk around it. A pile of clothes sat against the back wall, freshly cleaned and dried and waiting to be folded and put away. As I stepped closer to my destination, the floor creaked beneath my foot. *CRAP!* I stepped on the loose floorboard and its creak felt so loud that it went right through me. I froze, I couldn't move.

CRAP! I'm going to get caught!

I quickly lifted my foot off the floor and heard it creak again. I was just a couple of steps away from the wardrobe.

Turn back, Sal! Turn back!

No! I've come this far, I may as well keep going.

Besides, maybe they didn't hear the creak. My parents' bedroom was above our living room, but if Mum was cooking, she and Feroza would be in the kitchen. I got to the front of the wardrobe. It was built into the wall, with big oak wood doors. Through the glimmer of light coming through the curtains, I could make out where the handles were. I reached up and suddenly, the growling moans of a freshly cleared throat boomed in the room. I stood still, unable to will my body to turn around.

As I cranked my neck, there was Dad, sleeping in bed. *CRAP! CRAP! CRAP!* I had totally forgotten that he was working nights, so was sleeping. As he began to turn, my body dropped to the floor, crawling my way out the room. Every movement was like a cat, slinking around undetected. I crawled past the fireplace, working my way quietly around the bed. Dad didn't move, but one wrong creak and he was going to catch me. As I made my way past the pile of clothes, the light from the landing seeped through the open door frame. I saw a piece of fabric, sticking out of the pile of clothes on the floor. It was a rich, purple fabric that didn't go with any of the other clothes. I pulled at it, and it slowly revealed itself to be a chiffon scarf that belonged to one of Mum's Indian dresses. I quickly balled it up and got out of the bedroom.

By the time it was six in the evening, Dad had gone to work, and Mum called me out of my room to tell me that she was going to see my aunt.

'I won't be gone too long, alright?' Mum said.

'Where's Feroza?'

'She's gone out for a bit, but I'll only be an hour or so. I just need to drop some food off.'

'Okay, Mum, I'll see you in a bit.'

She left the house and I watched as she walked away.

Yes! I've got the house to myself!

I pulled out the scarf that I had stuffed under my duvet, letting it run between my fingers as I wafted it gently over my head. I put my cassette in the tape deck and pressed play. The flute began its sweet introduction and I lifted the scarf gently and turned to face the mirror in my bedroom.

Once the music kicked in, I danced as hard as I could, swinging the scarf from side to side with every sound that came flowing out of my Hi-Fi system. I felt so beautiful. I didn't need to say a word, all I needed to do was dance.

The years went by and as I got older, my life became cluttered with emotional baggage. As a result, I lost focus on the moments in life that gave me a sense of excitement about my culture. I no longer bothered with watching Bollywood movies because I started to lose touch with the good experiences in life as I was constantly fighting my way through the bad ones. Mum always had a Bollywood movie playing on the television whenever my Grandma was at the house, but I was becoming more and more distant from life in the build up to making the decision to transition. I felt a distance not just from my Indian culture but from everything in life. I was merely existing, not living.

Towards the end of my high school days, I can't count how many times I was asked the same questions over and over again.

Are you Muslim? Are you Indian or a Paki?

Straight away, I'd have a conversation with them, asking why a fellow Asian person needed to know this and what wanting to know if I was Muslim had anything to do with whether I was Indian or Pakistani. It was frustrating because I didn't like being asked about my religious beliefs as though that was the best way to figure me out. In my experience, being brought up in a Muslim community put a stranglehold on me and I was made to feel as though I was embarrassing my family and the community because I had the "nerve" to behave differently. I was fortunate enough not to experience this from my immediate family, but growing up in Blackburn meant growing up in a large Muslim community that did not take kindly to people who are different to them. I accepted being gay when I was young, but in order to do that, I had to deal with a lot of prejudice because who I was would never be socially accepted in the Muslim community I grew up in.

I've known plenty of people who are gay and transgender but end up conforming to what their family expects them to be. It's horrendous to think that people believe they have the right to prevent an individual from being who they were born to be in the name of religion. No religion has the right to tell you who you should be. Every single person has the right to discover their identity and come into fruition with a sense of pride and acceptance, knowing that who you are is not a product of anything else but your own self-discovery.

Chapter Six

Blackburn, 1999

I sat in the front room, waiting for the counsellor to show up. It felt weird, a counsellor coming to my house to talk to me instead of in an office somewhere, but I guess after what happened with the school counsellor they probably thought this would be better. Besides, I liked sitting in the front room. It was the one room in the house that people rarely used, so it felt like my own room. Sharing a room with Fareed, we were always falling out and frankly I was getting to a point where I couldn't stand being around him. We just didn't get along.

Sitting in the front room, I felt alone, which I liked. I never felt lonely, which is what a lot of people think you are if you're alone. I enjoyed being by myself because it meant nobody could say anything, nobody could do anything, nobody remembered I existed. I loved everything about the front room. Even though it was next to the living room, I could sit in there and not be disturbed. Sure, every now and then Mum would check to make sure I was okay, but other than that I was free to be alone. I even loved the decor. The light green carpet that complimented the green sofas, the faux coal fireplace that heated the room up with its glowing amber flames. I felt comfortable here, at my safest.

As I waited for the counsellor to arrive, I stared through the net curtains and out of the large bay window across from me. I wasn't looking at anything in particular, I was merely focused in my mind and staring blankly. I thought about the meetings I had with the school counsellor or "mentor" as they called them at Pleckgate.

For as long as I could remember, I kept a diary to record my thoughts. In high school, I had a gold leaf diary with a panda eating bamboo on the cover. I treated it as my Bible. When I went to my first mentor appointment, she asked me to bring my diary to our next session. From the moment I met the school mentor, I couldn't stand her. Her clinical tone and painted smile made me uncomfortable from the beginning, like I was a test case to practice on. I was reluctant at first to bring my diary in to school because I didn't like this woman at all. I wasn't comfortable letting a total stranger read my most intimate thoughts. I decided to bring my diary to the second appointment and read excerpts from it, rather than let her rifle through it.

When I brought my diary in, I sat outside the box room opposite the Head Teacher's office waiting for her to show up. I sat there trying to think of what pages to read out loud to her. I found myself staring at the panda on the cover, as if I was asking him what to do, but my mind was completely blank. I felt a hand on my shoulder and looked up to see her standing above me, her lipstick cracking as her smile grew, revealing her crooked teeth. I felt so uneasy around her.

I sat in the box room, tense, when she asked if I could read something from my diary. When I unlocked it with the small metal key, I opened it to a random page. I couldn't decide what to read to her, so I thought it best to read the first page to which it opened. I unlocked it, opened the diary and looked down. My eyes focused on the page and a heavy feeling descended in my stomach. I hesitated to say the words, but I felt compelled to stick to my guns and read what was on the page. The page only had a few words written on it in green highlighter, nonetheless, I didn't know if it was appropriate to say them.

The mentor asked me in her clinically positive tone to read her "a little something" from my diary. I swallowed the lump in my throat and said the words scrolled on the page…

I Fucking Hate My Life

The room felt dense for a moment, and I saw the smile on her face begin to fade, slowly hiding her teeth. She didn't know what to say or do. She muttered a few words under her breath and told me to put my diary away.

After that, I wasn't treated as a test case. I wasn't spoken to with the same sense of plastic intrigue and overtly false demeanour of happiness that I saw right through. Instead, she became passive and showed little to no interest in what I had to say. I tried my best to explain why I wrote that in my diary and how much the homophobic taunts I was subjected to on a daily basis were breaking me down inside.

I wanted someone, anyone, to understand how much I was drowning and to help pull me up from the water. I thought that maybe if I revealed to someone how I actually felt, I could be saved.

Instead, she looked me straight in the face and only had one response for me.

'Just laugh it off, Sal. It'll be easier if you laugh with them.'

'What?' I said, my voice weak from astonishment.

'Laugh with them. Laugh at their jokes!'

'I'm not a joke!'

I couldn't hold it in any longer. I was so outraged with what she said. I stood up and stormed out. How dare she tell me to agree with them! How dare she make me feel like I should succumb to other people's narrow-minded and malicious judgements. She made me so angry. As I left her office, I bumped into the Head Teacher who tried slowing me down by grabbing my arm. I turned and looked him dead in the eye.

The disgusting bastard. I hate you the most.

I pulled my arm from his grasp and yelled, 'GET OFF ME!'

I had a glimmer of hope when I first went to see the school mentor, thinking I could finally be able to talk about how I felt inside. I thought I'd finally be able to talk about the girl I felt I was and how I felt so confused about how to truly express myself. Instead, she made me internalise my true self even further and Sal became more vulnerable.

As the weeks went by, I found each appointment to be more of a waste of time. I sat across from this woman, feeling blank. I watched her lips move and her hands gesture with every syllable, but I heard none of the words that left her mouth. I felt no connection with the person sitting in front of me. She had no interest in me. She spoke a textbook language that was sterile and distant, like she was trying to relate to me through a sheet of invisible glass. I had no interest in telling her how I really felt. This frustrated her greatly.

Good! The school knew they were getting nowhere with me and decided it be best that I saw my General Practitioner about my "unsociable" behaviour.

I heard a knock at the porch door, breaking my concentration. The light thumping of Mum's footsteps from the living room travelled through the corridor and to the porch door.

'Sal. The counsellor's here!'

'Okay,' I stood up and heard the thud of my journal fall on the floor.

I'd forgotten that it was resting on my lap before I stood up. I bent down to pick it up when the front door opened. In came a young woman, late twenties to mid-thirties, I guessed. She was Asian, with long black hair tied neatly in a low ponytail. She wore a grey suit, stylishly put together considering she was a counsellor. I didn't really know what I expected to walk through the door, but I didn't feel nervous at all when she walked in. Mum swiftly excused herself and I sat back down on the sofa.

'Hello, I'm Bhanu. I'm here to talk about you and some of things that you're going through, if that's okay?' she said.

'Yep, that's fine,' I was unsure whether I should be smiling or being serious, which made my face distort from confusion.

'Bhanu. That's an interesting name!'

'It means the Sun. You have a lovely name too! Does your name have a meaning?'

'I'm not sure. I never thought to ask!' I instantly fell at ease.

'So,' Bhanu leaned back into her seat, 'tell me, what makes you happy?'

I was thrown completely. I didn't expect her to ask a question like that.

'I don't know,' I said.

'Anything at all. What puts a smile on your face?'

'I like making art, writing stories, stuff like that.'

'You like being creative?'

'You could say that.'

'And what's making you unhappy?'

I was silent. I didn't know if I had the energy to go through all this again. I was getting sick of talking about my feelings and nothing ever getting better.

Why should this be any different?

I answered Bhanu the best way I could, 'When people attack me.'

'Who's attacking you?'

'Everybody does.'

'Who's everybody?'

'People at school, teachers, friends, strangers, everybody,' I felt a lump in my throat that I tried to stop from growing. I didn't want to cry.

'Can I ask you something?' I asked.

'Of course you can.'

'Have you ever felt trapped with no way of escape?'

59

She paused. I could tell she was trying to think of the best way to approach my question.

'No, I haven't,' she replied

'Well, that's how I feel every day.'

'Why do you feel that way?'

'Because…' I hesitated.

Should I open up and say how I really feel?

'You've missed a lot of school, and your teachers have noticed that you've become a lot more isolated. I'm not here to judge you, my role is to understand what it is that's making you feel like you need to isolate yourself.'

I couldn't hold the tears back. I welled up, feeling the tears flow over the water crease and down my cheek. I quickly wiped it away with my palm.

'I can't explain how I feel. It's too difficult.'

'That's okay,' she said. 'I don't want to force you if you're not ready.'

It's so difficult to try and explain your thoughts and feelings when you don't understand them yourself. For most of us, talking about our problems and issues with others can help us understand them better and find a way to work through them. The problem I was having was the fact that I had absolutely no understanding of how I was feeling. Problems in life arise from a fundamental understanding of an issue that becomes problematic and you become incapable of working out the solution. For me, it was the fact that I had no understanding of my feelings that became the issue.

By my second meeting, I felt more relaxed. Bhanu saw that I was more susceptible to opening up, and talking with her started to feel more like a conversation than a counselling session.

'So have you had some time to think about what we talked about the last time I was here?' Bhanu cut right to the chase.

'I have, but it's hard. I get scared to talk about how I feel, because I don't know how you can help. People pick on me because of how I act. They don't like it. They call me gay, *khusra*, all sorts. I hate it. I like boys, but I haven't told anybody. If this is how they treat me now, I'm scared of what will happen if they find out the truth.'

'Has anybody ever hurt you?'

'Yes. Well, almost.'

'What happened?'

'I was walking home and some boys chased me. They cut some of my hair off right here,' I pointed to the front of my hairline. 'They fucking laughed at me. I told my mum that I did it, but it wasn't too noticeable.'

'That must've scared you.'

'It did. I didn't know what I did to deserve that.'

'Have you told your mum about you liking boys?'

'No. I haven't told anybody.'

'And you know that there's nothing wrong with liking boys?'

I stopped fidgeting with my hands. I looked up at her with a face of astonishment.

'No,' I said quietly.

'Well, there isn't. You can like whoever you want. There's nothing wrong with you.'

'Then why do I get treated this way? I hate being at that school. I walk to school crying, I hate it that much.'

'It's hard, but you need to try and focus on what makes you happy. If you only care about the negatives, that's all your life will be.'

She made sense. I was spending so much time focusing on all the bad elements that I wasn't making time for anything good.

'Do you have friends in the neighbourhood?'

'I have a friend called Kirsty. She lives down the street. She's at Pleckgate too.'

'Do you spend time with Kirsty at school too?'

'No, she doesn't speak to me in school.'

'Why not?'

'I don't know.'

The truth was, I really didn't know why Kirsty did that. At home, she always called on me and we hung out for hours. But at school, she didn't acknowledge me at all. Even if I tried to get her attention, she'd give me a quick glance and carry on with her friends like I wasn't there.

'What I want you to start doing is focus on what makes you happy. Whether it's painting pictures or writing stories, you do it.'

'I will. I promise.'

By the time I had my last appointment, there was nothing left for me in high school. I knew that if I stayed any longer in that place, I wouldn't survive. Thoughts crept into my head. Thoughts that scared me. I never had the strength to do something permanent to end my internal suffering, but the idea of doing so didn't scare me.

That was the very thing that scared me. I was scared of not being scared of ending the pain. I couldn't bear to live my life that way.

Don't let them win.

I knew that I had to get out of high school. I just had to. I didn't care about the fact that I wouldn't have any qualifications. My life, my sanity, was more important. Hating life took so much energy that it made me physically sick. I vomited on my way home from school from sheer exhaustion. It was as though my body was desperately purging the negativity out of me, in an attempt to cleanse me of my pain and heartache. But with every cleansing, a new day dawned and new pain was ingested.

Bhanu could see what was happening to me. She knew something had to be done. Art class was where I felt the most safe, studying the works of Escher and making pieces of art that I'd often show her.

By the time I reached my final year, Bhanu managed to get me out of school. Being one of the oldest students in my year, I was able to leave but not without a fight. The Head Teacher was not pleased, but I didn't give a fuck what he thought. Bhanu fought to ensure that I got out and I did.

After I finally escaped, I spent a lot of time reflecting. Bullying is a cowardly act, but discrimination is downright cruel. Whether it be physical or psychological, discrimination almost caused my demise. I was suffocating within the walls of Pleckgate, and nobody was willing to throw me a lifeline. Bhanu became my salvation. She saw that I was drowning and pulled me up above the water. Quitting school without completing my studies meant I had to do it in college. I just hoped my college days would be better than high school. They needed to be. They had to be.

The Gender Galaxy

Gender is a spectrum that spans over an entire galaxy. Back in the day, society had a binary view on the gender of just male and female with nothing in between.

Of course, as time progresses, so do our views on gender, but it's not always easy to understand the gender spectrum when you've secured yourself at a place on that spectrum. On one end of the spectrum are the male cisgender individuals that identify as male both physically and mentally, and on the other is end are female cisgender individuals. These are the two binaries we all recognise without question.

For a long time, we thought that these two binaries were the only accepted options. How wrong we were! What society didn't recognise is that between these two binaries are a whole range of people who find themselves placed at different parts of the spectrum. From transgender to non-binary to gender fluid, these are all valid on the spectrum. The galaxy is vast, and so is gender. We shouldn't eradicate gender, we should respect it.

Find your place on the spectrum where you feel the most authentic, and respect others for their position. It's that simple.

Chapter Seven

Blackburn College, 2000

I sifted through the photos on my coffee table, trying to find any pictures from my college days. I couldn't find a single one. As soon as I realised it, it suddenly dawned on me that I had destroyed any photos of me when I was around eighteen.

God I wish I didn't do that!

I suppose I did it because I was getting closer to the start of my transition and I didn't like seeing myself in photos. I hated it when anybody took pictures of me during my two years in college. After my year between leaving school and starting college had ended, I was still on my journey of understanding how to truly express myself fully, but I didn't want to hide from life until that day came. I made the decision to be a part of society and not worry about how I was coming across to others. For years, I attempted to adapt and change myself so not to draw attention, but all it did was make things worse.

September approached, and I was about to start college to complete my GCSEs. I never completed my last year of high school which meant it was my first attempt at passing and finishing my exams, plus I wanted to experience what life had to offer instead of constantly withdrawing into myself every time something negative happened.

Why should I be so scared anymore?

I had the right to live my life as much as anybody else and only I could allow someone to take that away from me. I wasn't about to let that happen. *Not again.* At college, I made the decision to come out as gay. I knew how I felt inside, but I had no point of reference for these feelings. I was at a stage in my life where I was unsure if feeling the way I felt simply meant that I was gay. Since I hadn't met any other openly gay people except for Matthew, I couldn't ask anyone if these feeling meant that I was gay, or whether it meant something else. I was attracted to boys and I was drawn to my feminine ways, but on the outside I presented as a male who came off very girly. I was so tired of trying to convince people that I was "normal" when I was growing up that I wanted to make a point when I started college to not apologise for the way I presented to society. I felt as though I needed to take ownership of life instead of letting society dictate how I should be. I knew that on the inside I was so much more than how I was presenting. I knew that I wanted more, that I could accomplish more, that I needed more from life. However, I had no idea how I was going to do it. I had no knowledge or understanding of being transgender, the only thing I understood was how I felt on the inside and how I presented were two completely different faces. I had no idea at the time that that feeling had a name.

Until the day came when I had that realisation, what to do? Do I hide away and isolate myself from everything and everyone? Or, do I open myself up to the possibility of living in society and have experiences and adventures that could possibly lead me to where I was supposed to be? I chose the latter. I chose to start college with a fresh outlook and not let the past drive me into a state of isolation. Although I felt like a girl on the inside, I had to be sure of my feelings. I had to find clarity in it all. In order to do that, I knew I had to expand my horizons and experience gay culture and seek out the answers that I so desperately needed. College life could give me the opportunity to meet new people, have new experiences and experience a different way of life.

My first day at Blackburn College, I headed to my Maths class and quickly realised that I was in higher Maths when I should have been in foundation. The teacher went straight into the deep end, covering equations and maths puzzles that I had no understanding of.

I have absolutely no idea what's going on!

When I asked, he checked his student sheet and saw that my name was not on there. He told me I didn't belong in his class. *You don't belong here.* Just the phrasing I needed to hear on my first day!

I excused myself and walked down the hallway to the foundation class. I walked in, glancing across a sea of new faces through the small window on the door. I was nervous to push the door open, knowing that all eyes would immediately fixate on me. I pressed my palm to the door and pushed, and as suspected, all eyes were on me. I managed to avoid a lot of the stares, but as my eyes moved over each person, they finally stopped when I saw a familiar one. Her name was Gillian.

I knew her from high school. She was tall with straight blonde hair that reached her shoulders. We knew of each other for years but never really spoke. I remember her hanging out with a bunch of girls and I'd hear stories in passing about them from the cackling cliques in school that had nothing better to do but put down other people. When I started Year 10, I chose Art as one of my main subjects to study as I knew that it was the one class I could go to and not worry about having to mingle with the other students so much. Gillian ended up being in the same class and we sat together, which was when I got to know her a little better. She had a great sense of humour and always had a laugh with me in class. I never met someone who had such an obsession with watching *Friends* and anything that starred Jason Behr from *Roswell*.

High school politics always creates a certain divide between certain social groups. As I was a complete outcast and spent most of my time away from social situations during breaks and lunches, I never really saw much of Gillian outside of Art class. I didn't feel bad about not being welcomed into the cliques in school because I always had something to look forward to when Art class came round. I enjoyed the company of Gillian. Art was fun, but the class sometimes got a little weird, in a funny way that is!

Our Art teacher insisted that we worked in silence, to a point where Gillian and I were the only ones deliberately dropping pencils and making noise to see if anybody looked up from scratching pencil to paper. Every now and then, we were allowed to play music, with a student being selected to bring in a CD to play. When my turn came around, I decided to play my album of the moment, TLC's *FanMail*. As the CD began to play, the intro started with its heavily auto-tuned opening monologue. Track two, *FanMail*, then started to play. I looked up from my drawing at the circle of students facing their own sheets of paper. I watched as shoulders started to bounce and heads began to sway to the beat.

Yaaaaas! Get into it!

TLC were everything to me, I listened to *FanMail* incessantly to a point where I couldn't go through a day without playing the album from start to finish. When the next track started to play, the reaction wasn't as enthusiastic as it was for the title track. I guess a song with a title like *Silly Ho* might need warming up to, but by the time the song ended and the guitar intro to *No Scrubs* started to play, the whole class instantly started jamming to it, singing along to the track. As the song got closer to finishing, I realised something that was surely not going to go down well.

'Oh shit, Gill!'

'What?' she said, looking slightly concerned.

'The next song! I need to skip it!'

'Why? What is it?'

'Seriously, I'm going to get in so much trouble!'

No Scrubs ended, and the next track started to play. The song began sweetly, with Chilli's soft serenade and the sound of a summer ocean that the class found pleasing.

Sunny days. Birds singin' sweet soundin' songs of love.

'Oh shit!' I said under my breath.

'What's up? What's about to happen?' Gillian said, barely containing her urge to chuckle at my disposition.

The song continued on.

As we walked hand in hand, just kickin' up the sand, as the ocean laps at our feet.

The class was grooving with every note, listening to the splashing waves and cool melody.

I'm in your arms, and all of your charms are for me…

'Oh fuck!'

Suddenly, the song flipped from a calming serenade, to a full on hip-hop TLC vibe that snapped everybody out of their daydreams.

I NEED A CRUNK TIGHT N***A
MAKES SEVEN FIGGAS
LACED WITH A PLATINUM
NOT THE SILVER SHIT N***A
AND STILL SEEK HER
TEN INCH OR BIGGA
KNOW HOW TO LICK IT AND STICK IT WHA WHAAT—

The whole class gasped and laughed. The teacher, hearing the lyrics blaring loudly from the sound system, came running in from the back room and promptly pressed stop.

I died of embarrassment. *How the hell did I forget that song was on the damn album?*

I only listened to FanMail like every day! I even had the FanMail poster on my art folder. Gillian and I watched as the teacher returned to the back room, his eyes of judgement fixated on me. As soon as he disappeared, Gillian giggled.

'Well,' she said. 'He won't be letting you choose music again!'

When I saw her in that classroom on my first day at college, I was instantly relieved. It was so nice to see a familiar face and not feel as alone as I thought I would be at the beginning of the year. I sat beside her and leaned in to talk to her.

'Thank God, you're here!'

'I know! So good to see you!' she said.

It turned out we had a few classes together, which made college life seem a little easier.

See, I told you college would be different for you!

Gillian and I shared the same Maths, Chemistry and Biology classes. I was only able to choose five GCSEs in college, so for the remaining two classes I chose to study English Literature and English Language.

In English Language, the first main focus was to review full-page magazine advertisements, discussing the language used to sell the product in question. We had to work in pairs, so I worked with a girl I sat next to in class called Isabel. She was a bookish girl with brown hair and glasses who mostly kept to herself. When we started working together, she came across as shy but was always ready to work.

As time went on, I got to know Isabel and she was the sweetest person. I found that she was interesting and intelligent but could tell that she too was trying to find her feet with college life. Gillian and I had built a tight bond, and I knew she would get on with Isabel as much as I did. During our lunches, or when we wanted to blow off Chemistry, Gillian and I ducked out of college to go to The Grapes, an old pub in the centre of town. It wasn't too far from college but far enough so we wouldn't get caught if we were skipping a class. We spent most our time shooting pool, ordering up a basket of onion rings and having a laugh.

At the end of one of my Language classes, I was meeting Gillian at The Grapes for lunch. I noticed Isabel packing up her college material in her bag.

'So what you doing for lunch, Isabel? Anything good?'

'I don't know, really, urm, I was just going to go the library,' she said.

'The library? For lunch!' I was a little confused.

'Yeah, to study.'

I couldn't have that. *No bloody way!* I knew she needed to break out a little. I could tell she was so much more than a bookworm who thought it best to study on her lunch break.

'No, you're not, Isabel,' she looked at me, thrown. 'You're coming to lunch with me at The Grapes. C'mon, grab your stuff!'

As the year went on, Gillian, Isabel and I became dear friends. I was accepted and treated like a real person by both of them, which was exactly what I needed. We started off a typical day with our morning ritual of a buttered currant teacake and a hot chocolate at the college cafe. I loved the experience of day-to-day life with friends who actually cared about me, who wanted to know me and felt comfortable being around me. I felt like one of the girls.

Gillian and I enrolled in an evening Law course, which was where we met the fourth member of our clique, Leanne. Leanne was outgoing, confident and had a certain fiery savoir-faire that was similar to my own. She soon became part of our circle and the more we got to know her, the more we loved her.

They became my sisters, and they treated me the same way. I look back at those days and smile because although I was working through my own journey to my true self, Gillian, Isabel and Leanne always stuck by me and treated me no differently. I was able to live life and actually enjoy the good times that came along when I was with my friends.

Outside of college life, meeting my girls at Puccino's, a café in Blackburn town centre, was a Saturday afternoon delight. Ordering up a New Yorker sandwich with a bit of girl time was the highlight of my weekends. I felt safe and wanted when I was with them, never thinking that I had to put on a face or a persona in order to fit in. *One of the girls.*

Being with Gillian, Isabel and Leanne allowed me to let go of the separate identity called Sal and come to the surface to experience life alongside them. The best part was that I didn't even realise it was happening at the time. I'm sure we've all had that friend or group of friends that just get you, without ever having to explain what you're about. For some reason, everything clicks into place perfectly and makes sense.

I never did any serious dating in college, but I never felt left out when I was with my girls. We talked about boys, and by "we", I mean mostly Gillian. She'd tell us about guys she thought were cute, and we'd joke and kid her to go ask a guy out instead of obsessing so much. It was so nice to talk about every day norms that I felt so detached from in high school. I never wanted to fit in when I was in high school, and even when I tried to, I ended up detaching myself from everything. It's so hard to find a way to connect with society when all you know is isolation. My girls changed all of that. They embraced me, without question, for who I was. It was as though they saw past the body I presented and saw the real me. That was one of the reasons why I felt so able to be myself around them. Gillian, Isabel and Leanne all had qualities that I also had, and I was able to relate to them on so many levels.

In college, I encountered my fair share of familiar faces from high school, most of which I could have done without seeing. I wanted a fresh start, as both myself and Sal. I was still a long way from discovering how I could be my true self and I was about to embark on an extremely scary chapter in my life. I knew how I felt inside, but I still didn't understand what it meant. Living in Blackburn, I had no exposure to gay culture or the gay community, so I had no idea what it meant to be gay. I felt like a girl inside, but I became concerned that I was mistaking feeling like a girl with being gay.

Am I a girl, or is this just what being gay feels like? I had no idea. I needed answers. I needed to open myself up and look for the answers, because waiting for the answers to come to me clearly hadn't worked. I was so sure of how I felt inside, but there was a thorn in my side that needed to be pulled out. A thorn that was plaguing me with confusion, with uncertainty and fear. Fear that I was interpreting how I felt inside completely wrong. As a result, I knew I couldn't find the answers I so longed for by hiding within myself. I had to come to the surface and learn what being me really meant. My true self didn't have a name or a label to explain where I fitted in, but I couldn't deny how I felt. Society saw me as Sal, but I didn't care. It wasn't me, I knew that, but it was still my cover while I sought out answers. Because of that, I didn't mind people calling me Sal.

At the age of eighteen, I came out as gay. I was so proud, but it happened unexpectedly instead of how I thought I would've done it. I remember it like it was yesterday. I was with my girls finishing up a class and making our way to the college café when a bunch of girls started loud mouthing about a hot guy they saw.

One of the girls, a blonde with a voice like a foghorn, called out to me and asked what kind of girl I'd go out with. 'Go on, Sal! Who'd you get it up for, eh?'

I could feel my cheeks getting warm as the loud girls all turned with stupid grins on their faces, waiting for a response. But then, the most magical thing happened. I felt the words rise up in my throat. I thought at first to try and stop it from happening, but soon enough the words were in my mouth, crossing my tongue and reaching my lips.

'I'd rather have a hot guy, thanks!'

The girls' faces were stunned as they did a double take in my direction.

'What, are you gay, Sal?' one of them said with a scrunched face.

I confirmed it, and the girls went silent for a moment, then went about their business like they never asked me the question in the first place. It felt liberating to hear the words come out of my mouth. For so many years, Sal was treated so badly because of how he came across. The one thing Sal never had was control. He was never able to control the situation because I was so scared of letting him validate what society was saying. It's one thing being called *khusra* and gay boy, but it's another to actually confirm that what they are calling you is true. The community tried to drum it into my head that being gay was disgusting, so I was petrified to actually come out as gay as I feared what might happen to me. I couldn't live like that anymore. I didn't want to be scared. I wanted to understand the essence of my identity and where the path of discovery would lead. In order to do that, I had to let go of the fears I once had and face life head on, unafraid.

When I told those college girls I was gay, I was telling the truth. At the time, that's who I thought I was because the only thing I knew about being gay was that boys were attracted to other boys. I was attracted to boys and I presented to society as a boy, but there was so much more to me that was unexplained. It was for that reason that I made the decision to seek out the gay community in Blackburn and learn more about gay culture. I knew that if I could just meet other gay people, I would finally be able to understand my feelings and thoughts and find answers. Gillian, Isabel and Leanne had no idea how I was feeling inside, but they somehow saw right through me and accepted me for who I was. I never came out to my friends because I never felt the need to. They knew who I was and never questioned me. Never judged me. They embraced me and let me be one of the girls, even though I didn't present as one.

Understanding my purpose and finding answers became so important that it consumed me. It was a fire so bright that I no longer felt the daily taunts and abuse I received. Somehow, it no longer brought me down. I was about to enter a culture I knew very little about and discover an entirely different world. I was so scared but that wasn't going to stop me. Living in Blackburn, I didn't know if any LGBTQ community even existed to seek advice about what I was going through. It was difficult living each day with so many questions that I needed to ask, but were afraid to ask them. The community I was surrounded by was unforgiving when it came to anybody who strayed from the social norms. If the boys weren't wearing a Ben Sherman jumper and tan coloured Rockport's with joggers tucked into their Donnay socks, then you weren't part of the social norm.

I had friends who accepted me for being gay, but I was too scared to tell anyone how I really felt. I was scared to tell anybody that I felt like a girl inside. Even if I wanted to explain it to my family or friends, I didn't know where to start. It almost felt like being a toddler. I knew what I wanted to say but when I opened my mouth the words just wouldn't come out.

I met a girl in college that changed all that. She was an unexpected beacon of light that helped to guide me to the answers I was searching for. Her name was Kayleigh. I met Kayleigh during my first year at college. We were in the same tutorial class and sat a couple of seats apart from each other. Every day, I noticed her in the room but never spoke to her. I didn't speak to anybody in my tutorial full stop.

One day, our tutor wanted us to start a small assignment. The assignment was to create a leaflet that explained the importance of recycling. It was that type of assignment that felt like a complete waste of time, given that the leaflets were going to end up stuck on a wall and not bothered with ever again. Nonetheless, we still had to do it. All the students in class paired up, leaving Kayleigh and I without a partner. I shuffled up a few seats and asked if she fancied partnering up. She agreed and we began creating the leaflet.

When I first met Kayleigh, there was something about her that I really liked. Her long dark brown hair that hung the entire length of her back, her full lips and smoky eyes. She was so beautiful and had a quiet confidence that didn't require any explanation. I could see the vibes pulsating from her, instantly intriguing me. The boys in tutorial tried so hard to catch her eye, but failed in their efforts as she toyed with them silently. She was a free spirit who didn't care what anyone thought of her. She was exactly how I wanted to be. I needed a friend in my life that had that same taste for life as I did, that wanted to have fun and not apologise for living in the moment. Kayleigh was that friend.

'So, are you as over this as I am?' I said as the tutor handed us pieces of paper and coloured pens.

'Fuck yeah. I can't be arsed with this,' she said smoothly. I chuckled under my breath, as did she.

It turned out we also shared a couple of classes, and as time went by, we became close friends. We'd ditch class and go to The Grapes, spending hours sitting and together talking. I listened intently as she told me her relationship dramas and be secretly fascinated with her life. She was so unafraid to express herself and never cared if someone had something to say about her. She knew who she was and was completely unapologetic if she encountered adversity. I wanted to be just like her. When I looked at Kayleigh, I saw myself. I knew that if I was born as the girl I felt I was inside, I'd be just like her. Witty, beautiful, sexually charged and oozing with confidence.

As our friendship grew stronger, we began working together at a bar in Blackburn called Barlife. It was the standard bar full of scantily clad girls with orange tans and post-pubescent boys in Ben Sherman jumpers looking for some action. The main bar was downstairs and the upstairs bar was tucked in a corner near the stairs. There were always two bar staff to one till. Kayleigh and I always wanted to work together, and it was never a dull shift when I was with her. She'd arrive at work and take off her tan faux fur coat and even in the hideous metallic grey shirts we had to wear, she always looked hot. My shirt was a size too big which made me look like a scrawny kid. I hated how it accentuated the body that I felt so uncomfortable inhabiting. Barlife was only open three nights a week, but I always enjoyed working with Kayleigh. We'd always have a laugh as we watched the horde of drunken students pile in and attempt to sexy dance to "Pretty Green Eyes", failing miserably.

When I told her that I wanted to experience the gay scene, she was happy to come with me. I knew that no matter what, we would always have fun together, so it was a comfort to know that she was happy to come with me. We started off at little pubs around Blackburn, the camp kind that had 60 years old drag queen DJs playing *Around the Old Camp Fire*.

It was fun to be out with Kayleigh, but being new to the gay scene, I didn't want to spend my nights out in pubs full of middle-aged men. I wanted to meet people my own age. Kayleigh and I soon began going to Never Never Land, a club in Blackburn that had a gay night once a week. I was so excited to go and see what it was like. *Who would I meet? What would they be like?*

I was ready to try and get some answers, and possibly get some enjoyment in the process. I was nervous before going to Never

Never Land. I walked to the club in the evening wearing a long dark coat, keeping to the quiet streets and avoiding eye contact with anybody that passed in my direction. I never wanted anyone to see where I was going, as I was so scared of getting hurt. Whenever I went to Never Never Land, I made sure to get there as quickly as possible. As soon as I made it through the heavy locked door, paid the admittance fee and had my hand stamped, I felt an instant sigh of relief. It's almost as if I held my breath for the entire journey to the club and exhaled as soon as I was inside.

The music blared through the speakers as I climbed up the steps to the main dance floor. I remember the first time I walked up the staircase. With each light step I took, my heart beat harder and harder. I swear by the time I was at the top of the stairs my heart was ready to break through my ribs. I'd always meet Kayleigh at the club, but the majority of the time I arrived before she did. My first time at the club, I glanced around the main floor which was empty. *It's only early.* I couldn't see Kayleigh. I felt exposed. Naked. I wasn't sure what to do with myself. I saw a few guys at the bar getting drinks and laughing amongst themselves. I went to the bar and got myself a drink but was too nervous to try and talk to anybody. I looked up and saw that the club had a balcony area with tables and chairs. It was completely empty so I quickly made my way up there. I sat at a table facing the main staircase and waited for Kayleigh to arrive. More guys began to show up and I watched their behaviour. Some were quite masculine, while others were feminine. It interested me to watch them as it gave me more insight on gay culture. From a distance, I could picture myself as one of them. I wondered if maybe this was who I was. *A gay boy.* Maybe this was the answer.

Kayleigh always showed up for a night out, and when she did, I always felt safer. Being in Never Never Land, I was able to cut loose and have a good time. I'd have a dance and meet new people that came to talk to me and Kayleigh. It was exciting to be in a room full of people who on some level I could relate to. I didn't have to hide the fact that I was gay, I was free to celebrate it.

As Kayleigh and I began to frequent Never Never Land, I began to yearn for a connection. I watched the circle of friends we made constantly make out with each other, never going home alone. I didn't feel a connection with anybody there. I still felt like an outsider, like I didn't belong. Being the person that I felt inside was the most important thing to me. There was nothing I wanted more. Then, a thought crept into my mind. *Do they feel the same way as I do? Are they hiding who they are as well?* I decided to let people in and get to know someone without instinctively putting a guard up. If I was going to try and learn more about myself, I needed to let go a little.

Kayleigh and I frequented Never Never Land on a weekly basis, always hanging out with the same group of people. Once I let my guard down, I actually started to have some fun! I made the effort to dress up in tight tank tops and combat pants and meet up with Kayleigh, admiring all the gorgeous outfits she'd pull out for the night. We'd go to the club, drink blue WKDs until our teeth developed that furry film and cracked jokes until our sides split. I absolutely loved being out with this gorgeous creature. Occasionally I'd get up and dance with one of the boys, mastering the slut drop that every fresh gay on the scene inevitably picked up. I can't deny that it was fun having other friends who were gay. At first, I didn't feel comfortable being in an environment I knew nothing about, but the more I went, the more I loosened up and accepted that it was okay to let go sometimes.

One night, Kayleigh and I were sat together at a table situated near the downstairs bar. We were facing the dance floor and could see all our friends dancing and having a good time. I was perfectly happy chilling with Kayleigh as she was always comforting to be around. Suddenly, Kayleigh caught a glimpse of a young man who was standing by the edge of the dance floor, staring at me. I saw a smile form as she took a swig from her cold drink.

'What are you smiling at?' I said with a curious laugh.

'That guy over there is *totally* checking you out!'

I tried to look over casually, which everybody always tries to do and fails miserably and saw that she was right. There was a guy staring right at me. *He's so cute!* My heart began to race as I turned to Kayleigh. I had no idea what to do. Every now and then, my eyes locked with the guy looking over until eventually I managed to hold his gaze long enough to smile. He smiled back and made his way over to me.

At the end of every night at Never Never Land, I always felt a little empty. I had fun dancing around when the music filled the room, but as the lights came up and the music stopped, something felt weird. I'd see everyone pair up and leave with a companion, sneaking kisses and touches as they left the club for a fuck fest, and I was always alone. I never yearned to be loved or craved affection, it was more the fact that I wanted to make a connection with something real, something tangible. I wanted to express my true feelings with someone without fear of being laughed at. I wanted someone to look me straight in the eyes and see who I really was and smile. I never felt lonely because it wasn't a relationship I was seeking. I had no desire to have a significant other to share my life with because I was too concerned with myself. I saw the couples in the club argue and create petty dramas worthy of daytime soaps and was exhausted just watching them. That's not what I wanted.

Everyone has that certain friend that gives you that extra boost of confidence. That friend that encourages you when you need it the most and always reassures you that they will be there should you need them when things don't work out.

Sitting in Never Never Land, Kayleigh gave me the confidence to smile at the guy who was looking at me from across the room. For months I had gone to that place, but never felt a connection with anyone. I was so tired of it.

If I can't find a connection in a place like this, where am I going to?

I was beginning to give up. I knew that I had to do something. I was attracted to this guy and he seemed different to anyone else I had met in the club. He approached me, confidently, and grabbed my hand to lead me to the dance floor. As I got up from my seat and followed him, I turned to Kayleigh and swooned. Kayleigh had the biggest look of excitement, encouraging me to go for it. He put his arms around my waist and I lifted mine onto his shoulders. We must've looked pretty stupid, slow dancing to Tatu's *All the Things She Said* whilst everybody else proceeded with their drunken, pill popping sleaze dancing ritual.

'What's your name?' the handsome stranger said.

'Sal. What's yours?'

'I'm Craig. You fancy coming home with me tonight?'

Wow. Talk about cutting to the chase!

I wasn't quite sure if I should. I mean, I had only learnt what his name was! Maybe I should just do it!

'Why don't we see how the night goes, shall we?'

'Okay then, how about a drink?' he said, smiling.

The night continued, and Craig and I got to know one another. As the club lights came on and the music stopped, I made a choice and accepted his invitation to go home with him that night.

The next morning, I felt different. I felt empty somehow, like something inside me had disappeared. Having sex with Craig was enjoyable, but I didn't feel at all happy. I couldn't understand why. I wasn't a virgin before I slept with him, but sleeping with Craig made me feel like I'd given up something more than just my body. I was so confused. I thought that I had made a connection with him in the club. We really hit it off and had some great conversations. Although I was fully aware that it wasn't going to blossom into a full-blown relationship, I thought that we really connected on some level. After having sex with him, I couldn't have felt more disconnected from everything. It was the first time I had ever felt lonely. I felt lonely because I didn't know where I belonged anymore. I didn't fit in with all the other gay guys, but at the same time I couldn't be the girl I was inside with my best friends in college because I didn't know how to. I felt so far away from any type of connection.

When one feels that way, it's easy to look inward for solace and shut the world out. I spent many nights doing just that as I slept on the bunk bed I shared with Fareed. I felt tears streaming down the side of my face and staining my pillows, trying my best to hold back my sobs so not to disturb my brother's sleep. I was lost. I didn't know what to do, so I did the only thing I could do. I picked myself up and kept on moving. I didn't want to slip into a state of depression and fear just because I didn't find the answers I was looking for. I had to believe that the answers were out there. I was just looking in the wrong places.

I saw plenty of transvestites when I went to Never Never Land, men who enjoyed dressing up as women, but I didn't see myself in them. I didn't want to just dress up like a girl. I *was* a girl. All the camp gay guys, drag queens and transvestites I encountered all enjoyed how they were and what they did, but inside, they were happy being men. That wasn't how I felt. I couldn't relate to them because they couldn't relate to how I felt inside. The only person that I felt any real connection to at that time was Kayleigh. Whenever I was with her, I felt completely free to be myself. She was the only person I was comfortable enough to be the confident, sexual, outspoken person I really was without worrying about what she might say. She never judged me.

One night at Barlife, we worked a shift together on New Year's Eve and it was a very busy night. As the new year rolled in and the party crept to the early hours, Kayleigh and I were able to have a spare moment to relax and enjoy the night with a drink. I sat with her in our silver Barlife shirts, enjoying each other's company. She grabbed my hand and looked into my eyes.

'I love you, Sal.'

I paused, feeling my emotions build up. Feeling her hand in mine, I began to smile.

'I love you too. You mean the world to me, babes. You're the most beautiful person I've ever met.'

Her beautiful smile grew bigger. It was at that moment that I found what I was looking for. Kayleigh made me realise that the connection I was looking for was inside me all along. I always knew that I was girl, but society kept telling me that how I felt inside was wrong, so wrong that I tried to hide away. I tried to find the answers in the gay scene because of how I presented. I was in the body of a boy, so I thought it be best that I associate with other boys who were attracted to men and see if I could understand myself better.

I realised that while I was trying to find my path as a gay male, my true journey began with the very thing I had been saying to myself for the past nineteen years. *I am a woman.* That night at Barlife, Kayleigh told me that she loved me, and she saw me for who I was. I saw my reflection in Kayleigh and saw the beautiful woman I knew I was supposed to be. As time went by, I learnt that I was transgender and that what I was feeling inside had a way of coming forth. Kayleigh was the first person I told about my plans to transition. She told me she was proud of me and that she'd always be there for me. For the first time in my life, I saw hope. Hope that the day would finally come when I can be who I was born to be. It was time to start a new chapter in my life, only this time, I wasn't afraid. I was ready.

Chapter Eight

Blackburn, Lancashire, 2004

Before I could start my journey of transition, there was one important task I needed to do. Tell my family who I really was. Still living at home and sharing a room with my brother, I finished college and got my first full-time job at a call centre in Preston, sitting at a desk taking calls about credit card activations. Dull as pig shit but easy money nonetheless.

Working at Barlife became a bit pointless after getting heavily taxed due to my full-time job, so I decided to quit. I'd miss working with Kayleigh, but I certainly didn't miss serving shit-faced men who commented on how femme I was and watching girls getting so steamed that their apparent dance moves went from mildly raunchy to the inevitable sloppy "come fuck me" dance you can only do when you're drunk off your tits. Yeah, didn't mind quitting Barlife.

Working in Preston was okay, but I needed to get a better paying job. I decided to try my luck in Manchester and found a call centre job at a bank that had better pay and more opportunities. Now that I knew what path I needed to take to finally be the girl I knew I was, I was determined to reach my goal and not let anything hold me back. The commute to Manchester wasn't too bad, just a 45-minute train ride but getting up early and making my way to Blackburn train station was tiring. Coming home from work, I spent more time in the front room downstairs. I had a nice little set-up with my TV video combi, my DVDs and my books. It felt like it was my room. Mum didn't mind me using it, as nobody else was. I started sleeping on the sofa, bringing my blanket from upstairs to wrap myself in. It was nice having a private space to call my own.

Mum was the first of my family members that I told of my plans to transition. I hadn't even come out as gay to Fareed or Feroza. I had only told my mum initially. I figured, it wouldn't matter if they didn't know because it was private, but I didn't like lying to Mum every time I went out to Never Never Land. I hated lying to her full stop. She always taught me to be honest. But this, starting to transition, I couldn't hide from anyone. My family were going to see the difference, no doubt about it. They had to know. I sat down with Mum and told her my truth. The conversation went a lot more smoothly than when I told her I was gay at eighteen.

When I told her was gay, I was shopping with her in Preston, answering all sorts of questions she had for me. She was intrigued about my life as I gave her a glimpse of something she had no real insight on. This time around, she was completely different.

'I always knew you'd say something like this to me.'

'You did?' I said, surprised at her lack of shock.

'I've always known there was something different, ever since you were little. All you can do is be yourself. I never wanted to hold you back.'

'It's hard. I don't know where to start,' my eyes were beginning to well up.

'Just be yourself. I never wanted to tell you who you are, you had to learn that on your own. But don't hold back who you are. Be yourself.'

'And you're okay with me?'

'Of course I am!' she said ecstatically. 'I don't want you being sad because you think you have to please me! As long as you're happy, that's all that matters. Besides, when I'm dead and buried, who will you be pleasing? Don't waste your life, Sal.'

I knew on some level that she always did see me for who I really was, but she too was waiting for the day when I would come to her and tell her what it all meant. She'd tell me stories of how she heard me playing outside, letting out girlish screams and being feminine. She always left me to be me. Of course, she didn't know how I would turn out as I grew older, but the most important thing was that she let me find that out on my own. She never tried to steer me into being anything other than myself.

When I told Feroza, she also didn't see it as much of a surprise. She didn't try to tell me anything different and was happy to support me and be there for me whenever I needed her, as she'd always done growing up. Feroza and I had a good relationship, but being five years older than I was, she had her own life that was a million miles away from mine. That said, she always had time for me and I'd sit in her bedroom countless times for hours talking about all sorts. Being very strong minded for as long as I could remember, Feroza always had her own life dramas to deal with. It was nice to check in with her every now and then and spend some time with her, but our paths were completely different. At the time, I was grateful to know that if I ever needed my big sister, she would be there no matter what.

I hadn't seen my doctor or been referred for any treatment yet, but I knew without a doubt that transitioning was what I needed to do. In order to do it, I had to completely change my look. I was going to work in Manchester, dressed in what I called my "Sal Uniform". It composed of a black shirt, black V-neck sweater, charcoal pants, POD boots and my curtain hair that was gradually growing longer. I needed to completely change my look from drab to fucking fab! Nobody at the bank knew that I was going to transition, and after working with them for several months, I knew it was going to be a shock. I was nervous at the thought of suddenly going into work as a different person, but at the same time I was excited to go into work and let my colleagues see the real me. I'm sure they already had an idea that something was going on, given that they didn't call me Sal in the office.

On my first day, me and a bunch of other newbies sat in the training room, doing the compulsory and incredibly cringe worthy icebreakers that most big organisations do. One by one, a new recruit stood up, introduced themselves and told the rest of us an interesting fact about themselves. As each person stood up, my turn was getting closer.

I contemplated what I was going to say. *An interesting fact. What the hell am I going to say?*

'You're up next!' the trainer said, looking directly at me. 'Hi, everyone. My name is Saleem…but everyone calls me Yvy.'

The room looked confused, giving each other glances.

'Why do people call you Yvy?' the cute newbie said, dressed in his tailored jacket and pants that hugged his crown jewels.

'Urrm, I don't know, it's just my nickname. It's pronounced Evie though.'

'Would you prefer us to call you Saleem or Yvy?' the trainer asked.

'Yvy,' I said, smiling. 'Call me Yvy.'

Since then, everyone called me Yvy. It was perfect because I knew that when I finally began my transition, there wouldn't be any confusion over what to call me. I'd always be known as Yvy. With that said, it was going to be a major change from my Sal uniform to the actual Yvy coming to the surface. In order to do it, I had to change the way I presented. I wanted to look different, but where to start? I had no idea what I needed when it came to make-up.

Mum seldom wore make-up so it wasn't something she was very clued up about. We frequently wondered around all the make-up counters in Debenhams, trying to pick up ideas on what kind of make-up I needed. I was way too nervous to ask one of the sales girls what I needed for my skin tone. I still had to shave every day to keep the facial hair away, and standard foundations were no match for a five o'clock shadow! I played around with a few cheap liquid foundations and powders, but none of them did what I needed them to do. I wasn't too bothered about contouring my face. There was no need to change my face structure, as I had very feminine looking features to begin with. Plus, this was way before the Kardashians made contouring a necessity in every girl's make-up routine. All I really needed was a foundation routine that gave me even coverage and lasted throughout the day. I built up a fabulous collection of eyeliners, lipsticks and blushes, but I was never too concerned with wearing eye shadows as my eyes had a natural smoky tint.

I didn't want to look too clownish so I decided not to bother with painting myself like a peacock. I was an amateur when it came to make-up and didn't know any good tricks to give myself a professional look. The days of YouTube make-up tutorials were yet to come so I didn't have much in the way of expert advice on make-up application.

I heard of a shop in Manchester that catered for the transgender community on the internet. A shop that apparently sold everything a trans person needed to build the aesthetic they wanted. It was an easy tram ride from Victoria station, so Mum and I decided to venture out and see what it was all about. We found the shop easily, as it was located on a main road that wasn't too busy. It appeared small from the outside, with the windows covered up with logo photos so we couldn't see the interior. As we walked to the front door, we saw another security door beyond it that we had to get permission to enter by ringing the bell. A friendly woman greeted us and we began looking around at what the shop had to offer. Mum's first impression was slightly underwhelming. She felt the clothes on the rails were incredibly dated and didn't feel like they suited me at all.

As we glanced around the shop floor, we saw an array of pills and potions with gold labels, promising amazing results that both Mum and I were quite intrigued by. The decor of the shop was very old fashioned. Every photo was of a heavily airbrushed trans woman posing nude on a cream rug and sporting the classic '80s' overly sprayed hairdo that could withstand a hurricane. Definitely a look that I didn't relate to. I wasn't interested in any of the clothing, as it was mostly black PVC miniskirts or animal skin boots that looked tacky. I was more interested in the pills and potions and what make-up they had for sale. With it being a shop catering mostly for trans women, I assumed that they had the best make-up available for the coverage I so desperately needed.

'Can I help you with anything?' the sales girl asked politely.

'Yeah, actually, I'm just looking at some of the sprays here,' I pointed at the locked cabinet, presenting an array of colourful sprays and creams in plastic bottles.

'Yes, we have tonics and ointments that can help feminise you and feel more comfortable. Like for instance, this spray here can help develop tissue in your hip and thigh area.'

'Excuse me? Really?' I was stunned at this revolutionary spray that I had no clue existed.

'Oh yes!' the sales girl said with an enthusiastic smile. 'To activate it, you just shake the bottle then spray on your hips twice a day. You can usually see results after six weeks!'

'And what about these facial creams?' I picked up a small white tub.

'This cream helps slow facial hair growth.'

'You mean, it can stop my hair from growing?'

'It won't stop it from growing, it'll grow back slower and weaker.'

I was stunned. I was amazed that there was so much on offer. I was so happy.

'I need a foundation that can cover my beard area too. The ones I've tried don't seem to last.'

'Yes, you'll need a foundation that can give you maximum coverage. This one will do, it's small, but you don't need a lot so it will last,' she handed me a small pot, covered in a gold label.

We sat down on a floral sofa while the sales girl made us a cup of tea. I glanced around the store, with its display of synthetic wigs and gel breast forms. Toward the back of the store was a set-up that looked like a make-up station, draped in a thick curtain.

'That's for people who want to do themselves up or get a makeover.'

'Do you get many people for makeovers?' I asked.

'We do. A lot of women feel comfortable getting ready here before heading into Manchester.'

As I looked around, I figured this was a pretty great place for someone who is transitioning to come for a little solace. A place where they wouldn't be subjected to ridicule and can in fact be made to feel like a human being. The sales girl packed up the spray, the cream and the foundation at the till.

'That'll be £170.'

I looked up from my wallet, slightly thrown. *How fucking much!!*

'Errm, do you take credit card?'

'Yes, that's fine.'

As she buzzed the security door and we walked out the shop, I turned to Mum, trying to keep a straight face, 'This better bloody work!'

For weeks, I practiced my make-up skills, getting better and better at blending it all in. The day when I was finally going to work as myself was getting closer and closer, and I wanted to make sure everything was perfect. I wanted to give the facial hair cream and hip spray a chance to work on me so I could look my best when I went to work. As time went on, I used the products as directed on the package. To my dismay, nothing happened. My facial hair continued to grow and my hips remained the same. I was so disappointed and upset. I couldn't understand why it wouldn't work on me.

After four months of using what I bought, I went back to the shop in Manchester. I went through the security door, but this time I was greeted by a different woman. She was older and less pleasant than the first sales girl I met. As I walked in, I saw another group of customers, perusing through the clothes rail. They were older than I was, maybe mid-50s. The sales woman responded to them, leaving me to look around the shop by myself.

I looked at all the pills and potions inside the locked glass cabinets, promising amazing and fast results, and remembered that feeling of excitement when I was here with Mum. Of all the possibilities of things to come if I used them. This time around, I had no such feeling. None of the products I spent a fortune on worked for me. The facial hair cream did nothing but give me a slight tea tree tingle every time I applied it. The hip spray, which apparently activated if I shook it like mouthwash, did nothing but absorb into my skin and disappear. I felt cheated. I glanced around the shop once more, and I felt as though I had stepped back in time.

The clothing, the pictures on the wall, the jewellery, everything looked incredibly stale. I overheard the sales woman talking to the women near the salon area in the back and could see she was getting them to try on PVC boots and synthetic wigs that didn't suit them at all. I could see that they didn't feel comfortable wearing the outfits but were being told it was the "in thing" and that they looked great. It made me angry. I didn't feel like she was helping those women at all but rather taking advantage of women who wanted nothing but to be themselves. I didn't want to spend another moment there any longer and asked to be let out of the front door.

***

I still hadn't told Fareed about my transition. I was worried about how he might react. Although I loved my brother, his tendency to be unpredictable when it came to his temper made me reluctant to tell him the truth about me. I never knew the right time to tell him. Fareed and I fought viciously over the years, but I was always the timid one who couldn't quite stand up to him in the way I wanted to. We were on such different wavelengths. When he was happy and got his own way, Fareed was fine with all of us. However, as soon as something didn't go his way, he was like a lit fuse travelling closer and closer to the bomb. When the bomb went off, no amount of talking would get through, he simply went off. It intimidated me so much to a point where I feared what he might do if he found out the truth. I wasn't ready for that. I wasn't ready to tell him.

I sat with Mum, as I did most nights, in the living room. The lights were dimmed and two hot cups of tea sat in our laps. We were always alone in the evenings. Feroza would be in her room and Fareed was always out with his friends until the early hours. It was getting closer to me starting my transition. I'd booked two weeks off work to prepare. I decided that after I took some time off work, I should just go for it and walk into that office as Yvy. There was just one little thing I was struggling with. I was fucking petrified.

'Of course you're going to be scared. Is that going to stop you?'

'No, I know that. But I'm still shitting it!' I said to Mum, grasping my tea in my hands.

'Once you've done it, that's it, you've done it. It's all the waiting that's making it hard.'

'I know. I just hate having to hide. I mean, how am I going to leave the house to go to work?'

'If you want to cover up, wear a long coat.'

85

'Forever?'

'Then leave here.'

I looked at Mum, confused. *She wants me to leave?* I didn't understand.

'Leave? You don't want me here?'

'Did I say that? No. I don't ever want to see my children unhappy. This town is making you unhappy. Don't stay here if it's stopping you from being you. You already have a job in Manchester, so move to Manchester! You'll be free to be yourself instead of being stuck with all these backwards bastards you have to deal with every day!'

She was right. Blackburn had done nothing for me except bring me down. *What am I staying for?* I was so scared of the thought of leaving home and starting my life by myself. I had never lived away from home before.

'What if I can't make it on my own?'

'Of course you can. Look at me! If I can do it looking after you three after your Dad left, you can easily manage. Besides you won't be on your own, you'll have me. I'm not going anywhere.'

'You really think I can do it?' I said with a half-smile.

'You already know you can. You don't need me telling you. Don't forget how bloody strong you are for doing what you're about to do'

'What about Fareed?'

'You'll have to tell Fareed at some point. But if you're not ready, then tell him when the time is right. In the meantime, do what you have to do to make it work. Don't think hiding yourself is you being ashamed. You just be yourself, and in time, things will improve.'

'Why are you so bloody bastard good, Mum?' I said with a chuckle.

'Because I am de bloody Queen of the de family and I know everything!!' she said jokingly, flailing her arms up like a diva.

As the hour crept toward midnight, Mum and I retired to bed. She made her way upstairs and I went into the front room. The fire was crackling, illuminating the room. I sat in front of it, feeling the flames heat my hands and face. I began to clear my mind, hoping to see the future.

A future of possibilities.

A future I could actually be happy in. A future that scared me. Of course I was going to be scared, but at the end of the day, isn't that what entering the unknown does to you? And more importantly, should that stop me? I opened my eyes and stared into the flames.

It's time, Yvy. Come out and play.

Mum and Baby Yvy

School picture with Feroza

Me and my brother, Fareed

Sisters in the making

Feeling fabulous!

Sal and Isabel, Blackburn

Sal and Gillian, Blackburn

Sal and Kayleigh, Barlife Blackburn

Me and Mum, London, 2007

Arriving at Euston, 2007

A Rose by Any Other Name…

How did I come up with the name Yvy DeLuca, you ask? Well I'd love to give you a deep, meaningful story of how I searched into the chasm of my ancestry and came across a name that held a sacred significance to my being. Instead, I can only tell you that I got the inspiration for my name from the cycle three winner of America's Next Top Model, Eva, during a period when I was obsessed with modelling!

I recorded every episode off Living TV and studied every single photo shoot. Watching the girls pose and model, looking elegant and fierce at the same time, I dreamt of one day being just as fierce. *Mission accomplished!*

I wasn't born a DeLuca. That too was a name of my choosing. I got my surname from *Pretty Woman*. I know, a girl loving *Pretty Woman*, shocker! DeLuca came from watching Julia Roberts leave a package for her hooker girlfriend at the hotel reception saying, 'I'm leaving this for Kit De Luca.'

So you could say my name represents a place somewhere between a supermodel and a streetwalking whore. A realisation I was *very* comfortable with!

Chapter Nine

Manchester, 2005

Making the decision to transition was the first big step. How I was going to start was the next one. I built up a nice selection of outfits and shoes, had all my make-up prepared and felt ready to finally begin my journey. Still living in Blackburn was becoming such a headache, but I planned on moving to Manchester once I saved up enough money. I wanted to do it right. The last thing I wanted was to move away, only to struggle and have to move back home. I had credit card debts to clear and a new chapter in my life to start. Whatever I could do to make this next step as easy as possible, that's what I wanted to do. I didn't want that to stop me from transitioning though. I couldn't wait any longer. It felt like I had been caged for so long and now I was finally given a key to unlock the door and express myself in ways I never thought I could.

Even though I hadn't told Fareed, I wanted to begin my transition straight away, even if that meant doing it from Blackburn. I had to keep it all a secret from him as I was too scared of how he might react. I knew that if I began my transition in Blackburn instead of waiting until I moved to Manchester, it was going to be fucking hard. With that said, I couldn't stay in that cage any longer.

I made friends at the bank but classed them more as work friends rather than actual friends. We never socialised outside of work, and I only classed one of the people I worked with as a real friend. His name was Sheds. He was my age, Asian, well built and had a great sense of humour. We clicked pretty much straight away and became really good friends. Out of all the people in my training group, he was the last person I thought I'd connect with. I thought I'd end up making friends with a bunch of girls, not the Indian guy who was built like a wrestler. It was a very welcomed surprise to get to know such a smart, witty guy whose company I actually enjoyed. He was very easy on the eyes too, with his discreetly filthy personality and ability to bench press a rhino with those arms of his.

For the first few months at work, I got to know Sheds more and more and found that he felt very comfortable opening up to me about his life. I was still wearing my Sal uniform, yet it felt like he was seeing past it and looking directly at me, Yvy. Every morning before we logged on for our daily shift on the phones, we joked and laughed as if we were flirting. He wouldn't care what anybody said about us, he was perfectly comfortable being around me. I was close to starting my transition, and he turned out to be the first person I told at work. It happened on a minibus to Liverpool when we visited another site office. A bunch of us went, around ten or twelve, and we crammed in the minivan and made our way.

I sat with Sheds and our conversation led to an unexpected confession. I never spoke of my sexual orientation at work. Hell, I imagined everyone just looking at me with my perfectly straightened hair and feminine demeanour and guessed that I was gay. I knew there was more to it than that, but I wasn't ready to discuss it with anybody. I sat looking out the window of the minivan, letting the breeze from the open window blow wisps of hair across my face. The rest of my colleagues on the bus were laughing and talking amongst themselves, but I remained peacefully silent.

'You okay, Yvy?' Sheds said quietly.

'Umm-hmm,' I said, turning to him with a half-smile.

'No you're not. What's up?'

'Have you—' I hesitated.

'Why'd you stop? Have I what?'

'Have you ever gotten tired of being something you're not?'

'Have you?' he said sincerely.

'Every day.'

'Why don't you just stop?'

'It's not that easy, Sheds.'

'Then make it that easy. Fuck what anybody thinks, just do you.'

I faced the window, looking out at the cars passing us by. I knew he was right, but I also knew it wasn't going to be as easy as I'd like it to be.

'Are you gay?' he said.

I turned to him, looking him dead in the eyes.

I saw no judgement there. He was completely open to me.

'I'm transgender.'

'Fuckin' there you go. Nobody died, did they? Do you want some of my Fanta?' he said, as if I told him something trivial like I was going vegan.

It didn't faze him whatsoever. He completely understood where I was coming from; I found it really admirable. It was fantastic to know that when the time came, I always had a friend at work who supported me.

I took my two weeks annual leave to fully prepare mentally and physically. The night before I was due back at work, I had everything laid out. I sat in the front room, looking at the outfit I picked out to wear on my first day as the real me. I chose a white cotton blouse with lace trim, beige pants with tan sandals and a cream silk scarf hanging loosely around my narrow waist. I decided to wear my hair up, as I didn't feel confident to wear it down due to its short length. I was never a fan of wigs as they always looked too synthetic, so instead I worked with what I had. I laid down on the carpet in front of the fireplace, the flames warming my skin. I turned the lights off and watched as the flames created dancing shadows on the patterned ceiling. I stared up, feeling a tear rolling down the side of my face.

Tomorrow's the big day. Are you ready for this?

I began to pray. Not to God, but to my brother, Tariq. He was the eldest of Mum's children, who passed away when he was just a few minutes old. None of us got the chance to meet our big brother, but I always felt him with me. From time to time, I spoke to him. I laid down in the middle of the night, and just start talking. The night before I started my transition, I spoke to my big brother.

I know this is going to be hard, Tariq. I know it is. I don't expect this to be easy, but I know for sure that this is who I am. This is who I am. This is who I am.

I breathed in sharply, letting the tears flow as my breath became shorter with every inhale.

Just watch over me, please. No matter what happens, please keep me on the right path. I have to get through this. I'm sick of living like this. I refuse to give up. Please keep loving me.

The morning of my first day back at work, I woke up extra early to prepare my make-up. I had to be very careful not to draw attention to myself when I made my way to Blackburn train station, so I applied my foundation, but left off any eyeliner or lipstick. That could wait to be applied once I was at work. I began to dress and put my bra and tucking panties on. It felt so good to feel the softness of my bra on my skin. The tucking panties on the other hand hurt like a motherfucker as I pulled everything back into a tight, painful sling. Being so flat chested, I decided to use gel fillets as they gave me a modest size without looking like a bimbo. I put on my outfit, made sure I had my lippy, eyeliner, gel fillets and sandals in my satchel and prepared to go to work. I decided to wear a long navy coat to hide what I was wearing underneath. I didn't want to draw attention to myself as I walked to the train station and I certainly didn't want any of Fareed's friends to see me. *What if they tell him?* I kept my head down and never made eye contact with anyone on my way. *Just get to work, Yvy, safe and sound.*

When I got to the train station, it was just after 7 am. The train had already arrived and the doors were open. As I got on, I found a seat near the back by the window. The doors closed and the train began to move, a sudden rush of fear washed over me. Nobody except Sheds knew at work what I was about to do. Nobody knew that this was the day and that I would no longer be wearing that fucking Sal uniform ever again.

As the train continued to move faster and faster on the tracks, I realised that there was no turning back. *This is it. You have to do it now.* My heart began to beat so hard with ever-growing nerves as the train got closer to Salford Central station. It was only a short walk from Salford Central to work, maybe five minutes, but this time it felt even longer. I got off the train and made the rest of the way to work by foot. I was more aware of my pace and tried to slow it down. Every second I could save gave me that little bit longer to prepare myself for what was about to happen. Before I let anyone see me, I had to make sure I looked the way I wanted to. I walked into the building and headed straight to the accessible toilets on the ground floor. I was unsure whether I could use the female toilets and felt too uncomfortable to use the men's.

Since the accessible toilets were single rooms, it was easier for me to prepare privately. I locked the toilet door behind me, took off my big coat and looked in the mirror above the sink. My skin was warm and clammy, developing a shine around my t-zone. I used my make-up brush to blot the shine away and smooth out my foundation. I applied my lipstick, Rimmel Coffee Shimmer and my kohl black eyeliner. I made sure my tuck was securely in place.

After putting the finishing touches to my outfit, I was ready to face them all. I took one last look in the mirror, readjusted my lop-sided boob and unlocked the toilet room door. I walked confidently past reception towards the lifts. The floor was polished and gleaming white. With every step I took, my heels echoed through the air. Hearing the click clack of my heels against the hard floor gave me a surge of confidence. There's something very empowering about walking in heels. I strut past the reception desk and felt the security guards' eyes on me. When I walked in the building in my big coat and my head down, they never looked up once to acknowledge me. Now, I was walking with a newfound confidence that radiated off me in waves. The reaction from the guards was something I'd never felt before. I caught the eye of one of the guards and he began to smile.

'Morning, love!'

It felt so nice to be called "love"!

I walked onto the call centre floor and felt all eyes on me. My palms were sweating, the reaction of feeling a tonne of pressure fall on me in an instant. I was so nervous when I made my way to my desk. I saw Sheds sitting at his desk as he looked up and saw me, with a big smile across his face. My teammates were completely floored when they saw me.

'Holy shit! Yvy? Is that you?' one of them said.

'Hi, everyone! Yes, it is me. This is the real me.'

They couldn't believe their eyes. The questions began to fly out of their mouths and I explained that I was going through my transition. Funnily enough, I felt more comfortable telling them dressed the way I wanted to dress. The old uniform was a symbol of my past, of oppression and fear. Whereas now, my style and the way I presented was bold and confident. I wasn't hiding in the shadows anymore.

I knew my colleagues had questions, and I was fine with that. It didn't bother me if they were curious, because I would be too. The difference between being genuinely curious and being malicious is sincerity. I could always tell when someone was being malicious or hurtful towards me and didn't have any genuine sincerity. If I knew the person, like my mum or Feroza, I understood that if they asked a personal question, they weren't doing it to make me uncomfortable or hurt my feelings. I knew that they genuinely cared and were simply wanting to get a further understanding of who I am. *That* I'm fine with. The moment a person becomes malicious, I switch off. My work colleagues weren't being malicious. I knew they had my back and were thrilled that I was being myself. I wanted to talk about it. *Hell, I've been wanting to talk about how I felt for years, why hold back now!* Of course, there was a fine line that I had to make sure they didn't cross but for the most part my colleagues respected that and most importantly, respected me.

Unfortunately, not everybody was as welcoming. For weeks, the work floor was buzzing with whispers. I could always tell when someone was talking about me, by every side glance and hushed tone when I walked by. With every person who made up a lame reason to walk past my work pod and get a nice long stare at me whilst I was working. I can't count how many times I saw people stare at my crotch as I walked to the photocopier in the hopes that somehow they could figure out what was actually between my legs.

Many of my work colleagues just couldn't let it go and began to ask intrusive questions. Questions that didn't require an answer, as the way the question was delivered blatantly showed that they had already formed an opinion of me. I didn't want to entertain people's morbid fascination with me if they didn't actually want to learn anything about who I was. All they wanted to know was what little tasty nuggets could they get out of me so they had more to gossip about. Some of the questions really were mind-numbing.

'So if I looked between your legs, what would I find?'

'If you were gay before, do you still prefer anal?'

'Do you have a vagina now?'

'What does your fanny look like?'

I was stunned at how some of my work colleagues thought it was appropriate to ask such questions. I'm not the kind of person who offends easily, but back then, I didn't have a clue how to respond to such intrusive and inappropriate questions. I decided not to play into the hands of gossip and pretended I didn't hear them. I hated trying to explain why asking such questions were offensive to these people, as it was like trying to explain particle physics to a fucking nectarine. All they wanted was gossip. They didn't want to educate themselves and get to know the real me. They wanted fodder about the Indian tranny they knew at work. I wasn't about to be a part of that. For some, they took that as being ignorant and decided to completely blank me in the workplace. I began to notice more and more people distance themselves from me like I was contagious. It really upset me at first but then I soon understood that their issues with me were exactly that. *Their* issues, not mine. I wasn't about to waste my energy hating them the way they were with me. Instead, I respected their decision to distance themselves and carried on with what was important to me: being myself.

Time went by and work life wasn't settling the way I'd hoped it would have. I'd walk into the office and eyes would roll up and down my body like clockwork. I didn't want to hide away but those feelings of wanting to disappear started creeping back. The only time I ever got a little peace was when I went to the print room. Even if I wasn't printing anything, I excused myself for a few minutes to go in the little cubicle area in an attempt to compose myself and stop from caving inward. I always saw an older woman in there, I didn't work with her, but she seemed nice. She'd see me go in the print room and flash me a sweet smile without saying anything to me.

One day, she saw the exhaustion on my face. She put her hand on my shoulder, prompting me to turn around. With her sweet, whispery voice she gave me a little advice.

'Soon you'll be yesterday's news, and you can face tomorrow. Every day will get easier,' she walked out of the print room, and I realised that she was right.

I left the print room feeling somewhat optimistic. I mean, I'd come this far, it would be stupid to stop now.

Still, the constant eyes on me were hard to shake. Every time I used the women's toilets, I received looks of disgust from female colleagues on the same floor as me. Feeling rejected is one thing but being rejected for using a toilet was so dehumanising. The men at work seemed to be fine with me for the most part. I noticed a couple of new men on the office floor who gave me coy smiles every now and then. One in particular was very handsome. Tall, sharply dressed and a smile that was almost too adorable. He always smiled at me when I came in the office every morning. I never knew his name and I guessed he didn't know mine, as we were on opposite ends of the room. I didn't mind engaging in a little harmless flirtation.

Then, one day, the smiles stopped. I saw him at lunch, buying a hot meal in the cafeteria with friends and watched as they all looked at me at the same time. They were throwing looks, trying to intimidate me. *I guess the cat's out of the bag.* I tried not to look at them, but you can always tell when someone is staring at you. That intrusive stare that gets under your skin like an infection. I attempted to ignore it and get on with what I was doing.

My end of the workday routine was pretty much my start of the day routine in reverse. Before leaving the office, I sneaked into the cubicle restroom to remove my make-up and breast fillets, change my heels and put on my trainers, wrap myself in my floor length winter coat and head to Salford Central station. After working an evening shift, I logged off at 9 pm and got my things together to leave work. I glanced over the office, seeing an abundance of empty chairs and the few colleagues who were also working the late shift. On the opposite side of the room, there he stood, the guy with the adorable smile. Only now, he wasn't smiling. He was alone, but he was still throwing me intimidating looks sporadically.

Just ignore him, Yvy.

I picked up my bag and coat and headed to the lift. As I waited for the lift doors to open, the office door flung open and out he came. I jumped in my skin but didn't turn to face him.

Keep looking forward, Yvy.

He walked past me and took the stairs. As soon as he disappeared, I let out a forced exhale. The lift doors opened and I made my way to the restroom in reception. The security guards weren't at their usual post when I got there, but I didn't pay it any mind. I arrived at the toilets and reached for the door handle. Just when I did, I felt a strong grip on the collar of my navy blue blouse. It was him. I let out a sudden gasp as he pulled me towards him and opened the restroom door. He pushed me into the room and walked in, closing the door behind him.

Not 'Passing' Isn't Failing

It's so tiring to battle with the constant struggle for society's acceptance, when all it causes is unhappiness. I never expected people I interacted with each day to act or dress a certain way that conforms to society's binary views.

The way I presented myself during my transition was a result of my own personal style. I had too many encounters with people who felt the need to invade my personal space and let me know how I made them uncomfortable. It took some time, but I realised that passing shouldn't ever be a priority when it comes to transitioning, because being transgender has fuck all to do with trying to fit an aesthetic relating to a certain binary, it's about being the person you are no matter what.

Trans people battle with social acceptance on a daily basis, and the fact that the focus seems to be on needing to do more to pass as the gender they identify with as some sort of necessary requirement is ludicrous. Instead, the focus should be on the people who need to open their minds and realise that nobody should have to "pass" as anything other than themselves.

Chapter Ten

I spent nearly six months commuting from Blackburn before I was in a position financially to start looking at moving to Manchester. I paid off all my store cards and credit cards, I saved up a deposit and was ready to start looking for a flat. I wasn't familiar with Manchester, except for where I worked, so I sought help from my work mates about possible areas to live. A friend of mine told me about an area in Greater Manchester called Chorlton, where she lived. I had never heard of it before, but she told me it was a really good area and would suit me perfectly. I found a flat for rent in the Metro newspaper in my price range and decided to go and view it with Mum.

When Mum and I got to Chorlton on the bus from Piccadilly, we were an hour early for our appointment to view the flat. We located it easily so decided to walk around and check out the neighbourhood. We instantly fell in love with Chorlton. Everything I needed was literally on my doorstep. When we viewed the flat, we were both overly excited after seeing what Chorlton was like. We entered the property and made our way to the top floor. It was an old house, converted into three flats. The flat I was viewing was in the attic.

When I walked in, I felt a certain energy wash over me. I saw the modest living room that included the kitchen area on the back wall, and I could see myself living here. *My home.* Mum felt the same way and really warmed up to the place. Although it wasn't very big, it was the perfect size for me. It didn't take long for me to snap the place up and sign on the dotted line at the estate agent. I was so thrilled about having my own place to live, so much that I couldn't recall seeing a sink in the kitchen when we went to view it. I felt silly that I couldn't even remember if there was a sink in the flat, especially as I just signed the contract to move in! I asked Mum if she could remember seeing a sink in the kitchen and even she couldn't recall. Thankfully, my worries were quashed when I moved in and found a silver sink and drainer in the kitchen.

The day before I moved to Chorlton finally came, but before I did, I had to tell Fareed about my transition. I didn't want him to hear it from anyone else but myself. We may not have seen eye to eye on many things, but he was still my big brother. I still loved him. I sat in his room in the morning before I went to work and told him about who I was.

'I need to tell you something before I move, Fareed.'

'Okay,' he said.

'I'm not sure how best to tell you, but I'll explain it as best I can. For years, I've struggled with who I am. You know I'm not like you, and there's a reason for it. I was born in the wrong body, and I've decided to change it. I'm a girl, Fareed. I'm not a boy, I've never been a boy.'

Fareed looked at me, surprisingly calm but with a puzzled look on his face, 'It doesn't matter to me. Whatever makes you happy.'

'I know it's hard to get your head around, and I understand that it's not easy to process. That's why I'm moving away, so I can do this my way.'

'Yeah, yeah, I understand that. Don't stay in Blackburn, it'll be shit 'ere for you. So, does that mean you're gonna be girl then, like, from now on?'

'Well, I've always been a girl, I'll just look more like one from now on.'

'Okay, well, I'll still love you.'

Even though I knew that he wasn't fully grasping the concept of what I was telling him, I gave him a hug and took his words as an indication that he still loved me. I didn't need to go into detail, as I knew that it was a topic Fareed didn't have any knowledge of. I didn't want to confuse him by going into my life story and how I felt, I mean, I never had that kind of relationship with him growing up in the first place. It was no different now. All he needed to know was what I was doing, not necessarily why I was doing it. He wasn't ready to know at that time, it was too much for him to get his head around. The possibility of him throwing this in my face or finding it a shock to the system was a definite possibility, but I decided to deal with that if and when that time came. After talking to my big brother, I headed to work.

***

I finished my shift and headed to the reception restroom. As I was suddenly forced through the door, I tripped on my coat and cracked my elbow on the hard, tiled floor. My collarbone hit the edge of the metal bar beside the toilet. I tried to gather myself when I heard the restroom door close and lock. I turned around on the floor and saw his face. The adorable man that used to smile at me every day. His face didn't resemble that warm expression I was used to seeing. He was cold, void of emotion. I picked myself off the floor, brushing the hair out of my face with my hands.

'Let me out, now.'

'Look at you.'

'Please, just let me out,' I said abruptly.

'Fucking look at yourself!'

He advanced towards me, grabbing the shoulder of my blouse, forcing me to face the long mirror attached to the wall. I gasped again, tears streaming slowly. I looked at the mirror and saw my face, petrified. I didn't want to look at him, so I avoided it.

'You're fucking disgusting. Say it.'

'No,' I said, sobbing.

'Fucking say it now.'

'NO!' I screamed, ripping his grip from my shoulder.

He pushed me against the wall, grabbed my crotch tightly, and put his hand across my mouth. His stare violated my soul. I saw nothing in his eyes. In that moment, I was saturated in fear.

'You. Are. Disgusting.'

He wiped his hand across my cheek, smearing my lipstick. He cleaned his hand on my coat, staining it in foundation and left the restroom. As he left, I rushed to the door and locked it. I collapsed on the closed toilet lid and began to hyperventilate. I felt like I couldn't breathe. I looked at myself in the mirror, my make-up destroyed and quickly rummaged in my bag to find my wipes so that I could erase the face reflecting back at me.

The room started closing in on me, the walls began to blur and my head was too heavy to hold up. I rested my forehead in the palm of my hands, applying pressure to my eyes. *Don't you cry. Don't you fucking dare cry.* I looked at my watch and saw that it was just after 9:30 pm. I'd missed my train. I couldn't stay locked in the restroom all night. I had to get out of there. I didn't think to check if my assailant was still around, I just had to leave.

I gathered myself and opened the restroom door. The reception was clear, not a single soul. I walked towards the large glass double doors that led outside. As I stepped forward, the click of my heel bounced across the room. My heart skipped and I froze on the spot. *Shit!* Any thought of strutting confidently in my heels were long gone, now I wanted to disappear. I carried on walking towards the glass doors, my pace quickening with every click. I pushed the doors open and a cold gust of air hit me in the face, filling my lungs. I lifted my hood up and hurried to Salford Central.

It wasn't long until the train to Blackburn arrived. I stepped on and found that it was surprisingly busy for a late train. Then I remembered, it was Friday night. I found a vacant aisle seat and made my way toward it. I didn't like sitting in an aisle seat, being exposed to prying eyes. I much preferred a window seat where I could spend the whole trip looking out the window and not worrying about people staring at me. I had no such luck this time. I sat beside an elderly woman and figured I was on my way home and that's all that mattered. The engine began to rattle the carriage and we slowly began our onward journey to the next stop. I leant my head back and closed my eyes. All I wanted at that very moment, was to see nothing but black.

'What is that?' a passenger whispered.

'Fuck knows!'

'Look at it! Is it a girl?'

I held my breath for a moment. As I opened my eyes, I saw a group of youths sitting at the table across from me. They were dressed up for a night on the town, on their way to Bolton or Blackburn as the other stops were all small places that didn't have much in the way of nightlife. I pretended to not see them, but I caught the eye of one of the boys and my heart sank. *Fuck's sake!*

'It's a girl! Look at its shoes!'

I tried to tuck my shoes under the seat, but there wasn't much room. *I knew I should've changed my fucking shoes before I left.* I glanced around discreetly at the other passengers, who were blissfully ignoring the bunch of teenagers. I closed my eyes, pretending to be asleep.

'It's a fucking boy!'

'Go ask it, go on!' one of the girls said, laughing.

It. They referred to me as It. I wasn't even a person in their eyes. I was nothing. I listened as they continued talking about me, feeling the anger building inside me.

'Oi! What the fuck are you?' a male voice shouted.

Their friends continued to laugh at my expense.

'Don't fuckin' pretend you're asleep!'

'LEAVE ME ALONE, YOU BASTARD!' I yelled.

I stood up strongly and walked right to them. I stood at the table and looked them all in the eyes.

'Who the fuck do you think you are? You're all a bunch of cunts! Now shut your fucking mouths before I fucking shut it for you!'

'Fuckin' try it, ya tranny!' one of them said. He got up from his seat, trying to intimidate me.

'Okay!' I lifted my fist and swung it straight at his stupid, ignorant face. My fist struck him and he—

And that's when I opened my eyes. I was still in my seat, slowly dying of embarrassment as they threw their taunts at me. I didn't have the strength to confront them. I felt pathetic. Weak.

You are weak, Yvy.

Nobody said anything as the group became more rambunctious in their cruelty. I stared at the seat in front of me, trying to focus on something else and block out what was happening. My breath became shallow and I found it hard to breathe. I felt like I did in the restroom, the train walls closing in on me. I wanted to disappear. I wanted to die. The train stopped at Bolton, but the group of people didn't get off. As the train approached the next stop, one of them walked over to me. She was dressed in a black mini dress and stunk from consuming copious amounts of Stella, the cans mounting on the train table.

'Excuse me,' she said. 'What are ya? Are you a boy or a girl?'

The train began to slow down. *The next stop.* As it came to a halt, I willed my body out of my seat and nudged past her to get off the train. The group laughed as they watched me leave, shouting obscenities behind me. I stepped off the train and watched as it continued its journey without me. I sat alone on a bench, feeling defeated.

Here I was, sitting at a train station that wasn't even my stop, scared off by a bunch of drunken fucks who felt the need to attack me, not knowing I had been attacked already. I was done. If this is just the beginning of my journey in life, I didn't want to stick around to see if it got any worse. I was wounded. The lump in my throat was so heavy it was choking me, but I didn't let it out. I wasn't going to cry over this. I didn't want to let it out, I was too scared that if I did, I wouldn't be able to stop. It was an hour before another train to Blackburn showed up and took me home. Thankfully, the train I got on was empty, but to be completely honest, I didn't even notice. I felt numb as the train made its way to Blackburn.

It was just past 11 o'clock by the time I finally reached home, and all I wanted to do was disappear. I unfolded the thick duvet and laid down on the sofa. My body was still shaking, filled with shame.

This is it. This is my life. I'm never going to escape it, am I? Mum heard the front door and came in the room to find me already in bed.

'Where have you been? I've been ringing you'

'Sorry, Mum, my phone died. I missed my train so I got a later one.'

'Okay, as long as you're alright.'

'I'm fine, I'm just knackered.'

'You excited about tomorrow?'

I hesitated for a moment, trying to figure out what the hell she was talking about. *You're moving out tomorrow, Yvy. You're leaving.*

'Yeah I am, Mum,' I said with a sombre tone. Mum looked at me with slight concern.

'Has something happened?' she said.

'No, I'm fine, really I am. I'm just tired.'

'Okay, then, goodnight,' she knew something was wrong but knew to leave it for the time being.

Once she left the room, I got out of the blanket and looked for my phone. I flipped it open to see she had tried to call me several times. I didn't even hear it. I turned on the heater and sat in front of the flames, staring blankly.

You don't belong here, Yvy. This world isn't for you. You shouldn't be here.

'You're wrong.'

Please, don't kid yourself! You're not fooling anybody! You are a joke!'

'Shut up.'

I mean look at you! Running away, moving out and for what? So you can live perfectly in some shitty attic? The problem isn't Blackburn. It's you.

'No it's not, there's nothing wrong with me.'

All that will happen is you'll deal with the same shit in a different place. Today proves it. You can't get away from what you are.

'I'm not gonna listen to this.'

You have no choice but to listen. All you have is your thoughts. I'm not going away! But you can.

'That's what I'm doing. I'm leaving.'

For fuck's sake, you're even stupider than I thought. You really think that flat is the answer? Ha! You're wrong!

'I can get through this. I'm strong.'

You are weak, Yvy! If you had any strength in you, you would have stood up to that fucking arsehole at work and those cunts on that train. And what did you do? What you do best, you coward. You got scared and ran off. You're pathetic! You're disgusting!

'Leave me alone!'

YOU WON'T LET ME! YOU'RE THE ONE WHO WON'T LEAVE ME! BECAUSE YOU'RE WEAK!

'Be quiet!'

Do yourself a favour and just DO IT! You don't want to be here anyway. Always wanting to fucking disappear. Well, here's your chance. Do yourself a favour and get the fuck out!

I looked down at the four boxes of co-codamol, filled with blisters of pills. I couldn't even remember sneaking into the kitchen and grabbing them from the medicine cabinet. A tear began to fall down my cheek as I contemplated what my mind was pushing me to do.

You hate it here. Your whole life you've had to fight and for what? You don't want to stick around to see how bad it gets, do you? You're a freak. You don't belong here. YOU DON'T BELONG HERE!

I pulled the blisters out of the boxes and laid them out in front of me. Judging from the boxes, there was at least twenty to thirty pills. Mum had a stash of medications built up over the years.

End it all. You'll be better for it. There's nothing here for you except misery. Why stay? It's not worth it. You can make it all go away.

Chapter Eleven

The sunlight warming my skin made me feel beautiful as I stood by the sea, looking over the horizon. The white sandy beach stretched for as far as I could see, untouched. I stood with my hands by my side, feeling the ocean air caress my body with loving care. The palm trees rustled and the sound of birds tweeted a sweet lullaby. The sun was beginning its decent, slowly setting the sky on fire.

I walked along the sand, leaving footprints with every step. The ocean resembled blue ice as the waves kissed the sands edge. An eternal depth of treasures. I walked slowly, wearing a two-piece bathing suit and a silk sarong that flowed behind me. As the sun got lower, the air began to cool. I made my way over to the rocks nearby and stood on the highest one, looking down at the crashing waves. I leant forward and prepared to let myself go. I could smell the water with every crash against the rocks. My head was clear of thought, no cares or worries to speak of. All I had left was clarity.

My body went limp and I fell through the air, suddenly finding myself submersed in the ocean's beauty in a mighty collision. The world went silent and all I could hear was the water. A deafening silence. I floated to the top and lay bathed in the ocean, watching the night sky slowly paint over its orange brilliance. The moon was full, shining its pale moonlight on the waves clapping against my ears. My body felt light as I felt the current pull me further away from land. I didn't care, I felt free. The water was refreshing, holding me up. Stars began to appear, twinkling in my eyes. As the water cooled, so did my body. I felt a shiver down my spine. The sun had set, and I was left to float in darkness. A noise in the distance caught my attention. *A siren? A boat, maybe?* I couldn't see through the darkness.

I tried to swim, but my body was too cold. My limbs were fused in position, floating in eternal night. The sound continued in the distance. I called out, but I heard nothing. My voice didn't carry across the dead air. I missed the warmth of the sun, the white sand, the blue water. I missed the light. I didn't want to remain in darkness. The siren got louder. It wasn't a siren, it was more like the chiming of bells. I tried to turn my neck to see what was making those noises, but I couldn't.

All I could do is stare at the stars, my body frozen in the water. With every chime, the stars began to disappear, one by one. A sudden rush of sorrow consumed me and my heart began to break. My eyes welled up with tears that ran down my face, into the water. My sorrow was becoming one with the ocean, forever and eternal. The chiming was so close I could practically feel it next to my ear. Before I could attempt to call out again, my body sank under the water, into the black abyss. I couldn't breathe, but I wasn't dying. The black depths of the ocean took me over, pulling me deeper and deeper. My eyes were stinging, my limbs went limp and I struggled to reach above the water. The chimes were everywhere, constant. Louder and louder…

My tired eyes opened, looking up at the front room ceiling. The sunlight was blaring through the bay window. The chiming of my phone alarm sounding beside me. I lay shivering on the floor, next to the boxes of pills. I sat up and looked for a blanket to wrap my cold body in. I turned the heater on and picked up the blisters I laid out on the floor, the co-codamol pills still intact. I bundled them back into their boxes and put them back in the medicine cabinet.

It was finally time to leave the house and move to Chorlton. Getting all my stuff together and into the hire van was done quicker than I expected. Funny, I thought packing up my entire life would take longer than 30 minutes. That said, saying goodbye to living at home took longer to process. It felt strange, leaving the house I grew up in since I was three years old. I was conflicted. I didn't know if I was happy or sad about it, but I guess a lot of kids feel that way when they fly the nest. I hated having to leave Mum. I loved having her around and I was about to go from seeing her every day to living by myself.

I knew she didn't want me to leave. If she could, she would've asked me to stay. But she knew better, as she always does. That's the thing about Zohra, she always knew what was the right thing to do. When she gave me advice, I always took it. Even if I hated what she was saying, I knew deep down that her advice was always right because she was the only person in my life that had my back. She wanted nothing but to ensure that I was happy and safe. I was going to miss being able to sit down with her in the evenings with a hot cuppa and talk. It wasn't like I was never going to see her again, but at the same time, I wasn't moving round the corner, I was leaving for a completely new city. A city where I had no friends, as in real friends, no support system. It was just going to be me.

Feroza and her boyfriend helped get me to Chorlton. I rode in Feroza's silver Corsa and watched as she got increasingly pissed off as she watched her fella constantly switching lanes on the motorway, making it difficult for us to stay behind him. He was driving the van with all my stuff, and all I kept thinking was *if you break any of my stuff I'll kick you in your fuckin nutsack!* We arrived at the flat safely, and they helped get my stuff upstairs to the attic. I unlocked the door to the flat, which immediately opened to a steep flight of carpeted stairs that led to the attic.

At the top of the stairs were high walls and a rectangle-shaped window on the ceiling. To the right was the narrow bathroom and the box-shaped bedroom. To the left, the living room and kitchen area. The living room had a small, worn two-seater sofa and a foldaway dining table against the sloped wall, with two sets of dining chairs stacked on each other. The kitchen had next to nothing, except for a few sponges and some cleaning products. I hadn't got a chance to stock it with food, so the compact fridge under the kitchen counter was empty.

'This is nice!' Feroza had never seen the flat until now.

'I like it, it's perfect for just me.'

'Do you have any food in the house?'

'No, I'll do some shopping in the morning.'

'You want me to get you some stuff from somewhere? You need to eat something.'

'No, it's fine. I'll just get some takeaway tonight.'

Once all the boxes were in the flat, Feroza stayed a little longer and then headed back to Blackburn, leaving me to get settled. I latched the door shut and went back upstairs as she and her boyfriend left. I walked around the flat, my fingers running along the wallpaper. *I live here.* It was a new chapter, one that I wasn't sure if I was prepared for. I opened the bin bags full of clothes and started hanging them in the built-in closet. I set up my stereo system and made the bed, putting my duvet and pillows on the bare mattress. I set up my television, placing it on the oval mahogany coffee table in the middle of the living room that was the perfect size for the television and DVD player. I lined my collection of DVDs in the storage cupboard on the back wall, finding an ironing board and an old vacuum cleaner the previous tenants must've left behind.

The living room had a fireplace but no actual heater. Instead it was just a mantel, painted white with dull coloured tiles covering the fireplace area and the hearth. I placed a pair of candlesticks on each end of the mantel and unwrapped my mirror to place in the middle. As the mirror was set in place, I was immediately faced with my reflection. I looked at myself, examining every detail. My hair that I wished were longer. My nose that I wish looked more delicate and less like my father's. My jawline showing the irritated areas from excessive shaving and the sadness in my eyes.

Feeling sad, feeling anything negative to be honest, seemed to come so naturally. Only 24 hours ago, I was assaulted, ridiculed and belittled. I hit rock bottom and felt the foundation collapse, falling fifty feet below and landing so hard on the ground that I contemplated ending it all. And yet here I was, still standing, looking at a courageous creature in the mirror. Then suddenly, it dawned on me, like a light switch was turned on in my head.

You're not going to give up now, Yvy.

That night in the front room was the only time I'd ever thought of doing something so final. You're probably wondering why I didn't do it. *Why didn't I swallow all those pills?* The truth is, I really don't know. Actually, screw that, I do fucking know why I didn't do it! I didn't do it because if I did, if I took my own life, I would never know what could have been. My curious nature always propels me fearlessly into the unknown. I'm forever wanting to push myself to my highest potential and see where it leads me. If I had followed through, it would have gone against everything I was. Doing something so final takes a strength I cannot comprehend, and truth be told, I don't hold that type of strength in me.

Did the idea of killing myself scare me at the time? No, it didn't. Did the fact that it didn't scare me, scare me? Abso-fucking-lutely! I hate feeling scared. I guess nobody likes being scared, but I physically hate it. I hate being made to feel afraid, because it makes me feel weak. But what I didn't realise at the time was that there's nothing wrong with having a weak moment, because that doesn't make you weak. What makes you weak is if you let it consume you. If you lay bathed in negativity, sooner or later it's going to drag you under and it won't let you go until you suffocate. I didn't want that for me. I wanted more from life and I wasn't ready to give it up without a fight. I looked in the mirror and saw how beautiful I was and loved the idea of one day being the real me, inside and out. After moving away from Blackburn, I was able to let go of all the insecurities of being seen and I was able to understand who I really was. For months, all I cared about was making sure I got from Blackburn to Manchester without being noticed, quickly changing in the restroom, doing my job and then going home. I never stopped to truly look at my life and who it is I wanted to be as a person. I'm not talking about gender, I'm talking about the person.

Who am I? Who do I want to be?

For years, I had ideas of who I wanted to be growing up. I always felt like a girl, but the type of girl I wanted to be forever changed as the years went by. When I moved to Chorlton, I was finally free to do whatever I wanted. I could be anyone I wanted to be. So the question remained. *Who do I want to be?*

I knew one thing for sure, I didn't want to be scared. Only I could change that. I spent the weekend unpacking and prepared to go to work the following week. There was one thing that laid heavy on my mind. *The assault.* I was torn about what to do. *Should I report him? Should I tell someone? Should I confront him?* I didn't know.

Since the first day I stepped into the office as Yvy, I was still dealing with the gossip and side glances. Management were useless at dealing with people who treated me this way. After using the women's restroom for the first time at the office, a group of girls lodged a complaint about me. Apparently, me using a closed cubicle by myself was offensive to them. *Go figure!* When they raised their complaint, I was called into a meeting by management to discuss their "concerns".

It didn't take long after I started my transition at work for all the bullshit to come up. In fact, I was only into my second or third week when this happened. I walked into the meeting and was greeted by three managers. One I knew from another team on the office floor, but the other two I didn't know. One was a woman in her forties, wearing a grey pencil skirt with matching jacket. The other lady looked slightly older, or more worn if she was the same age. She too wore a grey suit but with pants. *HR people!* As the three began to talk, it was eerie. Everything they said seemed perfectly rehearsed, as they all managed to know how to finish each other's sentences.

'Saleem, we'd like to speak to you about concerns that have been raised,' one of them said matter-of-fact like.

'My name is Yvy,' I said, my face expressionless.

'Excuse me?' the one in the skirt replied.

'She prefers to be called Yvy,' the manager from my floor said, feeling the need to break the tension.

117

'Oh, of course. Well, we've received some concerns from members of staff about your usage of the women's toilets.'

'What about it?'

'Well, some feel uncomfortable with you using the female facilities and we'd like to discuss—'

'I'm sorry,' I interrupted the room's increasingly irritating tone. 'Are you telling me that you've pulled me into a meeting to ask me to stop using the ladies' room?'

'It might be beneficial for your comfort to use the single toilet facilities to avoid—'

'Avoid what? Making other people uncomfortable? Do you realise what it is you're actually saying to me?'

'We understand this may seem insensitive, Sa-Yvy, but we want to ensure that we maintain a harmonious working environment for both you and everyone else.'

I was getting so pissed off. If this is how management thought it best to "handle" this ridiculous complaint, I was completely stunned. *Am I really making people that uncomfortable?*

'You might want to think about what you're asking me to do. I've done nothing wrong.'

The room didn't listen, only continued with their HR rhetoric about staff having rights to their opinions. I kept the peace and used the single restrooms, including the one in the reception. However, the night I was pushed into the restroom and threatened, I changed. I was sick of catering to people who didn't treat me as an equal, only to have a terrifying experience that was completely unprovoked. *Hell no! I'm not standing for that anymore.*

I can't deny it, my first weekend in my new flat was plagued with anxiety. I couldn't get my mind off the restroom incident and what I was going to do when Monday came back around. Soon enough, it did, and I had a choice to either stay home and hide or go into work. I walked into the office, wearing my black lace blouse and my baby pink Morgan skirt. I was sitting at my desk when Sheds turned to me.

'I gotta admit, Yvy,' he said with a grin on his face. 'You look good!'

'You always know how to cheer me up!'

'Why, what's up?'

'Oh, just some guy scared me last week.'

'What do you mean?' Sheds' face went from a smile to concern.

I told him what had happened. I trusted Sheds to listen to what I had to say.

'Who was it?' he said, looking stern.

'Leave it, I'm not going to make a fuss.'

'Who the fuck was it, Yvy?'

It's as if he heard me, because the bastard walked past the bank of desks opposite us. I nodded discreetly in his direction, letting Sheds know who I was talking about.

I don't know what happened, but for the next few days, Sheds didn't say another word on the subject. It was like I never brought it up. The following week, I went to print some letters in the print room when in walked the guy from the restroom. As he walked in, I heard someone call him by his name as they greeted him. His name was Paul. *Or was it Pete?* I wasn't too sure, the guy who greeted him said his name as he was walking past so I didn't quite catch it.

For argument's sake, I'll call him Douchebag. When Douchebag stepped into the print room and saw me, his face went pale. I didn't make eye contact and just carried on with what I was doing. I was calm and not intimidated by him. I wasn't going to give him that power. I wasn't going to be weak. To my surprise, Douchebag attempted to strike up a conversation.

'Do you know where they keep the letter headed—'

I didn't let him finish his sentence, I just opened the bottom cupboard door that housed the stacks of printer paper.

'Thanks,' he said softly.

I wanted to say something to him. I wanted to scream in his face *YOU'RE THE ONE WHO'S FUCKING DISGUSTING!* But I couldn't bring myself to say anything. At first, I thought it was because I was scared. *Weak.* But then it hit me, I couldn't say that to him because I'm not that kind of person. I wouldn't ever make another person feel that way. I was better than that. I was stronger than Douchebag because I didn't allow him to crush my spirit. He tried to break me down, and I was still standing. That showed him that I was the strong one, and he was the weak one. The moment I had that realisation, I felt at ease. It was at that moment that Douchebag did something I didn't expect.

'I'm sorry,' he said.

I was just about the leave the print room when he said that. I stopped and turned to him, my face void of emotion.

'I'm sorry about, well, I made a mistake.'

'It wasn't a mistake. You knew what you were doing,' I said abruptly, making sure he could see the bruise on my collarbone.

'I shouldn't have done that. I won't ever bother you again. I'm sorry.'

I walked out of the print room. I didn't want to accept his apology. I may not be the type to do what he did, but I can still take some pleasure from watching his sad face as I walked away. *Douchebag!*

I sat down at my desk with a smile on my face, sorting the printed sheets I had just collected.

'What are you smiling at, Mrs?' Sheds said.

'I just got an apology.'

'From?' he said, trying to contain his smug smile.

'Yeah, From!'

'Good! I'm glad he did,' he went back to typing at his computer.

'Wait a second,' I said, getting a sudden moment of clarity. 'Did you say something to him?'

'Would I do that?' Sheds gave me a mischievous brow raise.

'You said something to him, didn't you!'

'He won't try fucking with you again, trust me!'

Sheds reached out and put his hand on my leg. A momentary intimacy I hadn't experienced with my good friend. I laid my hand on his and locked our fingers. As we sat amongst a busy office, Sheds looked only at me and smiled.

Nunna Yo Bizness!

You know what really pisses me off? When a person believes that they have a right to know if someone is transgender. Who are they to think that I have to share my life so intimately out of obligation?

It's easy to blame this mentality on a person's privilege, but that's because it generally *is* due to their privilege status. I've had my fair share of white, cisgender males who think that if a person is trans they have a moral obligation to disclose everything.

Excuse me, bitch!

Now, don't get me wrong, I'm not saying every person is like this but a lot are. I commend anybody, including people I've known for a very long time, who believe that a person has the right to live their life without having the need to explain themselves to anybody. But unfortunately, a good chunk of people don't think this way. It's never an easy topic, but the issue of privilege still goes on.

Minorities are treated differently, queer people are misunderstood and trans people are being banned from using public restrooms. At the end of the day, who I am and what I've been through is none of your business, unless I choose to make it your business. Full Stop.

Chapter Twelve

Chorlton, Greater Manchester, 2006

After a long bubble bath, I felt relaxed and light-headed. In fact, my head was spinning, probably because the water was so hot it was more like a bubbly boil wash. I always loved the water to be hot but forgot sometimes that it goes to my head and my blood pressure. I stood up and wrapped the towel around me. The steam in my tiny bathroom was thick, making it difficult to see through it. My legs were feeling weak and ready to fall from under me. *I need to lie down.* I opened the bathroom door and let the cold air from the stairway hit me, making me shiver. I lay on the bed, covered in a damp towel, my skin cooling from the air gliding through the open window. Outside, the sun had already gone down and the night sky engulfed my bedroom; the moonlight casting a projection of my window across the pale walls. I closed my eyes and let my mind drift away with my thoughts.

As the heavy haze began to fade, I listened to my heartbeat, throbbing in my ears. It was beating so fast, making my chest bounce. I inhaled the cool air and felt my diaphragm expand, then slowly exhaled, calmly and controlled. The thumping in my ears started to slow down and I lifted my hands to my head, feeling my tangled, wet hair. I liked feeling the coldness of my hair against my cheeks. I ran my hands down to my chest and slowly loosened the knot of my towel, exposing my round, supple breasts. My nipples were erect as they were kissed by the cold air. My hands glided gently over them, barely touching, teasing them. My skin was still damp as my hands rolled down my stomach. I felt my abdomen expand and collapse with every controlled breath. I wanted to explore further. I spread my legs gently and slipped my hand further down.

BRRRRRRING!! I jumped and gasped as my eyes opened with a start. *Damn doorbell!* I quickly got off the bed and found myself naked in front of the bedroom mirror. I grabbed my nightgown and quickly flung it on but not before I took in a quick reminder of the body I was encased in. A body that didn't resemble the one I had just imagined I was touching. Every time I fantasised about touching myself, I never got the chance to experience the pleasure I so desperately wanted to experience. In my dreams, I was the woman I always knew to be, inside and out. In reality, I wasn't quite there yet. I had a way to go until my dreams became something I could actually achieve. I longed for my body to be the way I needed it to be.

The doorbell rang again with its insanely loud ringing. It was like a school bell every time it went off. I hurried down to answer it and found an old, Greek man at my door. *My landlord.*

'Hello, dahling!' he said sweetly.

'Hello, Mr Kyriacou.'

'I've come to collect rent!'

'Oh of course!' I completely forgot he was coming round to collect his rent. He preferred receiving it in cash, which didn't really bother me.

'Would you like to come in?' I asked.

'Oh no, dahling. My legs don't like these steep stairs.'

'No worries. Wait here then,' I went back up to the flat and got his rent money. By the time I was back at the stairs, he'd already made it halfway up.

'Feeling okay there, Mr Kyriacou?'

'Oh yes, dahling. I thought I'd give it a try!'

He made it up the stairs and we went into the living room. I brewed two teas and set them on the dining table.

'How you liking your home, dahling?' he asked.

'It's lovely! Nice and cosy.'

'Ahh that's good. I'm glad you settling in.'

'Me too,' I took a sip of my tea.

As the hot liquid touched my lips, I suddenly realised that I had no make-up on, no chicken fillets, just my nightgown. I started to panic. *Shit!* What if he sees the shadowing of my freshly shaved face? What if he notices that I have a flat chest? Mr Kyriacou blew the edge of the teacup and took a hearty sip of his brew.

'Can I ask you something, dahling?'

'Yes, Mr Kyriacou, of course,' I said.

Here we go, he's figured me out.

'Do you have husband?'

'I don't have a husband, no.'

'Why is a pretty girl like you who makes such nice tea have no husband?' he said, chuckling as he stood up and walked towards the kitchen with his tea.

'I'm not sure!'

'Well, I'm glad a nice girl like you lives here. You be happy here,' he sipped the rest of tea and placed the cup gently on the kitchen counter.

'I have to go now. Nice to see you!'

'Nice to see you too, Mr Kyriacou.'

He made his way down the steep steps, and I prayed he didn't fall down them. He held on to the bannister for dear life and refused any help from me.

'Bye, bye, dahling!' he said as he took a couple of steps down.

'See you soon.'

I watched as he took a few more steps, then he turned to me again, 'Bye, dahling!'

'Bye!' I said. *Oh my god! It's going to take him a week to get to the end of these stairs.* He only had a few steps left before he turned to me again as I stood at the top.

'Goodbye!'

'Bye, Mr Kyriacou, take care!'

He finally reached the end and left. I walked down the steps to lock the door. As I closed the latch, I heard Mr Kyriacou leave through the porch.

'Bye, bye, dahling!' he said to an empty porch as the front door shut firmly.

I sat on my bed, giggling at my landlord's sweet nature, when I looked up at my reflection in the mirror. I looked at my towel-dried hair, looking messy and sexy. My fresh face, all rosy cheeked from the hot bath. My body, covered in a grey, cotton nightgown. All I could think about was how much I looked forward to expressing my sexual side. My Kyriacou may have interrupted me, but truth be told, I would've snapped myself out of the fantasy and stopped my hands from reaching between my legs.

One of the biggest struggles I battled with as a transgender woman during the early stages of my transition was expressing myself sexually. I just couldn't bring myself to masturbate. For countless nights, I lay on my bed, sexually charged, dying to pleasure myself. I imagined feeling the sensation of caressing my round breasts and slipping my fingers into myself, slowly stirring into an orgasmic sexual release.

In reality, I was encased in a body I had no connection to. The last thing I wanted to do was use my body for pleasure, because I didn't want to associate myself with anything masculine. It just wasn't me. I wanted to come, sweet Jesus, I wanted to come so hard you cannot believe! But I couldn't. Every time I looked at myself in the mirror, I always made eye contact. I didn't want to see my naked body because it felt like I was looking at somebody else. That type of feeling messes with your brain, believe me! Having so much sexual energy with no way of releasing it sucks donkey dick! Every time I lay on my bed feeling horny, I got up and substituted my sexual frustrations by eating crunchy peanut butter right out of the jar in the middle of night and ordering three Chinese takeaways a week.

I couldn't relate to the body I inhabited in a sexual way, which made expressing myself sexually very difficult. It wasn't like when I was younger when I had sex, because at that time I was still searching for answers and living life as a homosexual. That was no longer the case. I was a woman, clear as day. I thought that if I could find a guy who saw me as a woman, but knew of my situation, I could possibly be able to find answers and be able to express myself sexually with someone I felt comfortable with.

***

It didn't take long for me to settle comfortably in my flat on Oak Avenue. I felt safe and secure every day when I took the bus home from work and locked the front door behind me. I fell into a daily routine that I was happy to do, as it finally felt like I had some real control of my life as an independent woman. I was living my own lifestyle without having to explain myself to anybody. When I got home at the end of each day, I was in my own little sanctuary. There was only one thing that became more and more obvious as time went on. I was always alone.

Manchester offered a wide variety of places to go and people to see. Being new to Manchester, I didn't really know anybody or had any real friends. I knew people from work, but they were just acquaintances. Although most were lovely people, I couldn't say that any of them were my real friends. Even with Sheds, who I considered to be my closest friend in the workplace, had a life of his own outside of work and we didn't see each other socially. I felt very much alone. Manchester was widely known for having a very big LGBTQ community, with its own gay village on Canal Street.

It was something I knew of from hearing the boys at Never Never Land talk about when heading to the Village to party some more. I'd been living in Manchester for a few months now, but I had no idea where the Village was or how to get there. I didn't know any other person who I could relate to, so I found it hard to reach out to the community. Getting to Canal Street would have been an easy task, but the last thing I wanted to do was wander around the Village by myself, hoping to meet new people, as if I was acting out a trans version of Queer as Folk.

I knew a couple of people from work who frequented the Village on the weekend, but once again I didn't have much to do with them socially. Plus, it was difficult to relate to anybody because I was the only person I knew who was transgender. I would have loved to open up, but they couldn't understand how I was feeling. It's not easy opening up to people who you think wouldn't understand you, let alone try to explain that you're beginning to have female sexual urges in a male body. It's understandable that most friends will listen to your problems and be a shoulder to lean on, but I knew nobody I could truly relate to. I didn't have anyone to ask questions or share experiences with. Nobody to talk about all the feelings I was having and how I could express them in a way that I would actually enjoy.

The internet can be a great place to meet people when other options seem limited. Of course, caution has to be taken, which can be said about any means of meeting people in a social setting. I was feeling isolated in my flat, not really going out or seeing anyone else other than the people I worked with. I wanted to interact with people and have adventures in the hopes that I could express myself sexually as Yvy.

Social media was nowhere near as big as it is today, so I used smaller social network sites like online forums and dating websites. I wasn't necessarily looking for a one-night stand, nor was I looking for Mr Right to fall in love with. I just wanted to talk to people about life experiences. I had sexual urges, but I wasn't impulsive to the point that I only wanted to get laid. I was very much in control of my impulses, or so I thought. Speaking to guys online gave me a sense of excitement and fun, whilst keeping some anonymity as safety. I wasn't blind to the fact that there are a lot of weirdos who troll the internet for naive people to take advantage of, and I was certainly not going to be one of them. I knew that if I got talking with anyone online, I would be able to stay in complete control until I was ready to possibly take any further steps.

After my fair share of oddballs who weren't quite my cup of tea, I got to know a few nice guys online to talk to. We met on different forums and eventually began conversing over MSN Messenger, which was better and faster than having to log into different forums to talk. I got to know a guy who seemed really interesting. I was never the type to be overtly sexual or vulgar with guys online, so it was quite easy to filter out all the guys who spoke to me with that type of attitude right from the beginning as it wasn't something that interested me. Yes, I had sexual urges, but I was also a lady who didn't really appreciate being spoken to in such a perverse way by a person I knew nothing about. I wanted to get to know someone a little, share a few laughs, have a conversation or two and then see where it might lead. One guy fit that criteria and we began to talk on a daily basis. His name was Toby.

Toby and I got on great and always had laughs with each other. We talked about all sorts, hobbies, work, likes, dislikes. It was nice to have light-hearted conversations about myself without feeling like I had to hold back. He knew I was transgender, and he knew I was pre-op. I was very open with him from the very beginning that I had not undergone any type of surgery and that I only recently began my transition. He was intrigued by me and wanted to know more. It was nice, kind of like having a pen pal I could talk to. Our conversations started off innocently enough, but that quickly evolved to borderline flirtatious, but I never felt pressured to make any sexual overtures. I didn't feel the need to be sexually forward in order to keep the conversation going. We both enjoyed being flirty, but we were also able to keep each other interested without trying. It was such a nice feeling. It didn't take long before my favourite time of the day was getting home from work and logging on to Messenger to talk to him.

One Friday night, I arrived home from work and opened my laptop to see if he was online. He wasn't. I settled for the evening, making myself something to eat and putting on some *Sex and the City*, when my Messenger rang. *It's Toby!*

'Hi, Yvy!'
'Hey! How's your day been?'
'The usual, really. Just finished work. What you up to?'
'Watching SATC and eating pizza.'
'Wish I was there! You got plans this weekend?'

'No, I'm not doing much. Just chilling.'
'Do you fancy meeting?'

I hesitated. *Should I meet up with him?* I don't even know what he looks like! I mean, he described himself to me before but for all I know he could be lying. Then again, he probably thought the same thing about me. My Messenger sounded with a new message.

'You still there?'
'Yeah, I'm here.'
'I'm just nervous to meet up.'
'We've only been talking for a couple of weeks.'
'I get it. I really want to see you though. Pic?'

I sent him a picture of me, with my hair tied back and my make-up on, I was nervous about his response. I waited for what felt like a really long time for him to reply. I had sent the picture and could see the notification alerting me that he received it. The little dots at the bottom of the conversation thread began to move, indicating that Toby was typing something.

Here we go. What is he going to say?

His reply appeared on the screen…

'Wow! You're a stunner!'

I felt butterflies fluttering in my stomach as I smiled uncontrollably at the computer screen. I couldn't control my happiness when I read those words. When he sent a photo of himself to me, I was pleasantly surprised to see that he was a very handsome man. Tanned skin, defined looks and dirty blonde hair that brought out the green in his eyes. I wanted to meet him, but I was still cautious. I wasn't about to meet up with Toby just because I thought it was what I *should* do. I wanted to be in control above all else, making sure that I was being smart about my personal safety. I decided that before I met up with Toby face to face, I should at least web chat with him.

At the very least, it would prove to me that the guy in the photo is real and that I'm not being lied to. I had nothing to hide so I wasn't afraid to web chat. Thankfully, neither did Toby. I got to see him on my computer screen, smiling and waving at me, which was a relief. I felt much more at ease with the idea of meeting up, so we decided to do so. Toby and I made plans to meet up the next night in Chorlton but not at my house. I wasn't comfortable with him knowing where I lived. I decided to meet him a couple of streets away near the centre of Chorlton, an area I was very familiar with and that was very easy to get back home from should our first rendezvous not go to plan.

Saturday night soon came and I needed a little time to get ready. It was already pushing 9pm so I told him to come and see me in a couple of hours. I showered, did my make-up and hair and put on a cute outfit. I didn't want to seem too obvious so I dressed in a nice pair of skinny jeans, tan heels and a bohemian poncho that fell off my right shoulder. He told me where he was parked and I made my way over to him. I was so charged and a little scared. I was afraid of the unknown, of not knowing if what I was about to do was going to turn out good or bad. My heels echoed through the air with every step on the pavement, as I made my way to his car. My attempt to walk softly so not to draw attention to the girl walking by herself at night failed miserably, so I began to walk slower.

Don't rush, Yvy.

I saw his car, parked outside the Turkish takeaway. He told me it was red, but under the cover of darkness, it looked blue. I approached his car and I saw the silhouette of a man in the driver's seat. I couldn't quite see him clearly under the dim street lamps. I was nervous to open the door in case it was the wrong car and I accidentally got into another man's vehicle!

As I peered over to the car from across the street, Toby flashed his lights, signalling that it was him. I was relieved that it was Toby rather than some random stranger sitting in his car at night. I gave him a little wave and walked over to the passenger side door and got in. It was warm and fresh smelling, like he'd just had it cleaned. The radio was on with the volume really low. I brushed the stray hairs out of my eyes and looked over at Toby. There he was, looking just as handsome in person as he was on my computer screen.

He leaned over and gave me a kiss on the cheek; the smell of his aftershave was inviting. He settled back into his seat and looked at me with a little half smile.

'Hiya,' I said softly.

'Hi,' a paused silence made the atmosphere awkward.

'Did you get here easily?' I said, trying to break the tension.

'Yeah, it was easy.'

'Good! I like it round here,' I turned and looked out the windscreen at the empty streets. 'I've only been here a little bit but I think it's great. Everything I need is round here so I don't go into town that much.' *Stop rambling, Yvy!*

I realised he wasn't really saying much. *Oh God! He thinks I'm ridiculous!*

'You okay?'

'I can't stop looking at you,' he said with a half-smile.

'Why's that?'

'You're absolutely beautiful.'

My cheeks flushed. I couldn't believe how great this was going. All my fears and worries were slowly beginning to disappear, relaxing my muscles. Before I decided to meet him, I felt so much anxiety about my appearance. I was convinced that if he met me in person, he wouldn't like me. I completely misjudged the situation.

'Can I kiss you, Yvy?' he asked.

'Yes,' I wanted to pounce on him, but I decided to be subtle.

He leaned in and kissed me sweetly. He felt warm to the touch as I placed my hand on his face. I leaned in, pressing his lips a little harder to mine. When we released, I saw that my coffee shimmer lipstick had stained his face. I wiped some of it away with my fingers.

'Can I kiss you again?'

'You'll get lipstick all over you!'

'I don't care,' he said. 'I want to taste you.'

I signalled my consent and I let him kiss me. Here I was, with a handsome and charming guy who thought I was beautiful, having an intimate moment in the still of the night. I wanted to take him home, I wanted to see where that night would take me. So I made the decision to let down my guard and asked him if he wanted to come back to my place. I didn't feel like that I was rushing things, I mean, we'd been talking online for weeks. Now that we both knew that we were telling the truth about each other and we were who we said we were, it almost felt like we'd already been on a few dates and were at that point in the relationship when both of us wanted to take that next step. He accepted my invitation without hesitation and we went back to my flat.

We walked up the attic stairs and into the living room. I sat on the edge of the sofa and pressed my heels against the fireplace, pushing my posture up. Toby made his way over until he was standing right in front of me. He leaned in and kissed me, only this

130

time, his kisses were full of passion. He leaned into me and I lost my balance, causing us both to fall onto the sofa. It was so unexpected that we went from kissing to rubbing teeth. We burst into laughter as we struggled to fit on the tiny sofa, inevitably landing on the carpet with an uncoordinated thud.

Once we were down there, we got our bearings and he began unbuttoning his shirt. Suddenly, my anxiety came flooding back. *Oh shit! He'll want me to undress!* My mind starting thinking in overdrive. *He's going to see the gel fillets stuffed in my bra! He's going to see the ugly tucking panties!* I put my hands on his shirt and pulled myself up from the floor, escorting him to the bedroom. I pushed him on the bed and mounted him. *Take control, Yvy. Just have fun.* Toby undid his shirt completely and I took my blouse off. My lack of breasts wasn't too noticeable with the lights off. We did the usual foreplay routine. You know the one, when the guy sort of signals for you to go down south and take care a business for a good ten minutes before getting down to fucking. When Toby whipped it out though, I was more than happy to oblige.

Damn! If I had pearls on, I would have been clutching them at that point. *Clearly he's been eating his fruits and vegetable to grow that piece!* I didn't mind servicing him, but every time he tried to service me, I felt awkward. I couldn't relax. I just felt, well, vacant. *Enough foreplay, Yvy.* Toby was a top, which was definitely fine with me, and we eventually got down to it. It felt nice, but I've never associated sex with being "nice". How did Charlotte York put it in *Sex and the City*?

Don't you ever just want to be really pounded hard? Like when the bed is moving all around and it's all sweaty, your head is knocking up against the headboard and you feel like it might blow off? Dammit, I just really want to be fucked! Just really fucked!

As he climaxed, I felt his warm body shudder behind me, his slow and steady breath heating the back of my neck as his fingers grasped my hips. I felt different, not like the other times I'd had sex in the past. It didn't feel as good as I thought I would. In fact, any sensation of erotica disappeared in an instant. I didn't feel beautiful or special, I barely felt like myself. My eyes were tearing up which prompted me to get up from the bed, throw on my nightgown and excuse myself to the bathroom. I looked at myself in the mirror above the sink, my make-up smeared and my hair all dishevelled. I fixed my foundation and ran a brush through my ponytail. I dried my eyes before going back into the bedroom.

'Is everything okay?' he said, sitting up on the bed, his naked body exposed.

'Yeah I'm fine, Toby, I, I just don't feel so well for some reason.'

'Can I do anything?' he was so sincere when he asked.

'I think I just need some sleep. It's getting late and I have work tomorrow,' I knew how I sounded. I sounded like an arsehole trying to get him out of my house.

'No worries, I'll get out of your hair.'

I watched as he began to dress, and I felt awful for treating him this way. I wasn't being rude, but it didn't change the fact that I was kicking him out and probably making him feel a bit used. He finished dressing and headed to the stairs. I followed him down and unlatched the door. Before I opened it, I kissed him.

'Can I see you again, Yvy?' he said. I looked at his sweet face and I knew I wanted to see him again.

'I'd really like that,' I gave him one last kiss before he left.

As the deadbolt locked, I turned my back on the door and felt my stomach churn. I thought I was going to be sick at first, but after I washed the make-up off my face and went to bed, I soon drifted off into a dreamless sleep.

It took almost a week to feel like myself again. I was so confused about my encounter with Toby. It all started off so well in the car when we kissed. It was full of seduction when I felt his lips against mine. I thought it would continue when I took him home, but everything changed the moment we had sex. For the first couple of days, I wasn't sure what made everything change. Then, when I was at work taking calls, it hit me like a punch in the gut and I realised what it was that upset me so much. I used my body in a way that no longer brought me pleasure. When I took Toby home and undressed for him, I presented in a male form. Toby fucked me, which was pleasurable for him, but I took nothing from it. Toby wanted to be with me not because of *who* I was, but *what* I was. He loved the thrill of being with a pre-op.

I didn't like seeing myself that way. Every day, I'd do the same routine of hair, make-up and body shaping to hide any resemblance of the body underneath it all. I never wanted to see myself any other way than Yvy. I was a woman, but it felt like I was living life as a female illusionist until the day came when I no longer had to and could walk the streets as the real me. It had nothing to do with being

132

ashamed of who I was, it was more about self-reflection. The person reflected in the mirror was not the woman I felt inside, so I had to work even harder to try and be the woman I was inside every time I walked out my front door.

When I met Toby that night and took him back to my place, I had nowhere to hide. I took off my clothes and exposed the body underneath I never wanted people to see. I didn't realise it at the time, but that was what made me so unhappy. I hated using my body in a way that I felt no connection to anymore. Toby and I met up a couple of times after that night, but I never went to bed with him. I could tell that he knew something was wrong, but I didn't even know where to begin to tell him how I was feeling. He was such a sweet guy and I really liked him, but I wasn't up for this kind of relationship. Toby was happy to be with a pre-op trans woman. Although that was the label I had to bear, it wasn't who I was. I was so much more than that. I had to tell him how I felt. He had a right to know and I didn't want to string him along when I couldn't give him what he wanted. It wasn't fair. When I told him why I couldn't see him anymore, he understood. He knew our paths were very different and that we needed to go our separate ways. A part of me wished I could've given him what he wanted, but I knew that I had to be true to myself and not give in to another if what I'm getting from the relationship isn't making me happy. Although it hurt to let him go, we both knew it was the right thing to do.

From then on, I never bothered looking for men to talk to online anymore. I knew from first-hand experience that although it is perfectly fine for men to hook up with pre-op trans women, it wasn't something I was interested in doing. I wanted to feel like the woman I was and not be used for the body I had no choice at the time to live in. Just because I was having sexual urges, it didn't mean I had to act on those feelings if it gave me absolutely no pleasure. I was better off not acting on them at all. That way, I could keep the dream alive that one day I would be able to express myself sexually in ways I've always wanted.

I took the positive from my brief relationship with Toby and learnt that I didn't want that kind of relationship. Being with the type of man I wanted wasn't an option for me at that time, but I didn't see the harm in dipping my toe in the pool every now and then. I was completely un-clockable when I walked down the street; nobody could tell that I was transgender. The people who didn't know the truth thought nothing of me. I used that to my advantage one night when I was at home watching TV and began to get a little restless. Living in Chorlton, I had a range of trendy bars on my doorstep that I hadn't ventured out to before.

I decided to get dressed and go out for a while to clear my head. I was getting tired of being in the flat by myself and wanted to be somewhere else. I wasn't necessarily looking to meet anyone, I just felt like a change of scenery. I was only a stone's throw away from home so I didn't have far to go and I could get there easily.

I went to an Australian bar on the corner near the flat and took a seat at the bar. I ordered a drink, took a sip and began to unwind as I glanced around the bar. It wasn't very busy, but it was still early so I assumed it would probably get more crowded as the evening progressed. As I glanced around the room, I caught the eye of a gentleman who was sitting at a corner table. He was very handsome, young and had gorgeous long brown hair. He had a rocker look with his studded denim jacket and a smile that caught my attention. He saw that I was also by myself and made his way over to the bar. He ordered a drink for himself and asked if it was okay to sit by me.

As the evening went on, we got to know each other a little. Nothing too personal, just the standard things one talks about with someone new. He had no idea I was transgender, which made me feel wonderful. I was being treated as a woman. I felt so relaxed with him because I wasn't being asked questions about what was between my legs, or where I was up to with my transition. I was able to sit in a bar with a man and just be Yvy, without anybody knowing anything different. I was starting to get a little tipsy from the vodka lemonades that I let down my guard and had a little fun. He kissed me unexpectedly, something I wasn't planning on doing, but I decided to let him carry on. We moved in closer and started making out. We tucked ourselves in the corner where nobody could see us. As I kissed him, my head was swirling with intoxication. I was so turned on. I was enjoying myself, so I didn't think much of it when his hands began to roam. He ran his hand along my thighs, my skin feeling warm and plump. Before I could determine what to do next, his hand was between my legs. I always tucked using binding undergarments whenever I left the house, but being touched meant my body reacted involuntarily. To put it plainly, I was getting hard.

He stopped for a second and asked what that was between my legs. My heart sank to my arsehole so suddenly like the gravitational pull one feels when you jump in your sleep. I was still tucked, but it was clear from his touch that I was beginning to form a bulge between my legs. In a split second, I told him I was on my period and he immediately thought that what he felt was the cushioning from my sanitary towel. He believed me which made me feel even more uncomfortable. He said not to worry and carried on kissing me. I went from feeling so turned on and womanly, to completely out of place. I told him I had to call it a night and made my way home. He asked for my number but I told him to give me his number to call, knowing full well that this was the last time I was ever going to see him.

I wasn't ready for sex. I reached a point in my life were I was finally coming to terms with who I was and starting a life changing journey to achieve what I've always wanted. I knew I was still presenting as male under the illusion of make-up and clothes, but I was still able to look past the body I was in and see the real me. I thought I was able to express myself sexually but when I tried, I quickly realised that I couldn't do it without using the body I so desperately wanted to escape. I didn't want to be that kind of girl. I made the decision then and there that I would not engage in any form of relationships while I was on my journey of transition. My journey was all that mattered to me, more important than a momentary thrill with a lover. Furthermore, I didn't want to give myself to someone who wished to sleep with me because I was something different or exciting. One day, I'll be able to express myself the way I really want to, but that day hadn't come yet. I refused to let the men of my present use me for what I was, and I wasn't able to let the men of my future see me for who I was.

Chapter Thirteen

Hammersmith, London, 2007

'I just want to be me.'

I sat in the waiting room of the psychologist's office at Charing Cross Hospital, feeling incredibly nervous. It was my first appointment in London, I wanted to make a good impression. After receiving a referral from my GP, I had to first see a psychologist in Manchester so they could determine if I was a "suitable candidate" to be referred to Charing Cross. It was a strange feeling when I went to see the psychologist, as it felt less like an appointment and more like an interview. One wrong answer and my goal of being referred to London could disappear. That was the process. You first see a resident psychologist who determines your suitability, then you're referred to Charing Cross Hospital who book a series of appointments with a psychosexual therapist that digs into your lifestyle and determines whether gender reassignment surgery is suitable.

Before any of that, I needed my GP to refer me. I registered with a GP in Chorlton who was extremely helpful and referred me pretty much straight away. My previous GP in Blackburn was terrible. When I went to my old GP when I was much younger and thought I was gay, he told me that what I was feeling was wrong and that I shouldn't disgrace my family. I was advised to play football and spend more time with my brother instead. Seriously, I'm not joking! Gaining the confidence to see my GP and talk about how I was feeling took so much and to be told that my cure was to play football was fucking bullshit. Thankfully, my GP in Chorlton was much better and I saw a resident psychologist in Manchester a few months after my referral.

When I walked into her office, the psychologist looked at me with a surprised expression. I took a seat opposite her, dressed in a pair of skinny jeans and a tan woolly jumper, my hair in a high, short ponytail.

'Very nice to meet you. Sorry, Ivy, is it?'

'It's pronounced ee-vee.'

'Oh, I'm sorry!' she said laughingly, hoping that I wasn't offended.

'It's alright, lots of people get it wrong!'

'It's rare that I see people presenting at this stage.'

I was confused by this remark. 'What do you mean?' I asked.

'Most people I see are only just trying to understand their feelings of gender dysphoria and most of the time attend appointments dressed in attire that match their current physical self.'

'Well, I'm not here to question whether this is who I am, I already know it is. I just need your help to get me to where I need to be.'

She instantly understood where I was coming from and didn't hesitate to refer me to Charing Cross. I was still living in Chorlton when I got my resident psychologist referral, but by the time my first appointment letter from Charing Cross came through, I had moved from my little attic to a one bedroom flat in Salford. It was more spacious and closer to my new job at Salford Quays. I was a little discouraged that there wasn't a hospital closer to Manchester that I could attend. I knew that there was going to be many appointments to go to during this process and going to a hospital closer to me would have been so much more convenient.

With that said, I knew this journey wasn't going to be easy. Mum offered to come with me to my first appointment. My appointment was early in the morning, so I wanted to get to the Gender Clinic with plenty of time to spare. *Nothing can go wrong tomorrow.* For my very first appointment, we stayed over at a cousin's house that I was close to growing up. Before we set off to Charing Cross, I got up at 6 am to get ready. Mum and I figured it was better to stay over in London the day before my appointment, that way we wouldn't be rushing.

I wore a black low-neck blouse with a faux leather knee-length pencil skirt, black faux crocodile skin boots, a faux fur coat and a pair of gaudy, gold earrings. I looked ridiculous, like I was doing the walk of shame after a night of hooking. *What was I thinking?* Due to the fact that my top was low cut, I had to use a lot more foundation than usual to ensure my skin tone was even. I hated wearing make-up to begin with, but on this particular day, I felt like a clown. I couldn't have felt any more uncomfortable, a feeling I really could have done without considering I was on my way to convince someone that this was who I was. But I figured looking as feminine as possible would be what they wanted to see. My mood began to change rapidly. Mum and I made our way from Bow to Charing Cross on the London Underground. As we made our way, my feet were killing me in my black, peep toed court shoes. The layers of make-up was already sweating under the sweltering heat outside.

Epic fail, Yvy!

I didn't want to go to this appointment, I was doing it all wrong. *This isn't me.* I had no choice though, I came all the way down to London and it was my foolish mistake to dress in a way that just wasn't me. I was going to have to walk into that clinic and act as though I'm the most confident girl in the room.

We got to the clinic with plenty time to spare. We sat down in the waiting room which was pretty much empty except for a couple of girls. My nerves started to build, waiting for my turn. Any moment now, I was going to be called into a room and answer questions to convince them of who I was. I was scared that I might say the wrong thing and give the wrong impression.

I can't mess this day up any more than I already have. I felt ridiculous, persistently trying to pull my skirt down to cover my knees, only for it to inevitably rise back up again. My fishnet tights looked so cheap. *Why the hell did I wear these?* Before I could spin into complete paranoia, the therapist came into the waiting area and called my name. *Yivy DeLusa!* I didn't want to go in the therapist's office by myself, so I motioned for Mum to come in with me. I left the fur coat in reception, thinking I could at least leave some of this ridiculous outfit behind before going in.

I sat down in the chair opposite the therapist, my mum sitting to my right. My palms were sweaty and I felt my cheeks getting warm. I should have gone to the ladies and had a quick once over with my foundation brush. *I guess I'll just have to deal with feeling shiny.* The therapist had a desk in his office, but he didn't sit behind it. Instead, he sat in front of me, his legs crossed and holding a folder in his hands.

I felt exposed. With my low-cut top and fishnet tights, I felt completely out of place. I wasn't ready at all to answer any of his questions. I wanted to kick myself for making my first appointment such an uncomfortable one. The therapist started with the standard greetings, but I barely heard the words that came out of his mouth. I could hear a loud ringing in my head that was starting to take over.

Calm the fuck down, Yvy.

Mum gave my arm a little squeeze of support, which calmed me down a little. She's always had that special motherly touch since as long as I could remember. I composed myself, got comfy in the chair and smiled at the therapist. I made it all this way, so whatever happens, I'll deal with it. Before he began the appointment, the therapist told me that it would just be a few questions to get to know me little better.

'So, why are you here today?'

'I just want to be me.'

The moment the words came out of my mouth, I no longer felt tense. My head stopped ringing and my mind cleared of any negative thoughts. I said those words instinctively without taking any time to formulate an answer. I said it because I meant it. Never a truer word ever left my lips, and if I responded any differently to that question, I would have been faking. I never imagined that so few words could hold so much weight in that very moment.

'That's great to hear,' he said. 'I usually get much longer answers to that question.'

A newfound confidence radiated from within. I no longer cared about the clothes I was wearing or the make-up on my face, because the real me was coming through it all.

'Well, if I can be honest, I'm not here to talk about who I think I am. I already know that. I need you to help get me there.'

'And that's what we'll determine during this process,' he said.

'Exactly.'

One of the criteria for gender reassignment surgery was having to live as my chosen gender permanently for a two-year period at the very least. I despised that phrasing. *Chosen*. It made it sound like I just woke up one day and chose to be Yvy. I never chose to be this way, it's simply who I was. None of us choose how we come into this world, but we make decisions along the way to either embrace who we are or deny it. Me embracing who I was wasn't simply choosing it but accepting it.

By the time I went to my first appointment at Charing Cross Hospital, I had already been living as Yvy for nearly a year, which went in my favour with the therapist. I changed my name by deed poll, I left the bank and was working for a reputable health insurance company, had my own flat and was living independently. All good on paper but still, that wasn't enough. I was required to attend appointments at Charing Cross when they came through, which meant more trips to Hammersmith and more questions to answer.

An appointment with the Psychosexual Therapist usually came every few months. Over the course of the year, Mum and I travelled to London and stayed overnight in bed and breakfasts near the hospital in Hammersmith. Travelling to London Euston by train was always the fun part. Mum and I would start off at Manchester Piccadilly and board the Virgin train for the two-hour journey. I loved going to London with my biggest supporter.

Our relationship was clear, she was my mother and I was her child. But as I got older, I began to see her as Zohra, the woman. She was powerful, beautiful and intelligent. Growing up, I witnessed how she had to endure being with a husband who never appreciated her. I saw how she had to handle my brother and sister when they got caught up in teenage dramas. I watched as she maintained a household, kept down a job and took care of her own mother, never asking for anything in return. I always tried to be the quiet one and not cause her any grief. Not because I thought she'd be sick of me but because I didn't want to be another worry for her. When I moved away from Blackburn, I didn't get to spend as much time with her as I used to, so doing these trips to London felt more like a holiday for the both of us.

The first bed and breakfast we stayed at was a quaint terraced house run by an Eastern European couple and their son. I found it online and booked ourselves in before we travelled to London. It was cheap and practically across the street from Charing Cross, which was perfect.

When we arrived, Mum and I walked into the hallway after being greeted by an elderly lady. I looked around and noticed that every picture frame on the walls and sideboards had cats in them. Not actual photographs but paintings. They were those old, grandma-style paintings that had that '80s tacky charm to them. Now, I'm a big fan of cats and loved having them as pets, but this place took it to a whole new level. As we were taken further into the house, they had an array of porcelain cat figurines, wall mounted cat plates and crocheted cat toys.

The owners weren't big on pleasantries and quickly signalled their son who was sat in the living room to show us upstairs. The staircase was narrow, with thick brown carpeting that led to the upstairs landing. We settled in our room, which was dingy as hell, with its one double bed and cheap built-in furniture. The room had no complimentary items like a kettle to make a brew or bathroom soaps, just a couple of musty bed throws sitting by the window under the stained curtains.

'This place is creepy!' I said, smiling. 'It's so weird!'

'Well, look at it this way, we're here for your appointments and nothing else matters,' Mum said, always being rational.

'Yeah, you're right.'

'I need the bathroom, I'll go ask them where it is.'

Mum disappeared for a while and I unpacked my toiletries and relaxed with some TV. Mum came back from the bathroom a few minutes later, looking annoyed.

'I just got bloody shouted at!' she said.

'W-what? What do you mean "shouted at"?'

'I used the toilet across from us and the bloody old woman told me off for using it?'

'Why!'

'She said that was the family toilet!'

'You're joking!' I couldn't stop laughing.

'It fucking said WC on the door, how was I supposed to know we can't use it? I mean, it's only a bloody toilet!' she said as she chuckled uncontrollably. 'Then I asked if I could have a cup of tea and she shouted at me!'

'You're fucking kidding!'

'She was like, "Eh! Go outside if you want a drink!" I even offered to pay the old bat and she still fucking said no!'

'Note to self,' I said to her. 'Fuck staying here again!'

We kept to ourselves for the evening, watching a rubbish television programme documenting Samantha Mumba's attempt at a comeback, making sure that whenever we needed the toilet we used the correct guest restroom which was apparently on the second floor. By midnight, we were both still wide awake. I'd only been to one appointment by this point, so I had no idea how this part of my transition was going to go.

'I'm so worried,' I said, my head lying on the hard pillow.

'Why?'

'I don't want to fuck this up.'

'You won't do, just keep doing what you're doing and you'll get there.'

'I know I will, but I hate the not knowing. It's all up to somebody else.'

'Yeah but look how far you've come. You did that yourself,' she said, and she was right. 'When I was your age, I couldn't bloody do nothing. If my mother was like me, I wouldn't have lived the life I did.'

'Do you ever regret having us?'

'No. I wouldn't change having you lot for anything. But when I was your age, all I wanted to do was move away and live my own life. Instead I was held back and then I was lumbered with your Dad. I had nothing but bad choices.'

Mum moved over to me and I snuggled with her, hearing her heartbeat in my ear.

'Ever since you were little, you could see so far into your future and you've never stopped reaching for what you believe in. I wish I had that growing up. Don't waste it.'

I closed my eyes and smiled as she wrapped her arms around me.

'I love you,' I said as I slowly fell asleep.

In the morning, we went downstairs for breakfast. We walked into the dining room to find the table laid out with cutlery and baguettes. The son was already sat at the table, along with a couple that looked slightly uncomfortable.

Don't fucking blame them!

We sat down at the table, and the old lady came out with a plate with two pieces of toast and a sausage. As she placed the plates on the table and walked back into the kitchen, I looked at my mum.

'Is this it?' I said in a hush voice.

'Let's just eat it and leave!'

The old lady came back with some scrambled eggs and piled it on our plates until we had to ask her to stop. The table was silent as we all began eating, making it one awkward breakfast. Once we checked out, we left the house and stepped outside.

'Did we actually stay there or did I hallucinate the whole thing?'

'I have no fucking idea,' Mum said, 'but let's not stay there again!'

***

Travelling to Charing Cross Hospital on the train every time I received an appointment letter throughout the year was slowly becoming a chore, and the appointments themselves felt like a waste of time. I was asked the same damn questions over and over again and my answers never changed. I was tired of talking about the same thing constantly, as if it was some sneaky attempt at putting me off having gender reassignment surgery.

Do you know the risks of gender surgery? Have you considered you might not be transgender? Do you need more therapy?

I fully appreciated that every transgender individual's journey was completely different, with some resulting in gender surgery and others not. It's a personal journey to find your authentic self and I knew without a shadow of a doubt that I needed to have the surgery in order to achieve my authenticity. Before I could have gender reassignment surgery, though, I had to undergo hormone replacement therapy for a certain amount of time.

Every time I travelled down to London and stayed in a bed and breakfast, I prayed that the therapist would give me the green light and prescribe the hormone medication. I hated sitting in front of him, answering question after question, reciting the same answers I already gave the last time I was here.

Please just give me the fucking hormones!

Months and months of appointments went by and still no hormone treatment was given to me.

Hormone replacement therapy consisted of an initial series of testosterone suppressants, followed by female hormone tablets, typically oestrogen, that acted as a substitute for the naturally produced hormones that had been suppressed. If a transgender woman decides to have gender reassignment surgery, the dosage of female hormones is lowered post-surgery and no longer requires testosterone suppressants due to the body not producing biological hormones. Nonetheless, once hormone replacement therapy commenced, it was a lifelong commitment required on a daily basis. I knew that once I was on the hormones, my life would begin to see some real changes. When speaking with the therapist, I was told that hormone replacement therapy can decrease the growth of facial hair and aid in developing breast tissue, among other benefits that can vary for each individual. The thought of no longer having to wear make-up thick enough to cement bricks or worrying about how I moved in public in case my gel fillet breasts made that squelching sound in my bra was too much to bear. I wanted, no, needed the hormones so badly. Every trip to London meant the promise of finally being prescribed the treatment and taking a huge step toward my true self.

Living in my flat in Salford was becoming increasingly difficult to manage financially. On top of that, I hated having to wear all the make-up at work and seeing my five o'clock shadow begin to come through as the day went on. I hated feeling the discomfort of feminising my body. Most of all, I was beginning to resent having to smile my way through it all and act as though this was the real me. Nobody knew about me at work, not like they did at the bank, so I kept it to myself. The thought of having to deal with arseholes again like I did before was not worth the time or energy. I was through with explaining myself to small-minded people. Every night after work, I rushed into my bedroom and changed into my comfortable clothes.

I started with my make-up, that was always the first thing to come off. I always took my make-up off by firstly wiping half of my face completely clean, leaving the other side still covered. I stared at myself in the mirror, examining the vast difference between both sides.

For a brief moment, I saw both reality and illusion at the same time. On one side of my face, I saw the make-up that covered my skin. It was a shade darker than my actual skin tone, and by the end of the working day, it looked greasy and uneven against the facial hair that began to surface underneath it. On the other side, I saw the truth behind the mask. I called my make-up a mask because that's exactly what it was to me. Some women love to wear make-up every day, but I wasn't one of them. Make-up wasn't something I wore to enhance my beauty, it was more of a necessity at that stage of my transition.

When I looked at the clear side of my face, I saw the real me. I saw past the imperfections and saw the woman I was. I realised that life was very much like looking in a mirror. A mirror reflects what's in front of it. There's no escaping its reflection. That's how I felt every time I walked out my door. I had no choice but to reflect the image of the body I was born into and how I dressed to feminise my features. Society looked at me and saw a girl who went to work, did her job, pretty much kept to herself and then went home every day.

Not one person knew how much effort and energy it took to do that. To exist. I had no choice in the matter. If I wanted to reach my goal of being the true me, I had to persevere somehow. A mirror reflects the facts but eyes see the truth. Nobody knows the truth about someone's life at a first glance. You may have an idea about someone or hear a story about them in passing but only they know the truth. For me, the truth was that I could see the woman I wanted to become and knew that one day I'd achieve it.

Wiping off the make-up gave me a glimpse of the real me, because I wasn't hiding behind a mask anymore. I was away from the public eye and I no longer needed to reflect the image of a girl I didn't feel very comfortable being. I wasn't a quiet, reserved girl who wore make-up every day to go to work. *No!* I was a vibrant young woman with a taste for adventure who wanted to be free to express herself the way she wanted to. But that wasn't possible. I wasn't able to be that girl and I had a long way to go before I could.

For now, I had to settle with wiping away the girl I reflected to the world and see the truth in the mirror through my own eyes.

I knew the day would come when I no longer had to conceal the real me, but jumping through hoops at my therapist appointments was pulling me into a state of depression, especially when I was still not given the hormone treatment I so desperately wanted to start. I fell deeper into depression and found it difficult to find reasons to get up in the morning. Every day felt like it was getting longer, and the thought of reaching my authentic self was moving further and further away. I felt drained of energy, trying to hold onto some resemblance of hope.

By the end of summer, I decided to leave my job and move back to Blackburn for a while. I was so unhappy in Manchester, so it didn't feel like I was leaving some great life behind. A bit of time at home with my family was what I thought was best. I was a different person from when I left Blackburn, so I knew that when I returned, I wasn't going to live the same way as I did before. I wasn't going to be scared or intimidated or ashamed of who I was. I moved back home to try and lift my spirits, as I didn't want my depressive state to consume me. Although I was going back to my hometown that had very little good memories, being at home with my family was what I needed. Funny, considering Blackburn was a fucking train wreck of depression for me in the past!

After I returned to Blackburn, Mum and I continued to go to my hospital appointments. We found a cute bed and breakfast round the corner from Charing Cross that was absolutely beautiful. It was tucked away on one of the side streets not far from Charing Cross station. It was welcoming, clean and had a refreshment table in the bedroom, with a kettle, tea bags and cups! After staying in that awful crazy cat bed and breakfast, this place felt like a five star resort!

Whenever we went to London, Mum and I walked for hours down every side street we found in Hammersmith to see what little gems we might find. Spending some quality time with Mum was always a comfort to me. She and I never had to hold back when we were together and constantly acted the fool in public. From cracking jokes, to taking pictures of each other hugging trees in the park, we were always acting crazy. It was just what we both needed. I needed to alleviate the tension that weighed down on me every time I came to London and release it so that I didn't take that energy to my appointments. I never wanted the therapist to see me face-cracked in case it made a bad impression. It angered me that I felt that way, but I knew that I had to suck it up.

From the very beginning, I told the therapist exactly what I wanted and how I needed him to help me achieve it, but he also had a job to do. He had to ensure I was making the right decision and that I wasn't rushing into anything prematurely. I fully understood that. He didn't know what my life was or what I had been through, and although I wasn't happy with how I was having to come all the way down to Charing Cross to answer the same questions, I had to believe that it was all for a purpose. I persevered and believed that everything was going to work out.

Mum and I checked into the fancy bed and breakfast for an appointment at the end of summer and went on a little adventure, exploring the streets to see what we could find. We came across a long stretch of road that was filled with high street stores, markets, blocks of flats and more. Mum was all excited as we both absorbed the hustle and bustle of the streets, picturing ourselves renting a cute flat right there and being perfectly happy. A dream we both would've loved to have come to fruition. It was so clear that my sense of individuality, independence and flare for creativity came from Zohra.

After we had something to eat, we called it a night and went back to the bed and breakfast. The next morning, we checked out and made our way to Charing Cross. It was just another appointment and I was beginning to feel like I was simply going through the motions with little to no expectations. We arrived at the clinic and sat amongst a packed room of eagerly waiting patients. I was rarely seen on time, which always worried me as I had a train to catch at Euston station in a few hours that was non-refundable.

This time, I was called in to the therapist's office on time. The therapist and I ran through the normal pleasantries and update enquiries. *Everything is the same. Nothing has changed.* Toward the end of the appointment, he put his folder down and told me that he had discussed my situation with the other therapists and the next course of action was to start the hormone replacement therapy.

What? Excuse me?

I snapped out of my mundane haze and registered what he said. He explained the side effects and benefits with me again and said he'd contact my GP with his recommendations to begin the treatment straight away.

When he asked me if I understood, a smile formed on my cheeks so big that it hurt. After we left the clinic, Mum and I let out a massive scream in the car park and began jumping up and down with joy. I was ecstatic. *YEEESSSS!* I couldn't believe that I was finally going to start the hormones. My life was going to see a real change for the better and I couldn't have been happier. This meant so much to me and I was one giant step closer to my true self.

And Where Is the Body?

Let's take a moment to address something real quick. Your body is the only thing in life that you truly own. As a result, you have every right to be body beautiful. Now, when I say body beautiful, I don't mean copying or imitating what society defines as beautiful. Body positivity has nothing to do with being flawless, because it doesn't exist.

Being body positive has to start with loving yourself. If you love yourself, it shows with how you see your body. Having a little extra meat on your bones or not much at all doesn't make you disfigured. Having stretch marks or scars on your body doesn't make you ugly. Looking different to someone else doesn't make you less beautiful. We need to stop seeing individuality as something we need to erase and start loving ourselves more.

Once we do that, it doesn't matter what we choose to do with our bodies. Whether you love wearing make-up, want plastic surgery, gain or lose weight, anything at all. If you're doing it for you, then that's all that matters. Don't let anybody shame you into thinking that you are not body beautiful. It's true how the saying goes, your body is a temple and larger than life is just the right size!

Chapter Fourteen

Blackburn, Lancashire, 2007

The last thing I wanted when I moved back to Blackburn was to sink back into the person I was when I left in the first place. I didn't want to spend my days hibernating in my bedroom and skulking around with my head down every time I went out in public.

I wasn't the scared, uncertain person that cared about what Blackburn thought of me anymore. I wasn't about to go back to registering the opinions of people that I couldn't give a fuck about. When I packed my bags and moved back to live with my family, I vowed to continue being the person I was when I lived in Manchester. If anybody didn't like it, including my own family, then tough. *This is who I am and I'm not changing for anybody!* The days of trying to fit in and cater to other people were dead and buried in a ditch, along with all the fucks I used to give.

Since I'd already used the downstairs front room as my bedroom before I left to live in Manchester, Mum gave me the room again as my permanent bedroom. At this point, sharing a room with Fareed was clearly out of the question. Mum moved the sofas that were in the front room into the living room, and I bought myself a new bed to sleep in and transformed the space into my own little sanctuary. It was nice to have a proper bedroom instead of sleeping on sofas. Moving back to Blackburn meant packing up my entire flat in Manchester and fitting it into one room. I didn't have any other furniture except for my bed, so I was pretty much living out of boxes and black bin bags.

Moving back meant proving to myself that this wasn't a step backwards. I wasn't giving up or failing by going back home, as my transition was still going strong. I wasn't giving up on the most important journey I had embarked upon. Of course, I had misgivings about moving back home again, but my confidence gave me the strength to believe that no matter what happened, good or bad, I would stay true to who I was. I started searching for work, mostly in offices and call centres but found nothing.

Getting a job was a necessity as I had my own bills to pay, as well as helping out around the house the best I could. A few potential roles came up here and there, but I grew more and more frustrated when I applied for countless jobs and received no response whatsoever. I tried to find jobs in small businesses. I didn't want to work with loads of people like I used to in Manchester. I couldn't be bothered with having to explain my transition again and again.

One of the most annoying things about applying for work during my transition was having to explain myself to the recruiter. Every prospective employer required a form of identification. It became the thing I dreaded the most when applying for jobs. I had no passport or driving licence, so I had to provide my birth certificate instead. As it had my birth name and sex on it, I had to also provide my change of name deed and provide full disclosure. Every time, without fail, the recruiter let out a gasp of surprise and told me they never would have guessed. It got old, real old. In the end, I had to accept that in order to get a job I had to go through this humiliating routine over and over again. It was too much to hope that I could find a job where I could get on with my work without feeling like I was on show as the "transgender one".

When I lived in Chorlton, I jumped from job to job, having to deal with the constant struggle of explaining myself to employers when applying. Once I got the job, I never told anybody about my transition. I figured that if they didn't know, it saved me time and energy having to answer questions or deal with small-minded people like I did when I worked at the bank. What I didn't realise at the time was that with every passing day, I began to evolve into the woman I was going to become. I started to feel uncomfortable with the thought of being labelled as transgender. I saw myself as a woman, just like I saw myself as a girl when I was a child. As a result, not telling people at work about my transition had nothing to do with being ashamed of who I was.

To the contrary, it was because I was beginning to evolve more and more into who I wanted to be, and the thought of telling people about my transition made me feel like I was holding on to the past, when all I wanted was for people to see me the way I do. That became a very hard thing to do when the first thing I was required to present at my new employer was a birth certificate that relates to my birth gender. I was labelled as transgender at the start and from that moment on, it was hard to break through the label when I knew that a bunch of people in the work place were aware of my transition. I'd catch my work colleagues giving me a sideways glance or bring their conversations to a whisper if I walked into the break area to fill my empty bottle with water. It was hard for me to relax in the workplace, as I always felt like I was on show, even when I wasn't. It's like when you're a child and you steal some sweets from the shop. Because you know something the shopkeeper doesn't know, you begin to believe that every glance or movement from them means they're on to you. They're going to catch you and you'll have to explain your actions. The truth is, the shopkeeper has no idea what you're doing, and it's all in your head.

Looking for work in Blackburn was becoming hopeless. I had a couple of temp jobs for a few weeks, but they never worked out. Mostly because I didn't like working for managers who treated me like something they scraped off their shoe in order to cater to their self-absorbed, power-trip egos. I reached my limit with bad workplaces. Mum then told me about a job she came across that was very close by to where we lived.

'A sex shop? Really?' I said.

'Why not? It's a job, isn't it?'

'Well, yeah, I guess. But a sex shop?'

'Listen, you said you wanted a job where you don't want to interact with too many staff. Well, this is perfect for you!'

'How do you know?'

'Because I went for an interview there and you'd be practically running the shop by yourself!'

'Wait a minute,' I paused for a second. '*You* applied for the job?'

'Yeah!' she said, with a smile on her face. I couldn't help but chuckle at the thought of my mum applying to work in a shop selling dildos and porn.

'I don't want to apply if you have, Mum, what if I get the job and you don't?'

'Listen, as long as one of us gets it that's what bloody matters!'

She had a good point.

I had walked past the shop a few times on my way home from town before, and in all honesty, it didn't really look like the normal type of back alley, seedy, blacked out window type sex shops that you'd normally expect. It was on the high street but outside of the main town centre. It had two large display windows which presented an array of sexy lingerie.

'What's it like inside?' I asked her.

'It's alright. You'd be working by yourself when the manager isn't there, so you won't have to deal with working with anybody else.'

At first, I wasn't too keen on applying for the role, not because of the type of shop it was, but for the fact that the hours were pretty minimal. Mum twisted my arm and told me to at least give the manager my CV and see if I got an interview. I walked into the store for the first time and was pleasantly surprised. The door sounded with an electronic beep as I pushed it open, entering into the main half of the store. There were racks of kinky lingerie and costumes made of lace and PVC. As I walked further towards the back of the store, I noticed the manager standing behind the sales counter. The counter took up most of the back wall, and I could see that the store was in fact split in two by a partition wall.

When I peered around the corner to the other half of the store on my right, I saw a massive collection of sex toys and porn. To my left was a set of stairs that led to a lower floor. *I wonder what's down there.* The manager was a woman in her mid-thirties, her hair tied back into a greasy ponytail. She smiled and greeted me to the store. I handed in my CV and walked back out again. Mum was waiting outside while I handed it in. I didn't have any type of retail experience, so it was highly doubtful that I was going to get an invite for an interview.

After a few days had passed, the store manager asked me to come in for an informal chat about the role. I felt a little bit bad about going, considering Mum hadn't heard back from the interview she already had, but she encouraged me to go for it. Like she said, it didn't matter who got the job, so long as it was one of us. I went to the interview feeling quite bland. I wasn't too fussed about actually getting the job and since I hadn't had much luck in the job department, I was pretty much expecting this one to turn out the same.

I arrived at the shop on time and was greeted by the manager again. The shop was empty, which was strange since it was a Saturday afternoon. It was then that I recalled that the shop was empty the last time I came to hand in my CV. The manager took me behind the counter and into the small office that was tucked away in the corner on the left side of the shop. I walked in the office, and noticed a window that provided a full view of the right side of the store. I sat down, took a sip of water and waited for the questions to begin.

'My name is Kerry, I'm the store manager. Is your name pronounced Ivy? Am I getting that right?'

'No, actually it's pronounced "ee-vee".'

'Oh I'm sorry! I didn't mean to get it wrong!'

'No, it's fine, I get it all the time.'

'So you haven't worked in retail before?'

Here we go. This was her subtle way of rejecting my application.

'No, I haven't,' I said, knowing full well I didn't have the job.

'What could you bring to this type of role?'

'Well, I have plenty of customer service experience, I can work on my own as well as a team and I'm not afraid of dealing with complex issues.'

I can't tell you how many times I've used that line in job interviews. It got to a point where I didn't even need to think of what to say when asked that question. It rolled off my tongue like a well-rehearsed script.

'Okay, good!' her tone seemed less than enthused. 'Let me ask you, this role needs a person with a very confident attitude and who doesn't discriminate or judge easily. How would you say you would fit that description?'

I paused for a second. I'd never been asked that before in a job interview. All of a sudden, I was intrigued by where this interview was leading. I took myself off autopilot and really thought about what I was going to say. Being confident and secure in myself was the very essence of who I was. I felt like this was the perfect opportunity to tell someone just how confident I was. *Just say it, Yvy.*

'Being that I'm transgender, I think I fit that description perfectly.'

I waited for the obligatory gasp of surprise to come out of her mouth when I told her.

'I think that's fantastic. It's great to see someone so secure in themselves. It's that type of person I'm looking for.'

I was thrown by her response. This interview was going in a direction I didn't anticipate, and I was very happy about that.

'I know first-hand what it feels like to be judged or discriminated against, and in my opinion, if how you're living your life is making you happy, who am I to judge you for that?' I said.

'I couldn't agree more,' Kerry replied with a comforting smile.

I could tell she was becoming more drawn into what I was saying. The atmosphere in that small box-shaped office was becoming less monotonous and more like two girlfriends having a chat. She offered me a brew and we ended up having a couple of custard creams while the interview continued.

'So, there is something I need to ask,' Kerry said with a little twinkle of humour in her eyes.

'This shop gets its fair share of odd balls who try their luck with you. Do you think you could you deal with someone who is getting a bit out of hand?'

'I think so. I mean, I'm a very polite person but I don't tolerate any form of threatening or unreasonable behaviour.'

'And when it comes to sex, you'll need to know or learn some terms you might find uncomfortable.'

'Oh, I'm not easily offended when it comes to sex!'

'Do you know what bukkake means?' she said bluntly.

'Erm, if I say yes, will you think less of me?'

Kerry burst into laughter as soon as I said that. All I could think was *what the hell did Mum say when she was asked that question?* After we both controlled our laughter, I answered her just so she knew I wasn't fibbing.

After the interview, she showed me around the store. We started off on the left side, going through the selection of lingerie from the cheap and tacky budget wear, to the more sophisticated and pricy items near the counter. Opposite the counter was a wall covered in bondage accessories. Everything from floggers, whips, handcuffs and gimp masks were on show.

I could definitely get used to working here!

I saw the stairs that went to the bottom floor and I asked what was down there. As I followed her down, I saw another entrance to the shop on one side and a metal cage covering an entire wall on the other. My eyes lit up when I saw that inside the cage was a set of dungeon furniture. In the centre was a wooden bondage chair with wrist and ankle straps. To the left was a black leather rope bondage table and a wooden whipping bench on the right. I was beginning to get excited at the prospect of working here. I loved the thought of being in a place that was so sexually open and being completely unapologetic about it. We went back upstairs and she gave me a tour of the other half of the store.

'The shop is sectioned into two halves,' Kerry explained. 'Some customers come in to buy lingerie and don't necessarily want to see the hard-core stuff.'

'That makes sense,' I said as we walked down the DVD aisles. 'So we start with girl on girl, and high cost production titles. In the corner we have amateur porn, gay and transgender titles and then on the other side is barely legal, fetish and extreme fetish.'

As she walked me through the aisles, I went past titles like "Little Fit'un", "RearEnders", "How I Fucked Your Mother" and the ever so inventive "The Porn Apprentice". The cover showcased a naked tangerine-tinted Trump lookalike pointing at the camera with the tagline, "You're Fucked!"

The back wall was covered in with an array of discount videos and boxed-up sex dolls. On the other side of wall was the office where I just had my interview, and I noticed that I couldn't see the window that I looked through before I sat down to answer questions. I quickly realised that it was a one-way mirror.

'That's so we can keep an eye on customers when you need to.'

'Do you have to do that a lot?' I enquired.

'Not a lot, but we do get the odd person coming in to try and steal a dildo or have a quick wank by the DVDs.'

'Oh! Well, fair enough!'

I definitely want this job!

We finished the interview with a pleasant goodbye and I made my way home. I was feeling optimistic, but like most job interviews, you can never be too sure just how well it really went. I told Mum all about it when I got home and that I should receive a phone call about the outcome in the coming week. After about an hour, I received a phone call from Kerry, offering me the job.

***

For years, I pictured the kind of girl I wanted to be when I grew up. I wanted to be free to live each day with confidence and happiness. It's a wonderful escapism to be able to close your eyes and imagine yourself exactly the way you want to. As I grew older and life became more intrusive, the girl I used to dream of becoming began to slip away. When I closed my eyes, the girl I once saw clearly became a distant memory that I could no longer bring into focus. I had to try and build a new vision of myself, only this time, it was a lot more difficult. I wasn't merely daydreaming like I did as a child, I wanted to build a picture of the woman I knew one day I wanted to become.

I knew that the road of transition was going to be paved with challenges I was going to have to face head on, but at the end of that road was the woman I was going to become. It wouldn't be a dream, it would be a reality. It's a difficult task to imagine something so personal without the added anxiety of setting yourself up for failure if the person you envision yourself becoming turns out to be completely wrong in the end. Getting the job at the sex shop was a big step, as it was the first job I ever had where I was dealing with the general public face to face since my transition. I wasn't sitting behind a desk and seeing the same work colleagues every day while talking to customers on the phone. In this job, I had to run the shop by myself and deal with new faces walking through the door. I had to bring the woman I envisioned to the surface. The confident, independent woman that saw each day as a new opportunity to show the world just how fabulous she was.

By the time I got the job, I'd been on hormone replacement therapy for a few months and was starting to see subtle changes to my body. My breasts had started to form and I no longer needed to wear those awful squelchy gel fillets in my bra anymore. It was the early stages of development, but I felt comfortable enough to wear an A-cup without feeling like my breasts looked like a couple of fried eggs.

I treated myself to a gorgeous black Calvin Klein bra that gave me a little bit of cleavage and made me feel fucking sexy. Mum told me to start wearing a bra all the time so that I get a nice shape to my bosom as they developed. I also noticed that my facial hair growth slowed down considerably. I found myself only having to shave every other day as the hair wasn't coming through as fast or as thick as it used to. I didn't need to pound on the make-up anymore, just a light foundation was needed.

The hormone treatment didn't stop the hair growth altogether like I thought it would, but the consultant at Charing Cross did tell me before I started the treatment that each individual is different and the results can vary. Seeing my face become more feminine looking without all the heavy five o'clock shadow and make-up gave me a newfound confidence that I never felt before.

My new job provided a work uniform, a plain black polo shirt with the company emblem on the right in hot pink. The same colours as the shops interior. Kerry explained that the colours were used to give the shop a female and couple-friendly vibe, so as not to get a reputation as yet another creepy-looking sex shop. The first couple of weeks were spent training in house, but soon I was working on my own every Wednesday evening and over the weekends when required. It didn't take long for my hours to increase and I started working more weekdays whilst the manager was away.

A typical day at work consisted of me opening up the shop, serving the customers and making sure the shop floor was presentable. After a while, my responsibilities grew and I had to display and catalogue new stock, balance the tills and deposit money, take orders for international stock and ensure that the handover each day was smooth.

I loved being able to take on such a big responsibility of running a shop. I had a sense of purpose in the workplace that I never experienced in any other job. Every day I arrived to work with my company polo shirt, low riding hipster jeans that hugged my hips, my long dark hair flowing and a smile on my face that needed little to no make-up. The woman that was once a thought in my mind was starting to take on corporeal form, looking back at me every time I paused in the mirror. I no longer needed to dream about the woman I wanted to become, it was already happening. I didn't want it to stop, I had to keep going. I was so excited to see where this was going to lead me.

I could see my path was preparing me for the next chapter in my life that was so close I could almost grab hold of it. I knew that there were a few things I needed to do to prepare myself for the next chapter, both internally and externally. The first was my facial hair growth. I wanted it to stop completely. The thought of having to shave my face after I had gender reassignment surgery just wasn't an option. I wanted to feel wholly as a woman and leave behind any aspect of my former self.

I heard about Intense Pulse Light treatment, or IPL, which apparently worked wonders for hair removal. I couldn't afford to go to an IPL specialist, so I decided to purchase an IPL machine and do it at home. After weeks of using the machine, it turned out to be a complete waste of time and money. I subsequently went to an IPL specialist in Blackburn to have my first treatment. Feeling the searing burn of the pulse light penetrate my skin and destroy the hair follicles was an excruciating pain. At the beginning, I had extensive IPL treatment across my cheeks, upper lip and neck area. It took months and months of costly visits, but eventually I saw that my skin was getting smooth and hair free. All the pain and soreness was completely worth it.

Working in the adult industry was something that I related to in certain ways. For one, I was not shy when it came to the subject of sex. I was fascinated by everything sexual and was always intrigued by the deviant delights and curiosities that came with sexual pleasures. Most importantly, I related to its unapologetic expression of being. Here I was, stood amongst rows and rows of pornography and I felt right at home. I loved the fact that I was a part of an industry that didn't need to explain itself. Instead, it sent a message out loud and clear that it will enjoy the pleasures in life and be exactly what it wants to be and if you don't like it, then don't participate. That's exactly how I felt. I no longer felt the need to explain myself to anybody. I loved being who I was and I refused to conform to what others felt I should be doing. I saw myself as a beautiful, intelligent, sexual woman and I was excited to see what the future held. It gave me the outlet to truly be myself in a place that was as free and unapologetic as I was.

I felt a change in me that gave me the confidence to let out a side of me that never really came out to play. I was flirty, sassy and developed a quick wit that I used to engage with customers. The shop saw all walks of life come through the door and each time it gave me a new opportunity to express a different side of myself. To my customers, I was Yvy. The gorgeous, young Indian girl that had a confident attitude and wasn't shy talking about sex. I loved it! I met some pretty interesting people at the sex shop. Some good, some bad and some, well, let's just say I got a crash course on just how sexually deviant some people wanted to be.

The Pakistani man I called "Creepy Hair Guy" came into the store one day through the downstairs rear entrance. I'd never seen him before, but Kerry mentioned that he came in infrequently to peruse the porn and leave after he was done trying to get away with touching himself in the corner. I was told to watch out for him because although he was harmless and didn't proceed to take his actions too far, you never know when someone might decide to take their touching to the next level and try to get away with masturbating on the shop floor. I was told he rarely came in the shop, no pun intended, so it wasn't too much to worry about.

He was tall, with short bushy hair and wore sandals with ill-fitting trousers that stopped just before his ankles. He never made eye contact and walked with caution. I could tell straight away before he headed to the porn, that he was scanning the shop in case there was somebody he knew already inside in case he needed to make a swift exit. Once he felt safe enough, he went straight to the lesbian porn section. He didn't notice me when he came in, as Kerry was at the till and I was sat in the office having a nosy at what he was getting up to. He picked up a few DVDs and put them down again, occasionally peering over at the till to see if she was keeping a watchful eye on him, which she was. He headed towards the stairs to leave through the back door when I stepped out of the office and brought some stock to the counter. He stopped in his tracks and stared at me for a moment. He gave a nervous half smile and scurried off down the stairs and left. After that, he began to visit the shop a lot more often. In fact, he visited every week on a Wednesday night for months. He'd come in, scan the shop, smile at me and head to the lesbian porn.

One evening, he plucked up the courage to speak to me. I was leaning on the counter, going through the weeks purchases, when he came over.

'Hello,' he said in a hush voice.

I looked up at his nervous face and instantly knew this was going to turn into an awkward moment.

'Hi.'

'You Pakistani?'

'No, I'm not,' I looked back down at the purchase sheet, indicating that I didn't want to carry on with the conversation.

'You Muslim, though?'

'Nope!' I said bluntly. I learnt from experience not to open that door when confronted with that subject with Muslim people, as it tend to get complicated and borderline confrontational when I said I wasn't Muslim. I found it extremely tiresome to explain to Muslim men how I can be Indian and not Muslim without them thinking I'm going to Hell. Standing there in front of him from behind the counter, I didn't want to open that can of worms and get a lecture on morals from a man who just spend the last 10 minutes readjusting his cock to lesbian porn in public.

He got the message and proceeded to take the conversation in another direction that I wasn't expecting. Had I known it was going to go in this direction, I probably would have happily talked about my ethnic background.

'You have pretty hair,' he said as he leaned onto the counter.

I didn't say anything. I just stood back from the counter and rested my back against the shelves lined with Poppers. I folded my arms and gave him a stern look.

'Please can I play with your hair, please?' he asked with a sincere tone.

'Errr, no!'

'Okay then. Goodnight!' he went downstairs and the beep of the back door sounded as he left.

The next week, he came back in, much more confident than before. His eyes locked with mine straight away and he said hello.

In my head, I already felt completely over it. I knew it was inevitable that he was going to ask me another direct question, his demeanour was a lot cockier than before. As suspected, he came over to the counter after rummaging through the porn and smiled.

'Hello!'

'Hi.' I was totally over the conversation before it even began.

'I had a dream about you.'

'Good for you,' I really didn't want to entertain him and tried to answer in a way that might end the conversation. Clearly, it didn't work.

'I put your hair around my dick and came on you,' he said with such joy in his voice.

I had no clue how to react. I honestly didn't know whether to kick his arse out of the shop or take pity on him and say something like, *Awww, good for you. Glad you had fun!* Before I could respond, he looked at me with an awkward gaze. His cheeks were flushed with embarrassment. He told me he had to go and waved goodbye. I never saw him again after that evening.

"Sunday Man" was a man who came in every Sunday morning with a smile on his face. I opened the shop at 10am and he came in minutes after I unlocked the door. Sometimes, I was still setting up the shop when he came in, like he'd been waiting in the gravel car park at the rear entrance for me to lift the shutters. He always entered the shop from downstairs and was always so enthusiastic. He was a perfectly well mannered gentleman in his late 60s who came specifically to buy porn.

Unlike Creepy Hair Guy, Sunday Man actually purchased stuff when he visited. He was very chatty, asking me who I was when I first started, always being polite and respectful. I didn't know his name, so I was unsure how to address him. When I asked what his name was, he asked if it was okay if he didn't tell me. I was perfectly happy with that, as he seemed like a decent enough person and if he didn't want to share his name then that's his choice. He was a short, white man, around 5'6", with silver hair and a sagging face. He always wore a long tan coloured raincoat, and I could see that underneath it he wore a light blue shirt. He had a thing for transgender porn. Kerry told me that he'd been a regular customer since as long as she could remember, and he only ever shopped for trans porn.

Every Sunday, he'd come in and Kerry kept a note of any new trans porn releases so he could have a look at before buying. When he decided on what he wanted, he asked that the DVD be put in a black case without the sleeve, insisting that he paid cash and be given no receipt. The following week, he'd come back to the shop with the same DVD and exchange it for another one. As we kept the DVD sleeve under the counter, Kerry put it back into the case and re-sold it at a discount price.

This was Sunday Man's routine. Every week, like clockwork, he came in. I looked forward to seeing him, because he was always talkative and became friendly with me and with Kerry.

'You're a very pretty lass! What you doing working in a place like this?' he asked with glee.

'What do you mean?'

'Well, you could be doing anything, instead you're 'ere talking to an oldie like me!'

'Awww, well to me a job's a job. So I don't mind talking to you.'

'I wish my wife was as talkative as you are, love.'

'Yeah? Why, do you and your wife not get along?'

'When you get as old as me, love, you learn when to not argue. You never win with women, lass!'

'You might be right there!'

'Anyway, that's why when she's off and away at church, I come here.'

'So, you watch—'

'She wouldn't understand, love. Besides, I'm not hurting anybody am I?'

'How long have you been watching these when your wife's at church?'

'Few year now, lass. She wouldn't understand. Back in my day, I'd 'ave been chucked out in the street if anybody found out. That's why I like it 'ere. You and Kerry are top gals. Never judge or 'owt.'

In some ways, I felt a little sad for him. I could only imagine just how long he'd been attracted to pre-op transgender women and was petrified to say anything to anyone. Although he wanted to uphold some form on anonymity, it was clear that he felt so at ease when he came to visit me or Kerry, as we didn't pass any judgement on him. He felt comfortable enough to be himself and could see it every time he walked in with a smile on his face.

I became a very fast learner on how to deal with the range of personalities that walked through the door. Young lads looking for cock rings and trying their best to embarrass me by asking which vibrators were the best. It never phased me, and on more than one occasion I recommended the most expensive vibrator, promising it would put their girlfriends in a come coma since they obviously weren't up to the task. Then there were the many, many, *many* older gentlemen who felt the need to show me pictures of their penises on their phones, as if I asked them to do it.

Word got out that an Indian girl was working in a sex shop and I began to notice a lot more Asian men visiting. Most of them did the same old dance of looking wary and uncomfortable, going straight to the porn, never buying anything and then leaving. And of course, I dealt with a number of men who spent an hour going through all the porn, then told me that I was going to Hell for working in a sex shop. The way I dealt with them was pretty easy, all I needed to do was remind them that I'm getting paid to be in a sex shop, so what the fuck was their excuse? That normally shut them up.

One day, a young Indian woman came into the shop. She was by herself, which surprised me. She was traditionally dressed and she came in through the street entrance on the high street. Normally, I found that most Asian customers came in the downstairs entrance to avoid being seen, but this woman seemed different. I watched as her hands moved through the lingerie with an inquisitive look in her eyes. As she moved closer to the till counter, she noticed the bondage wall and expelled a short gasp. I greeted her, but she seemed to be in a daze. She didn't respond at first, peering around the corner to the other end of the shop. I assumed she was doing what most customers did, checking if there was anybody she recognised around. I looked in her eyes and saw something that completely threw me. I saw complete and utter fear. I saw a woman who was frightened of everything around her, like a lost child who was unfamiliar with her surroundings, thinking everything was out to get her.

I approached her again with a calm tone and asked if she was okay. She turned to me and locked eyes with mine. She had beautiful brown eyes. I asked if she was alright, and she smiled and preceded to ask me some questions.

'I don't know what I'm doing here,' she said with a shaky voice.

'Well, is there something you're looking for?'

'I guess so. I don't know where to start.'

'Tell me what you're looking for and I'll help you.'

She paused. I could tell that she was trying to find the right way to say what she wanted to say. The words just wouldn't come out of her mouth, like her lips were forcibly sealed shut.

'Are you looking for something particular, or do you need some advice on anything?' I said.

'Yes. I need advice.'

I understood her perfectly, but I could tell that she was struggling with her English pronunciation through her thick accent, 'No problem, what do you want to talk about?'

'My husband want to try something with me, but I don't know what it means?' she said, her hands shaking.

'What does he want to try?'

'He say he want to do it anal with me.'

Working at the sex shop, I heard it all. I had a countless amount of people coming in and asking for all sorts of things, from adult nappies and self-ejaculating dildos, to enema porn and grandma sex dolls. It never phased me because I was comfortable at the thought that these people wanted these things for their own pleasure.

Not one person came across as uncertain about their particular appetites, and in some ways, it was quite nice to be trusted enough to be invited into their way of thinking, even if it wasn't my personal taste. When this woman walked through the door, I could tell that she was uncertain about something. The more I interacted with her, the more I realised that it wasn't uncertainty, it was fear. She had no idea what she was asking or what her husband was asking of her. She had no place to turn to and it suddenly dawned on me that it must've taken so much strength and courage to walk into the shop in the hopes to find someone caring enough to help her.

At that moment, I made the decision to take on that responsibility. She had no idea what anal sex was, so I had to think of the best way to explain it to her. When I told her what it was, she was floored. She was appalled that her own husband wanted to do that, as she had absolutely no idea people did that in the first place. I could tell that she was getting really upset so I made both of us a cup of tea and had some biscuits.

It didn't take long for her to relax. I got to know her and she began to open up about her relationship with her husband. I'd never been the kind of person to pry into other people's personal lives, I always thought that if someone wanted to tell me their problems, they would. Her name was Yasmine, and she was married to her partner for nearly two years. She moved from India when they married and she was daunted at the task of adjusting to completely new surroundings when she moved to the UK.

She insisted on standing when she spoke to me, inching left and right like she was preparing to make an exit. I asked if she wanted to sit down, if just for a little while, so she can at least sip her tea in peace. Something about her screamed out to me. I could see in her eyes that she was holding so much in but didn't have anyone to purge her thoughts and feelings on to.

As she sat down and cupped the mug in her hands, our conversation took an intimate turn.

'So, do men like doing it anal?' she asked, her cheeks flushing.

'Some men do. Some women do too.'

'Why?'

'It's about having fun. Having sex should be fun for both of you.'

'I hate it. I don't like it.'

I didn't know what to say. I tried to wrack my brain for something to say to Yasmine, but nothing sprung to mind. Here was a woman, sitting in a sex shop sipping tea, telling me that she hated sex and was scared of a sexual act that her husband was giving her no choice but to participate in. I felt for this woman. I wanted to say how I really felt about the situation, but I was worried about the ramifications of my opinion.

'What don't you like about sex?' I asked.

'Everything. I don't like how it feels. I-I don't know what to do for him,' tears began pooling in her eyes. 'My job is to be his wife, but I'm scared I cannot do things for him sexually. He take care of me, so I have to do things I don't understand for him.'

'No, you don't,' I couldn't hold my tongue any longer. 'You shouldn't do anything you don't understand just because he wants you to. If you don't want to do something, just tell him. Talk to your husband and let him know how you feel. If you don't want to do something, there's nothing wrong with that, but he won't know that unless you say something.'

Yasmine's hands began to shake as she put the empty cup down on the counter. She looked up and smiled. I could tell I was the first person she'd spoken to since arriving in Blackburn that told her she actually mattered. As she continued to tell me how her life mostly consisted of serving her husband with a silent tongue, her heartaches began to pour out like a fountain, leaving her feeling lighter. I tried to explain the best I could that being in a relationship meant both people are able to talk about how they feel, without being scared of how the other person will react. The trouble with that was the fact that I was fully aware of what a traditionally old school Muslim relationship could be like, and it doesn't always involve acknowledging a woman's feelings.

'Sex should be an enjoyable experience. It shouldn't be a chore.'

'I will remember that,' she said, as she picked up her bag to leave. 'You should come round my house for chai sometime! I would really like that!'

'Yeah, that would be lovely!'

She gave me another smile and thanked me for being so nice. She stood up and left the shop, giving me a wave before I heard the door close behind her. Later that night, I began to worry about what I advised Yasmine. For all I knew, her husband was a wife beating son of a bitch who didn't tolerate back talk from women.

What if he's beating her right now because of what I said to her?

I started to worry. What I advised her was the right thing, as I didn't point blank tell Yasmine to refuse sex, I basically told her to talk about it with her husband so they can work through their issues.

Maybe I was better off not saying anything at all.

For days, I stood at work thinking about Yasmine, but the more I did, the more it bothered me. I couldn't change what I said to her so all I could do was hope that things worked out for the best. Over a month had passed, and I was working a late Wednesday shift, when the front door bell chimed and I came out of the office to find Yasmine walking towards me. I had that sinking feeling, you know, that sudden feeling when you're walking down a flight of stairs and you miss a step.

I noticed that she was smiling, the biggest smile I'd ever seen.

'It's good to see you, Yasmine!' I said with a smile.

'Good to see you too! I wanted to come say thank you!'

'What for?'

'I talked to my husband and tell him how I feel. He was so understanding and felt bad for upsetting me.'

'That's great! I'm so glad he listened to you. So how is everything?'

'We are taking it slow pace, but he wants me to enjoy *it* too. I said no bum stuff though. That's for dirty girls.'

I chuckled when she said that. Yasmine gave me a hug and thanked me for letting her know that she had a voice. I never saw her again, but it felt so good knowing that I was able to help her through her struggles in my own way. I was happy knowing that the person I was and the person I was going to become was a generous and caring human being.

By the time the New Year rolled in, I finally got a date for my gender surgery and began counting down to the big day. I wasn't nervous at all, because I knew that everything I had done to get to this point was exactly what I wanted and needed.

Chapter Fifteen

Kensington, London, 2008

It's hard to describe how it felt, waiting at Piccadilly station for my train to London Euston to pull in. For months I had imagined how I would feel when I got to this point after I was given the date of my surgery. *September 16th.* Maybe I'd feel excited, or nervous, or even scared. It was a huge step for me. The final stage of my transition was upon me and all the years of struggling to achieve this was coming to fruition.

I thought I'd be filled with overwhelming emotion that would be too much to handle. I imagined my heart giving up and my body combusting from the build-up of energy that screamed to be released for so long. Instead, I felt something I never even fathomed. I sat in the train station with complete clarity. My mind was calm and void of all the baggage that cluttered my head for so many years. My thoughts and memories of the past were gone, and my mind was open to the possibilities of the future. The train pulled into the station and I knew that as soon as I stepped on, things were never going to be the same. Mum and I planned on making the trip to London together. She was with me every step of the way during my transition and always came with me to my therapist appointments. The only problem with this trip was how much it was going to cost her. It wasn't like before when we spent one night in a bed and breakfast, went to an appointment and came back home. This time I was going to be in hospital for two weeks, possibly longer.

'I'll be fine going by myself, trust me,' I said to Mum as I packed my bags for the trip to London.

'No, I'm coming with you.'

'You'll have to stay in a hotel for two weeks! That won't be cheap! Besides, you'll only be able to come see me during visiting hours. What will do the rest of the time?'

'It doesn't matter, you'll need someone there with you after the surgery.'

'I'll be fine! Seriously, you don't need to worry. You can come and get me once I can come home.'

'I don't like this. I don't like you going for surgery without me coming with you.'

I went over to her and gave her a kiss on the cheek. Her face was full of motherly concern.

'I'll be okay, Mum. I'll be back before you know it.'

I would've loved for Mum to be by my side, but I was in safe hands and I tried to reassure her that I'd be okay going by myself. I wasn't scared of going, I was more glad than anything. I felt as though I had already gone through all the struggle and pain throughout my life and now it was finally coming to an end. Nothing could bring me down. Mum had always provided such strong support, not just for me, but for Fareed and Feroza too. She always let us know that we could count on her for a shoulder to lean on and gave us sound advice. Mum's advice was always right. She always had my best interest at heart, so I knew that any advice that left her lips were always for my benefit. This time, though, I decided to go against her advice, and went to Hammersmith alone. I wanted this part of my journey to be just mine. I didn't want to share this with anybody. It had to belong to me and me alone.

Mum was devastated to see me go when I left the house for the train station. She wanted to come with me, regardless of how much money it cost her. She didn't care how much a stupid hotel cost, she knew what was more important. She couldn't stand the thought of me waking up in a hospital bed in Charing Cross all alone. She hated the fact that she would be so far away as I had such major surgery. Mum knew that there could be a real possibility that when I walked out the front door, I may never return. She didn't want to stay home and let her youngest child face something so huge without her mother by her side. I made my decision and I was fine going by myself. I could tell she was worried, but she kept her feelings in and ordered me to call her as soon as I arrived in London.

I arrived at Manchester Victoria from Blackburn and made my way to Piccadilly. The Virgin train to London Euston pulled in and I found my seat with ease. I wanted to be one of the first people to get on the train as it wasn't due to depart for another twenty minutes, thus avoiding the dreaded pushing and shoving to find my seat in the aisles as they filled with people putting suitcases away. I always booked a table seat for me and Mum in the past so we could both sit by a window that way, so I decided to do so this time. I knew Mum wasn't with me, but it was still nice to sit by a window and place all my snacks and drinks on the table. I put on my iPod and chose to listen to some Janet Jackson.

More people started boarding the train, seating themselves in neighbouring carriages.

I enjoyed the quiet on the train. I wasn't in the mood to be seated near screaming children or rowdy idiots who liked to shout for no reason for the duration of my journey. The train seats indicated whether they were reserved with a white card sticking out the top of the headrest. I was relieved to see that all the seats around the table were all vacant, which meant I had the whole area to myself. As the beat to *That's the Way Love Goes* kicked in, a man entered my carriage and found his seat on the opposite side of me. It wasn't a table seat, and I saw him struggle with his briefcase and sports bags as he attempted to put them in some kind of order before stuffing them into the overhead compartment.

He was tall, handsome and smartly dressed. He looked like he was in his forties but I could tell he worked out a lot as his build was more muscle than fat. He was the rough around the edges type that I always found attractive. He sat down on the aisle seat and placed his briefcase on the window seat beside him. As he settled into the groove of the cushioned padding and stretched one of his legs in the aisle, he let out an exasperated sigh and closed his eyes, tilting his head onto the headrest. Without thinking, I took out my earphones and asked him a question.

'You already having a bad day and it's not even 10 am yet?'

His head jolted up and he opened his eyes, regaining focus. He looked over at me with bemusement, not responding for a moment.

'Are you talking to me?' he said.

'Of course I am. We're the only people on this carriage, aren't we?' he smiled. 'Yes actually, it's been a rough start to the day. I missed the last train and First Class is full, so I have to sit here.'

'Well, you're not missing much in First, unless you prefer to pay extra for a free newspaper and a lamp on a table you don't really need.'

'What's your name?' he asked. His head tilted and his smile grew bigger.

'It's Yvy.'

'I'm John.'

'Nice to meet you John'

'How's your morning going, Yvy?'

'Not too bad, thanks, a few stress levels below yours by the looks of it.'

'Can I ask, do you make a habit to talk to strangers?' he said with a grin.

'You're not a stranger. You're John. The guy who missed his train and ended up talking to a girl who *didn't* miss her train.'

He sucked his teeth as he turned and faced me directly, looking happily perplexed at my quick response.

'Would it be okay if I sat with you?'

'Sure, the seats are open.'

He moved over with his briefcase and jacket. I assumed he'd sit opposite me but instead he sat beside me, which felt a little intrusive. His aftershave was a seductive, masculine musk that made his presence a little sweeter. As he relaxed next to me, he opened his briefcase and took out his laptop. The train doors shut and we started to move.

We're on our way.

For the first half of the journey, we got to know each other more.

'So, where are you off to?' he asked.

'I'm going all the way to London.'

'Me too. I'm down there for business. How about you?'

'I'm visiting someone. A friend who's in hospital.'

'Oh, I hope they're okay.'

'Yeah she's fine. So what type of business are you doing?'

'I'm in Public Relations.'

'Fancy! That must take you to some pretty cool places!'

'It does actually. I was recently in Monaco which was fantastic. A lot of corporate events to work, but I've been to the south of France a few times. It's one of my favourites.'

'Sounds like fun!'

'What do you do?'

Hmmm, how am I going to put this? Ahh fuck it, just tell him!

'I work in a sex shop.'

'No, seriously,' he said after a brief pause.

'Seriously. I work in a sex shop.'

'You mean like Anne Summers?'

'Err, no. Anne Summers is a pet shop compared to where I work. No, I'm talking the full deal. Bondage, R18s, sex dolls, the works.'

John's face lit up with delight. Any conversation about Public Relations came to an immediate standstill.

'So you must see a lot then?'

'I certainly do. Nothing shocks me these days.'

'You must get some interesting customers float your way!'

'You could say that!'

As the train continued its journey, I told him a few stories of some of the customers I had encountered. By the time we reached Milton Keynes, we began to talk more about ourselves.

'Being in PR means I have to be able to strike up a conversation with anybody. I find you fascinating though?'

'Why's that?' I asked.

'Because you beat me to it. It's been a long time since someone struck up a conversation with me. I like it.'

'I'm glad you're so pleased!'

'And if you don't mind me saying, you're a very attractive woman.'

'Thank you and no, I don't mind!'

The train reached Euston and pulled into the station.

'What are your plans for this evening?' John asked.

'Not much, really. I'm going to the hospital in the morning so I'll be having a relatively quiet night.'

'If you're free, I'd love to see you again later. Can I have your number?'

I paused, trying to contemplate exactly where this was leading but decided to throw caution to the wind. This was my last night before my surgery and I was going to spend it in a hotel room by myself, bored, anxious, possibly scared. That's not how I wanted to spend my evening. John seemed like a nice man, and if I played this right, I would be in complete control and have a little adventure tonight.

'Tell you what, John,' I said. 'You give me your number.'

'Here,' John handed me his business card. 'Call me tonight. I'd love to hear from you.'

I checked into the bed and breakfast in Hammersmith, showered and relaxed for a few hours. I called Mum to let her know I arrived safely and then took a disco nap. I love a good disco nap, you know, the type of nap that you wake up from so refreshed and full of energy…and ready for disco! It was creeping towards 7pm and John's card was still in my purse.

Should I call him? Would that make me look desperate? Maybe I should leave it.

I decided to text him instead. That way, I can avoid any awkward conversations and simply wait for his response.

'Hi John, it's Yvy.'
'Hello, there! Glad to hear from you.'
'What you up to?'
'Not much. I'm just with some associates.'
'Sorry if I've disturbed you.'
'Not at all. Would you care to join me?'

I wasn't too sure about meeting him and his "associates". For all I knew his associates were a bunch of sex crazed maniacs who were planning to lure me into their den of sexual depravities.
Wait, that does kinda sound like fun, Yvy!

'Where are you?'
'The Hilton hotel bar. Kensington.'

He's at a hotel. *Bad idea, Yvy.* Although, he did say he was in the bar, not a hotel room. If it was too scary, I could easily leave if I needed to.
Ahh just go, Yvy.

'I'm on my way.'

I arrived at the hotel in a black cab, dressed in a simple white maxi dress and my favourite pair of butterfly earrings. I walked into the lavish reception and made my way to the lifts. One of the staff members told me that the bar was on the top floor of the hotel. I pressed the button for the bar and the gold lift doors closed as I entered. I watched as the floor numbers flashed above me.

4, 5, 6, *maybe this is a bad idea*, 10, 11, 12, 13, *am I making a huge mistake?* 19, 20, 21, 22, *it'll be fine, Yvy, chill*, 25, 26, 27, 28, DING!

The doors opened and I walked into the bar. It was plush and extravagant, with a view of London that was absolutely breathtaking.

John spotted me walk in and called my name, I smiled and made my way over to where he was, sitting with a bunch of smartly dressed men. They were all drinking and laughing, standing up to greet me as I approached. It turned out that John really was having a few leisurely drinks with some work colleagues. I was a little nervous at first, as I wasn't quite sure what to make of the situation, but I soon calmed down when I realised that I was in a crowded bar and I could very easily dismiss myself and make an exit if I was feeling uncomfortable for any reason.

We all sat together, drinking cocktails and while they all talked about business deals, I sat with my frothy cappuccino. I couldn't partake in the cocktail consumption, given that I was being operated on in the morning.

'So Yvy...' one of the men said, 'do you work in PR with John?'

'No, I don't. But I have a feeling you already know that!'

'Why do you say that?'

'Because if I did, I wouldn't sit here for thirty minutes with nothing to say.'

He looked at me for a brief moment, not quite sure what to say. I leaned in slightly towards him.

'I'm just joking!' the group started to laugh, including John.

'Yvy works in the adult industry, you know!' John said.

'Really?' the men said in unison.

'Well, yes, but not in front of the camera, I'm afraid. Sorry, boys!'

The group continued with their shoptalk and I carried on nursing my cappuccino. I felt John's eyes all over me. He watched as I picked up the spoon and dipped it in the froth that sat on top of the cup. I knew he was studying me, so I brought the spoon to my mouth and slowly licked the cream off, delicately resting it inside and pulling it out, revealing a clean spoon. John bit his lip in excitement, knowing that I was teasing him. I had him under my control.

Before we knew it, it was already creeping toward 10 o'clock. The guys were beginning to leave the bar and I was ready to head back to my hotel and get some sleep before the big day. I had a pretty enjoyable evening, even though it was spent listening to a bunch of people talk about work.

Beats sitting in a hotel room by yourself!

All of the associates had left and I was gathering my coat and purse, ready to make my way back downstairs.

'Where are you going?' John said, surprised that I was leaving.

'It's getting late so—'

'Oh no, I've made reservations.'

'Reservations?'

'For supper.'

'At 10 o'clock at night?'

'You've never had a late supper before?'

173

'Not *that* late, John!' I said with a sarcastic tone.

John laughed.

'Trust me, you'll love it.'

His face gleamed as he put his arm around my waist and walked us over to the restaurant on the other side of the floor. The restaurant was pure decadence. I looked around, at the stylish women dressed in Chanel and YSL eating tiny portions of rich food on their glistening white plates. I saw men enjoying their company, dressed stylishly in suits and drinking expensive wine, with the occasional table ordering a chilled bottle of champagne that sat in a silver ice bucket.

Wow, talk about being out of my element!

The Maître d'hôtel escorted us to our table and I made myself comfortable, sitting by the window and taking in the view of the twinkling city beneath me. The table looked exquisite, with its crisp white linen cloth and sparkling glassware. I looked down and found a white serviette folded beautifully on a plate. An array of knives and forks sat on either side.

'You alright, Yvy?' John asked, giving himself an opportunity to brush his hand against my arm.

'Oh yeah, I'm fine, it's beautiful in here, isn't it?'

'Yeah, I have quite a lot of business meetings in this hotel so I like to dine here when I can.'

'Nice!'

The waiter came over and placed a breadbasket in the middle of the table with cups of humus. As he placed them on the table and left, I realised just how hungry I was. I picked up a piece of bread and dipped it in the humus. It was delicious! I made sure not to shove the entire piece of bread in my mouth and tore a piece off first before dipping it in the humus. Still, I looked over at John and he had a smile on his face that he was trying his best to mask.

'What?' I said, pushing the bread to the side of my mouth with my tongue.

'Nothing,' he said, still smirking.

'No, seriously! What are you laughing at?'

'You're supposed to use the spoon.'

'What spoon?'

He picked up a small, white spoon that was nestled in the breadbasket.

'Use it for what?' I said, genuinely unsure by what he meant.

'You use it to put the humus on the bread.'

'Why?'

'What do you mean?' John said. It was his turn to be unsure.

'Well, why use a spoon when you can just dip the bread in the humus?'

John paused to actually think of a reason why it was necessary to have to use a spoon.

'Oh, I see,' I said. 'This is a posh people thing, isn't it?'

The waiter brought over the menus and everything sounded so sophisticated and delectable. None of the dishes on the menu had a price next to it. *How are you supposed to know how much it is?*

'How do you know what everything costs?'

'Don't worry about it, Yvy. It's on me.'

'Oh, I know it's on you, but how do you know what the damage is?'

'You crack me up you do! I love your little dimple on your cheek when you smile like that!'

My cheeks flushed and I looked at the menu, trying to decide what I wanted.

'What do you fancy, Yvy?'

'I'll have the steak for my main…and for starters…I think I'm going to have…the lasagne, 'cause I've never seen lasagne as a starter before!'

'Good choice!'

The waiter came over and took our orders, leaving John and I to talk a little more.

'Tell me more about what you actually do, John.'

'Well, I've run my own PR firm for years, handling corporate function for high paying clients. It's busy work, but I love what I do. It's not as exciting as your job though!'

'Well, I wouldn't call my job exciting if I'm honest! I mean, it does have its perks, but it's just a job. It's not my career or anything.'

'Who do you want to be then?' *A question I've been asking myself for years.*

'I'm not sure yet,' I replied. 'But I've got plenty of time to figure that out!'

The starters arrived and the waiter placed the plate in front of me. My forehead wrinkled as my confused expression grew. On the plate was a round, pale blob, topped with a frothy white weirdness. It looked like it fell out of a baked beans can and kept its shape on the plate.

'That's a lasagne? I've never seen that before!'

I picked up a fork and dug into the lasagne. As the fork penetrated each layer, the shape of the lasagne fell apart, revealing a hefty amount of mince and cheese. Once again, John had an awkward look on his face that he was trying to conceal as he ate his calamari.

'What's up?' I said, shovelling lasagne in my mouth pot.

'It's nothing really; you're just using the wrong fork for your starter. It's adorable watching you, Yvy. I'm telling you!'

'Look, John, there's something you should know about me,' I said with a big smile on my face. 'I'm from Blackburn. Do you know where that is?'

'Yeah, I do, but I've never been there before,' he replied.

'Well, being from Blackburn, it doesn't take all *this* to woo me. I mean, I'd be happy with a meat and potato pie, chips, peas and gravy from the chippy honey! So if you're trying to impress me with all this posh stuff, believe me, you really don't have to!'

John's face lit up and he burst with roaring laughter. It was the sexiest thing he'd heard in a long time. I was confused at first, not sure if he was serious or if it was a not so subtle way of mocking me, but I soon realised he was completely serious. He became so fascinated by me that by the end of the dinner, I had him eating out the palm of my hand, metaphorically speaking. He was charming, and I was definitely attracted to him. He made no efforts to hide the fact that he liked me, finding any reason to gently touch me or rest his hand on my knee.

It was getting close to midnight, and we finished our delicious three-course meal. It had been such a magical night, that I didn't want it to end. However, I knew that our time had an expiration date. I went to the restroom on the other side of the bar to freshen up. I re-applied my lipstick and made my way back to John, who was waiting by the lift.

As he kissed me on my cheek, he leaned in intimately.

'I can't resist that adorable dimple, Yvy,' he said with a grin.

'I hate that you can make me feel shy.'

'Funny, I quite enjoy it!'

'I would never have guessed!'

'You ready to get out of here?' John asked.

'Yeah, sure. You going to tell me how much that meal cost you then?'

'Nope!'

We got in the lift together but before the gold doors could close completely, they suddenly opened again, letting in a bunch of people who pressed for the lift too. For the entire journey down to the lobby,

John and I were amidst a bunch of tipsy socialites, planning the next spot to visit on their night out.

Before we knew it, DING! The doors opened and we all poured into the hotel lobby. As we walked toward the entrance, John held me close, our steps moving in unison. We stood outside, my hair blowing behind me, when John stopped me in my tracks and pulled me towards him. I could feel his breath on me, wanting to kiss me. All I wanted in that moment was for John to kiss me. Kiss me so hard it hurt. He laid a sweet, gentle kiss on my lips. It was the sweetest kiss I'd ever experienced in my life. He pulled his lips away from mine and brushed the flowing hairs from my face.

'Would you like to come to my place for a nightcap?'

Oh, how I wanted to say yes. In that moment, I pictured going with him to his flat. I pictured making love to him. I didn't want this night to end. But Cinderella was getting closer to midnight. It was time to say good night to the dream before reality dawned.

'I'd love to, but I have to go. I had a wonderful night though.'

'Can I see you again?' John said as he laid another kiss on me.

'I'd like that.'

I pried my hand from his and jumped into a black cab. As the door slammed shut, John blew me a subtle kiss and the taxi pulled away from the Hilton.

Not exactly how I dreamed this night would end.

Chapter Sixteen

Charing Cross Hospital, Hammersmith, 2008

I sat in hospital ward reception, feeling a wave of emotions wash over me. I was so calm and focused on the journey here from Blackburn, I even felt calm on my date with John the night before, but now I felt as though any semblance of calm was out the window and on its way to a sunny destination, possibly the Greek Islands.

I arrived at the hospital at 10 o'clock in the morning, exactly when I was supposed to. The reception was completely void of any patients, just rows of empty plastic white seats nailed to the floor. I was glad to have a bit of quiet and sat with my bags at the far end of the waiting area. I wanted to collect myself and calm my mind so I could string some clear thoughts together.

As the hours went by, patients started filling the seats, but my name wasn't being called by the nursing staff. By 2 o'clock, the room was above capacity, and my head was stirring uncontrollably. I had no idea what was going on or why there was such a huge wait. I expected to be allocated a bed much earlier and have my surgery the same day. As the afternoon grew later, I realised that it wasn't very likely that I'd be having any surgery that day. The increasing sound of frustrated patients and angry relatives was unbearable, like a constant tolling of a grand bell hitting my temples.

When I finally got called, I was given a bed in a shared ward away from all the noise. I felt relieved at first, but as soon as the noise around me stopped, the noise in my head grew louder. My bones felt heavy, too heavy to hold up. I wanted this feeling to go away, but I couldn't just shake it off. I climbed onto the bed and rested my head on the thin pillow. Closing my eyes, I tried to rest my thoughts but realised it wasn't my thoughts keeping my mind racing, it was my feelings. My feelings were so chaotic, I didn't know how to process everything at one time. It was tiring to think or speak, all I wanted was to rest for a while.

The nurse walked in and interrupted my train of thought. 'Hello Edie.'

'It's Yvy.'

'Oh, I'm sorry, I didn't mean to—'

'No it's fine. Really.'

'Your surgery is set for tomorrow morning.'

'Oh, it's not happening today?' I said unsurprisingly.

'No we've had to postpone some surgeries due to others taking longer than expected.'

My heart began to beat harder. *Oh, God! Did something go wrong with someone's surgery? What if I'm next?*

'It's nothing to worry about,' the nurse said. 'These things happen all the time. A nurse will come see you in the morning to prep you and you should be in surgery by around 9 o'clock.'

'Prep me?'

'Yes, you'll need to have an enema at 6 am.'

'Oh, well, okay then,' I said, trying to hide my nerves.

The nurse left and I found myself alone in the wardroom. I looked at the three vacant beds around me, thinking that soon enough they too will be occupied by people like me, feeling nervous. It was then that I realised I was thinking way too much and I just needed to chill out. *Go to sleep, Yvy. Tomorrow, your life will change forever.*

It was an early start the next morning. By 9 o'clock I'd already gone through my pre-op flooding and I was squeaky clean for my surgery. The sleep did me a world of good, but I had a nagging feeling that something just wasn't right. The nurse came to wheel me to theatre and I laid there watching florescent lights flash before my eyes as the bed wheeled through corridor after corridor. When I got too flustered and felt short of breath, I'd close my eyes and let my thoughts take me places I didn't expect. The craziest images and sounds would swirl around in my mind, comforting me somehow. Even though nothing that came to mind made any sense, I'd lose myself in the craziness and let go of all control, feeling free.

Lying on the hospital bed, I wanted to feel that way, even just for a moment. My life was about to be put into the hands of skilled doctors, but for all I knew, I may never make it to that life changing chapter I so longed to achieve. The more I tried to control those thoughts and feelings, the more I realised it was an exercise in futility. So I closed my eyes, hoping that I could escape for a moment and saw something that caused my heart to thump hard in my chest. I saw Mum, standing in front of me. She was laughing and smiling, the way we do when we act a fool on one of our London trips. It was so nice to see her. I didn't bring any family photos with

179

me to the hospital, so seeing Mum right in front of me felt so warm and comforting.

The bed came to an abrupt halt and my eyes strained to regain focus on the harsh, penetrating lights as they opened. The image of Zohra vanished like a dream, leaving the reality of a cold, box shaped room with nurses prepping me for my surgery. I felt so lonely, which was a feeling I seldom felt. It was then that I realised what was missing. *Mum should be here.* Mum told me that she didn't care how much it cost her to come with me to London, so long as she could be here for me. I never understood where she was coming from, as I was blinded by the sheer excitement of finally having my surgery. Lying on that hospital bed, I understood what she meant. She knew that I needed someone to be there when I was wheeled to theatre. She knew I'd need someone to be there when I woke up.

I realised I made a terrible mistake by telling her to stay home and save money. All I wanted was for her to take my hand and feel her soft delicate skin. I felt tears well up in my eyes as the anaesthesiologist injected a milky substance into the cannula.

'Count backwards from ten for me, Ivy,' she said softly. *It's Yvy, damnit!*

10…9…8…7…6…

I woke up hours later in the hospital ward. My eyelids weighed a tonne and I felt sick to my stomach. My mouth was dry and tasted of copper. It took a moment before I noticed a woman standing at the end of my bed, smiling. *Mum, Mum is here!* The blurry haze began to fade and I saw the nurse standing at the foot of the bed. She smiled and proceeded to talk as she took my blood pressure, but I wasn't registering anything the nurse said.

All I could think of was I wanted to see Mum so badly. I wanted to call her to let her know I was alright, but I could barely hold my head up, let alone have a phone conversation. I heard my phone vibrating on the bedside table and buzzed for the nurse as she had already left and asked her to get it for me. I flipped it open and saw John's message, all four of them. *Whoops!* I mustn't have heard my phone go off yesterday.

'Hello, Yvy, so glad to have spent time with you.'
'How are you?'
'Can't stop thinking about you.'
'When can I see you again?'

It felt nice, knowing he was thinking of me, but the fifth message made me forget anything John had to say.

'Thinking of you. Hope you're doing okay. Love you!'

It was from Mum. I gulped down some water to sooth my scratchy throat and called her. I just wanted to hear her voice. It rang a few times and then, she picked up.

'Hello, my Pretty Zinta!' she said, happy to hear from me.

'Hello! Sorry if I sound like a basset hound! My throat is killing me!'

'Aww doesn't matter. How are you feeling? Are you alright?'

'Yeah, I'm okay, just really tired.'

'You're bound to be. Has the consultant come to see you?'

'Not yet, I've only just woke up properly so they'll probably come round later.'

'Ah okay, well, make sure if you're in pain to let them know. Don't lie there quietly. I'm glad you're okay though.'

'I promise I will do. I'm going to have a rest now but I'll speak to you later. I love you.'

'Love you, my precious gem!' Mum said with a giggle.

After we said goodbye, I felt so much better, like she'd taken away all of my worries and anxiety. Hearing her voice made it feel as though she was right there with me. I didn't tell her how much I missed her, but I could tell she knew it already. She always had a feel for what her children were going through.

When I first moved out, I received random text messages from her asking if I was okay whenever she was getting a weird feeling in her stomach. She'd tell me that her gut instinct was kicking in and she was making the rounds, messaging me, Fareed and Feroza to make sure we were all okay and not in any trouble. Most of the time she was right, and most of the time it was Fareed who was up to no good. But every now and then, she messaged me right at a time when I was feeling low or confused, and it was as though she was also feeling what I was. She must've been a witch or something in a past life because I swear that woman has powers.

I snapped my phone shut and lay comfortably until I drifted off again, feeling more relaxed. When I woke up a second time, the sunlight was no longer streaming through the windows. It was well into the evening and the ward had an eerie silence. I tried pulling myself up to a more comfortable sitting position, but the bandages hindered my movement. I wasn't in any severe pain, but I could feel the tightness of the bandages cutting into my skin around my hips.

I tried to get into a comfortable position without moving too much and noticed that I was no longer the only patient in the room. To the right of me was a girl, sat up watching a movie on a portable television on wheels. I couldn't see her clearly as the curtain was pulled halfway between us but could see she was blonde, around my age from what I could gather. Her gaze caught mine and when I smiled, she returned the same courtesy. I saw that she was watching *From Dusk Till Dawn*.

Ugh! One of my faves! I was tempted to ask if I could watch it with her, but given that she was probably here for the same operation as me, I highly doubted she was able to get up and move the television. I looked at the clock above the open doors and it was almost two o'clock in the morning. I shut my eyes and returned to sleep.

'Morning! Breakfast is here!'

My eyes opened to a brightly lit room and an overly enthusiastic nurse pushing a trolley with jugs of hot water, cold milk and boxes of cereals.

'Would you like a cup of tea?' she asked

'Urmm, yeah, please. Milk, two sugars,' I said, half asleep.

'What would you like for breakfast? We have cereal, toast, fruit—'

'Can I just have a couple of biscuits, please?' I was in no mood to eat a load of food. My stomach was still in knots from the anaesthetic during surgery.

'Can I have the same please?' the girl in the other bed said. I looked over and saw the curtain was pulled back all the way and was able to see her clearly.

'Sorry, you can only have liquids' the nurse said to her.

She leant back on the bed and rested her head on her pillow as the nurse poured her a brew too and then left the room to serve the other patients. We caught each other's gaze and I decided to introduce myself.

'I'm Yvy.'

'Hiya, I'm Jennifer.'

'Hi. You here for gender surgery too?' I asked.

'Sort of. I already had my gender surgery six months ago.'

'Oh, okay,' I was intrigued by her answer, but I wasn't going to push her into telling me why she had to come back.

'Where are you from?' she asked.

'I'm from Blackburn.'

'Did you come here on your own?'

'I did. My mum wanted to come too but I told her to come and get me when it's time for me to leave. Did you have to travel far to get here?'

'No, I live in London, I've had to come back here, let's see, this is my fourth time now.'

'How come?' the words just slipped out. I was hoping that wasn't being intrusive, but I felt like she invited the question.

'I had complications after surgery,' her face looked sad, almost defeated when she said that.

'I'm sorry, I shouldn't have asked.'

'No, it's okay. It's me who doesn't want to hear it.'

'I get that. I feel that way a lot of the time,' I decided to change the subject to break the tension.

'I was so jealous of you last night!'

'Why?' Jennifer asked. Her sad face soon turned to a bemused one.

'You were watching *From Dusk Till Dawn*! That's one of my all-time faves!'

'Awww, you should have said so! I would've rolled the TV your way!'

'Oh, nah, it was like 2 am, I didn't want to disturb you.'

'No please, disturb away! I'd rather have you disturb me instead of a nurse. Oops, speaking of which!'

The breakfast nurse came in, holding a clipboard.

'Lunch menu!' she said with her painfully cheerful tone.

'Didn't you *just* bring us breakfast?' Jennifer said sarcastically.

'We provide the best service here, Jennifer!' the nurse said. 'Well, I'm still nil by mouth, but please feel free to tell me about everything I can't eat. I'm dying to know, honey!'

For the first couple of days, it wasn't easy being bound in bandages, barely able to move. The day came for the bandages to come off, and I honestly couldn't tell if I was excited or scared out of my mind. In just a few seconds, I was about to see what I've always wanted to see when I opened my legs for the very first time. The bandages were unravelled, and I felt the sweet sting of pain as the pressure around my hips started to throb. The cuts on my side were exposed and the nurse had to clean and plaster them up. I didn't care though, it felt so good to be out of those bandages.

The nurse handed me a mirror and I slowly lowered it between my legs to have a look. Through all the bruising, swelling and stitches, what I saw was truly beautiful. A work of art. I was blown away, so much so that I didn't even realise that I was packed with gauze down there.

'Yvy, we're going to take the gauze out now. So it might feel a little strange.'

'Strange? Urrm, okay then!'

'Don't worry, it won't hurt, but try to relax as much as possible. Lie back, Yvy. You'll need to be flat.'

It's a known fact that when someone tells you to relax, chances are you're not going to. The pain and discomfort from the cuts on my side made it difficult to relax comfortably, which made this moment even more nerve wracking. The nurse found the end of the gauze and began pulling it out of me. At first, it seemed to be going smoothly, but as more iodine soaked gauze came out, the more I started to feel it tug inside me. It was a feeling I never felt before, I was totally freaking out in my head.

It was my first experience of my body as Yvy, the first time I had felt something so intimately surreal. It was so strange to feel something moving inside me for the first time. At first, it was just plain strange, but soon the sensation was quite pleasurable. The gauze continued to be pulled out, *Holy crap! How much can fit in there?* I felt the gentle tugs here and there as the nurse continued to make sure I wasn't in too much pain. I was in a lot of pain, but I was able to see past it. I'm not one to complain when something hurts, especially when there's not much I could do about it. Pulling the gauze out did hurt, but if I complained, it only prolonged the time taken to take it all out. Instead, I looked past the pain and found myself relaxing more. I became more aware of the sensation inside me, something I wanted to feel for so long.

The last tug of the gauze as it came to an end was the most painful. My body flinched and I felt the cool air fill me. Once it was over, my muscles loosened and felt less tense. Although I still had the catheter fitted, I could move my lower half much more freely. I looked at the massive pile of brown gauze and couldn't believe that all of it fit inside there.

'Okay, Yvy,' the nurse said, putting the gauze into the waste disposal unit by the door. 'It's time to start dilating!'

'What?' I was shocked. 'Already? I mean, it's only been a couple of days!'

'The sooner the better, love. It's really important to start early.'

Dilating is the most important process following gender reassignment surgery. The process involves using dilators to maintain the width and depth of the vagina. Dilation begins at a very early stage and is a lifetime commitment to ensure optimum results. Failure to do so can result in loss of depth, which in most cases is irreversible. The thought of dilating for the first time made my stomach crawl.

After taking out the gauze, I felt so exposed and raw, so the idea of dilating knocked me sick. I knew this was coming, as the consultant told me all about the necessity and lifetime commitment of dilating months before my surgery, but I just couldn't handle doing it in that moment. I was terrified when the nurse presented me with my very own dilators, or "say hello to your little friends" as she liked to put it, and a tube of sterilised lubricant. She handed me two clear Perspex dilators, one slightly wider than the other, but both the same size in length. Dilating for the first time was excruciating, but I knew that I had to do it. It literally felt as though I was stabbing myself with a sharp blade, the searing pain rushing through my nerves, causing my body to flinch uncontrollably.

'Don't worry, Yvy, it'll get easier the more you do it.'

'You sure about that?' I said as I took out the first dilator and prepared to receive the wider one.

'Definitely! Now up we go, Yvy!' the nurse inserted the lube-drenched dilator.

'Sweet Mother of fucking God!' the words poured out of me as I grasped firmly on the hospital sheets.

Once I completed my compulsory three times a day routine of dilating, I was literally wiped out. I had no energy at all. It took a lot out of me and I was feeling pains in places I never knew existed. The lights went out on the ward and I tried to get as comfortable as possible in my bed, putting a pillow under my knees to ease the pressure. As I started to drift off, I heard Jennifer, sniffling. At first, I thought it was just her having a runny nose or something but soon realised that she was sobbing. I looked over and saw her clutching her stomach. I couldn't see her clearly, but the lights from the hall were shining in and I could tell she was in trouble. I immediately pressed my nurse call button.

'You okay, Jen?' I was concerned.

'I can't move. I need—'

'I've called for a nurse.'

Soon after I said it, the nurse came in and saw that it wasn't me who needed help, it was Jennifer. Another nurse was called to assist and they helped her out of bed and to the bathroom. I looked at the back of her robe, stained with pale green patches. When they brought her back to bed, she seemed to be calmer, more comfortable. The nurses left, and Jen called me over to her bed. I slowly made my way over, leaning on the edge of the hospital mattress.

Jen looked so upset, trying her best to hold back the tears. 'I don't know how much more of this I can take, Yvy.'

'What's happening?' I asked.

Jen wiped her eyes and signalled for me to pass her some ice chips.

'My surgery had complications. During the first one, they had to take tissue from my colon to line the cavity. It led to my digestive system shutting down. I can't digest anything. That's why I can't eat or drink properly. My stomach spasms, and it clenches so hard I can barely breathe. I just want all this to be fixed. I hate coming back here.'

I didn't know what to say. There wasn't anything I could say. All I could do in that moment was hold her hand tight. She held onto my hand and smiled.

'Thanks.'

'For what?' I asked.

'For not spouting inspirational bullshit. I hear it all the time. Sometimes, I just want to get my feelings out without someone telling me I'll be fine.'

'No problem.'

I held her hand and felt her body relax. I could tell that she had so much on her shoulders, but in that moment, she was happy to sit with another person who could relate to everything she was feeling. Relate to what it must've taken for her to even reach this point in her life. As she closed her eyes, I made my way back to bed and went to sleep.

After a week, the catheter came out and I felt more comfortable moving around. Even though I no longer had any bandages or gauze, I still had to wear ever so flattering disposable nappy underwear. It's expected after the operation to produce a certain amount of discharge, which regular sanitary towels aren't as effective to handle, so it was easier to use the nappies, as it eliminated the need to change as frequently, and avoid possible infection. For the first few days after my surgery, I made an effort to walk around a little, but I was getting sick of doing laps around the ward like an old lady going one mile an hour. Once the catheter was taken out, I felt like I could do cartwheels!

The only thing that daunted me was going to the bathroom for the first time. I was told by the nurse that one of the things my body needed to get used to again was passing water. Considering the type of surgery I had, passing water was going to be a little messy until my body got used to the change and I was able to urinate in a steady stream. At first, going to the bathroom resulted in such a mess but thankfully my body adapted and it stopped being an issue. I hadn't showered since my surgery and since I was already dilating and my catheter was finally taken out, I felt confident enough to shower by myself. I gathered all my toiletries and a towel and locked myself in the bathroom. Before I showered, I decided to use the toilet first. I sat down to use it and before I even got started passing water, I felt a sudden stream of blood trickle out. I looked down and saw the clear water turn crimson.

Holy shit!

I panicked and thought it best to get in the shower and let it wash away. When dilating, I occasionally saw a bit of blood when cleaning myself up, but the nurse said it was perfectly normal to bleed a little. This was different, the blood was streaming out of me like a fountain. My first thought was not to panic too much and get into the shower.

It's just a little bit of blood, Yvy. It'll stop eventually.

I thought that if I just got in the shower and let the blood drain, eventually it'll stop and I'd be just fine. I lifted myself from the toilet and made my way to the shower, leaving a trail of trickled blood behind me, turned the shower on and let the hot water beat against my skin. My legs felt weak, shaking uncontrollably. The water felt so heavy that I was holding onto the handrail for dear life.

Suddenly, my vision became blurred. I tried to focus on something, the tiles, the shower head, anything, but I couldn't.

Calm down, Yvy, just calm the fuck down.

My head was screaming, I couldn't string a thought together any longer. I reached for the shower knob to turn the water off, but I couldn't find it. The room was filled with a hot, sticky fog that I couldn't see through. In a matter of seconds, I felt my legs buckle under the pressure and my body could no longer stay upright. I crashed to the ground, smashing my head against the hard surface. I looked up to see a blurry red triangle shape in front of me.

The emergency chord.

I held myself up and attempted to pull the chord, but it was just beyond my reach. Before I could scream out for help, the room faded to black and I lost consciousness.

My eyes opened and I saw three nurses kneeling around me. I was lying on the bathroom floor, naked, wet and draped with a towel. I looked across the room to the floor length mirror on the wall and saw myself lying on the floor.

Damn girl! Even when you're wet and half dead you look hot!

I couldn't help but smile at that moment, which seemed to break the panic in the room and the nurses began to smile and laugh as I perked up a little. It turned out that the blood that was trickling out of me was just excess that found its way through, and the hot water from the shower caused my blood pressure to rise dramatically, causing me to collapse.

Thankfully, no real damage was done and I spent the remainder of my hospital stay with a few extra bruises and unwashed hair. That same day, Mum sent me a bouquet of flowers and get-well teddy bear to cheer me up, which was exactly what I needed. It's almost as if she knew that I needed to feel her loving presence in some shape or form that day.

Eleven days passed, and I was ready to go home. The final day was getting closer and I couldn't wait to leave. Jen had already left a few days prior and I remained with a grumpy old lady across from me who arrived just before Jen's departure. Mum and Feroza were coming down to get me. I was so excited to see them after so long. Talking to Mum on the phone every day was comforting, but I couldn't wait to see her in person. I only imagined how worried she'd been since I was gone. The last few days went by pretty quickly and before I knew it, I was ready to go home. It was early afternoon by the time they were expected to arrive, so it gave me a chance to freshen up a little. I spent the last few days feeling pretty grubby, and my only attempt at a shower didn't leave me feeling so fresh, which didn't help. I resorted to giving myself birdbaths for the remainder of my stay, and I couldn't wait to have a proper shower and give myself a good scrub when I got home.

Mum, Feroza and her boyfriend arrived at the ward and I was all packed and ready to go home. It wasn't long before I received my discharge papers and I was free to leave the hospital. With every step towards the exit, I felt exhilarated. Any moment now, I was going to step out into the world for the very first time. The next chapter of my life was beginning with that first step. All I wanted to do was rush outside and breathe in the fresh air, soaking in the knowledge that Yvy had finally arrived, but walking fast wasn't something I was capable of doing just yet.

Baby steps, Yvy, don't push yourself.

It felt like an eternity of walking through corridors before I finally saw the hospital exit, my legs shaking with every delicate step toward the door. As I exited the hospital and felt the warm air touch my skin, I smiled. Mum continued to hold my arm as we made our way to Feroza's car. I turned to her, looking straight in her eyes.

'I did it, Mum!'

Mum rarely talked about her feelings, her actions always spoke louder than words. She saw the smile grow on my face and put her arms around me. I knew that was her way of telling me how proud she was.

It was time to go home, and I couldn't wait to get back to familiar surroundings. The journey home didn't quite go as planned though. At first, it was the little things that made the journey difficult. Sitting down in an upright position was incredibly painful. I wasn't able to fully recline in the back seat of the car. Instead, I had to try and sit in a position that put minimal pressure between my legs. Prior to the surgery, I never thought about the positioning of my lady bits. I didn't know that if I sat a certain way, I would literally be sitting on it! It's funny, I felt like a little girl learning about her body, yet there I was, a 23-year-old woman in a car, experiencing something about myself as if it was day one of my life.

With Mum sitting beside me in the back, I ended up having to hold on to the car door handle and hoist myself up as though I was levitating in order to alleviate the pressure. Little did I know that holding myself up in the car for the three-hour drive home was going to be the least of my problems. We pulled out of the hospital car park and departed through the streets of Hammersmith. The traffic was manic and every second felt like a minute as I continued to hold myself up. We were barely moving on the road and the cars were building up behind us. In front was a huge truck that took up so much space, other cars tried to steer around it, but the oncoming traffic on the other side was just as busy.

By the time we got out of the traffic, I felt relieved that we were finally making our way home. We weren't that far from the hospital when our luck decided to run out and the car stalled on a busy side street. Knowing absolutely nothing about cars, I had no idea what was going on. Feroza tried to start the car, but it was having none of it. My stomach felt heavy to the point of dread.

Of all the days for Feroza's car to give up on us, it had to pick today!

With it being a two-door Corsa, getting in and out of the backseat was very difficult so I decided to stay put until it was absolutely necessary to get out of the car. Feroza made a few phone calls, and soon after a tow truck came to take the car to a nearby garage. Mum helped me get out of the car gently, but my stomach went from feeling heavy to turning into a brick when I realised that I had to climb up into the tow truck in order to get to the damn garage.

This is where I'm going to die!

I was so bloody scared of climbing up in my long maxi dress and sitting in this dingy, uncomfortable truck. It wasn't a small truck, and it had none of the amenities that Feroza's Corsa had that could help me be remotely comfortable. I decided to sit in the middle between Mum and Feroza so that I could hold on for dear life as we made our way to the garage. As the truck pulled out and made its way, I felt like I was on a ride a Blackpool Pleasure Beach. Every little bump in the road was amplified by about a thousand, my body bouncing uncontrollably. I felt physically sick. My body was so sore, I was scared at the thought of pulling a stitch and bleeding into my nappy.

Oh God, this is absolutely where I'm going to fucking die in a nappy!

Mum didn't need to say anything, her worry for me was written all over her face. We were almost at the garage when suddenly, the tow truck stopped. I looked outside and couldn't see the garage anywhere. The driver got out of the car and gave us the bad news. The tow truck had broken down. *Kill me, kill me the fuck now!*

Mum climbed out of the truck first, then held on to me as I got out. I felt so high up as I turned my body around and lowered my foot down, trying to find the steel step just below the door. By this time, we had left the hospital an hour and half ago and we still hadn't left Hammersmith. A second tow truck arrived to take the car to the garage, which meant we had to climb into the new truck and leave the old tow truck behind.

By the time we reached the garage, I was in sheer agony. Climbing out of the second tow truck took it out of me and I barely had the strength to hold myself up anymore. Mum never left my side, holding on to me as my life support. Even though I was quiet and kept to myself, she knew I was screaming inside. I felt bad for Feroza, it was her car that broke down and she was royally pissed off. I felt guilty that it happened when she travelled for hours to come and pick me up from the hospital. All I wanted was to go home but instead we were all stuck here, miles from home, going out of our minds.

The Corsa needed some work done and it wasn't going to be fixed any time soon, so we had to arrange for a hire car to drive home. We finally set off to Blackburn and as you can imagine, the mood in the car was absolutely destroyed. None of us were in the best of ways but we tried to not let the ordeal completely break us. It was a long drive home and by the time we reached Blackburn, it was just after 10 o'clock at night. What should have been a two to three hour journey home in Feroza's car, ended up taking one car breakdown, two tow trucks and over eight hours total before I saw my own bed. To top it all off, I had to complete my last dilation of the day as soon as I got in.

Perfect. Just fucking perfect.

I was tired, sore and in no mood to dilate, but I had no choice in the matter. I had to do it. As I set everything up in my bedroom, turned the fireplace on and lay down on my soft bed, all my worries started to leave. I finally made it home, and tomorrow was another day of a brand new chapter. I thought of Jennifer and everything she had gone through. I'm sure she too was excited to start her new chapter when she first had her surgery, only to constantly be in hospital with complications. I laid on my bed, thinking just how lucky I was, and it made me realise what I had done. I fought hard to achieve my true self, to feel whole. I made it to the other side and I was ready to take on the next chapter of my life, with all its ups and downs, knowing that I could wake up every morning and greet each day as the woman I've always known myself to be. When I thought of things that way, I felt blessed to have finally made it home.

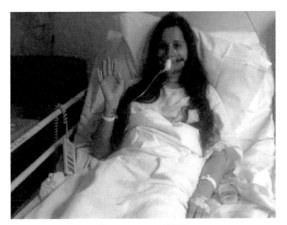

Post-surgery, 2008

Me and Feroza, Charing Cross, 2008

Vanilla, Manchester, 2012

The Thompsons Arms, 2013

Coyotes, Manchester, 2014

Gillian, Me, Leanne and Isabel

The love of my life

Volunteering for the LGBT Foundation

Manchester Pride 2016

Miss Sparkle Contest 2017

Hello, Missy!

There are so many names for the vagina. Some are all light and fluffy, like "tuppence" or "lady garden". While others like "beef curtains" and "axe wound" are pretty cringe-worthy. I mean, who the hell comes up with these? I do, however, love the word "pussy". Oooh, just saying it sounds so sexy, in a good way. I love it. The word just screams out to me. From listening to Khia in the early 2000's calling the ladies to pop their pussies, to RuPaul prompting queens to step their pussy up, the word just sings to me. *Pussy.*

Nonetheless, when it comes to Yvy, I never use the term vagina. It sounds like I'm back at school, watching one of those embarrassing videos in biology about anatomy. It's such a sterile word. Of course, I have a few personal references that I use from time to time, but that's something I'll keep to myself for the moment. A girl likes to keep a few things private!

Still, for the sake of this journey I'm taking you on, I want to use a vagina term that's pretty but also fitting. I mean, I have a lot to say moving forward about myself and I certainly don't want to shy away from it. I've been pretty forthright so far, it would be a shame to stop now. So, I'm going to use the term "Missy", named after my beloved pussycat that lives in Blackburn. She's perfect, she's beautiful...she's Missy.

Chapter Seventeen

Blackburn, 2008

I always imagined getting to this point, feeling a sudden euphoric sense of completion. An emergence from chrysalis to butterfly of which everything I once knew as dull and grey would magically become shiny and new. That wasn't quite how it turned out, which I was surprisingly unsurprised about. Having the surgery doesn't automatically mean the journey is over, far from it. The truth is, the real work came after the surgery.

Once the surgery was complete, I was forced to learn a whole new way of living. I was no longer working toward a greater goal, I had achieved it. Now, it was time to learn how to live. There's no preparation for that. The first and most important thing I started with was making a real connection with my body. Being back home again felt wonderful, but I still felt like a hospital patient. Movement was very limited. Missy still had a lot of bruising and swelling, not to mention internal and external stitches that were yet to dissolve. Even though there was no doubt or regret about my decision to go under the knife, life was not the bed of roses I had hoped it would be. It was more like a bed of thorns every time I attempted to sit down or when I curved my body sideways and rolled onto my bed like a beached whale with my legs spread. All the while, wearing my visually appealing nappy knickers. I was a few clouds away from nine, you can imagine.

With that said, I couldn't have been happier to feel like myself. I was no longer at Charing Cross, but I still had to maintain the same daily routine as I did back in London. Dilating became second nature and I tried my best to stick to a very strict regimen so I didn't find myself slipping and causing Missy any damage. Dilating had become slightly more tolerable after the first few days, but it still hurt like a motherfucker. It was like being stabbed with a large kitchen knife three times a day. Missy had so much healing to do, and dilating was an extremely delicate process, but I always tried to keep my spirits up and work through the pain. It was expected to still have a little blood on the dilators after use, which gradually decreased after leaving the hospital, but the consultant recommended dilating in the bath to help ease the pain and provide a little comfort.

I wasn't loving the idea of immersing myself in hot water for too long a period. I was worried I'd have another episode like I did in hospital and end up crashing to the ground in a blackout the moment I stood up to towel off. Still, the pain of dilating was starting to take its toll and I was willing to take the chance. I mean, at least I knew first hand that if I did end up collapsing, I'd look damn fine in a wet towel!

The actual act of dilating took around forty minutes, but that didn't include all the preparations of lubricating the dilator, gently inserting it, taking it out, taking breathers every now and then to try and relax, lubricating the second dilator and so on. I gave myself a good hour to complete the routine. Being in the bath for a whole hour wasn't very appealing. It's not like I was lying in a tub full of bubbles and a glass of wine in my hand. Too many red flags were swirling around in my head.

You won't be comfortable. The water won't stay hot. You'll be too tired to have a proper bathe and clean.

I decided to give dilating in the bath a try at least once, but I wanted Mum to sit in the bathroom with me in case something went wrong. Feeling self-conscious was never an issue when I was around her, so getting naked didn't bother me. I held onto Mum's arm and gently lowered myself into the clear bath water, making sure not to go too fast. I straightened my legs and balanced myself on my tailbone, making sure not to put any pressure between my legs. The hot water relaxed my muscles, the coils of my nerves unwinding, putting my mind at ease. I brought my knees up slightly and felt a sudden gulp of water enter me, which felt completely foreign. I noticed a little blood surfacing on the water, but it was nice not having to worry about cleaning and just relax. Usually, I had sheets on my bed and rolls of paper towels in case I needed them. Here, I forgot about it and relaxed.

'How are you feeling?' Mum said as she put the toilet lid down and sat across from me.

'Okay, just a bit cramped. I can't spread my legs as much.'

'Do you want to get out?'

'No,' I said, 'let me give it a try.'

Mum handed me the first dilator and I coated the top of it with sterile lubricant. I took in some air, which had warmed with steam, and gently expelled in a controlled breath.

Relax, Yvy, just relax.

As I lowered the dilator beneath the water and pushed it inside me, any comfort I once had completely disappeared. Most of the lubricant came off the moment I put the dilator under the water, which made Missy cry in agony. She was expecting a smooth entrance but got something she wasn't banking on. It didn't go in smoothly at all.

This is not going well.

I attempted again, only this time I applied a generous amount of lube and tried to get the dilator where it needed to be a lot quicker. I inserted the dilator and immediately felt the stabbing pain rip through my nerves. My body went from floating in the water to a heavy anvil crashing to the bottom of the tub. Mum knew how uncomfortable I was, but I told her to just keep talking to me.

'Talk to me. Talk about anything,' I said.

'You're doing well.'

I wanted to try and preoccupy my thoughts, hoping that I'd lose myself in conversation and get my mind off of what I was doing. After the first ten minutes, I gently took out the dilator and saw the bloodstained lubricant slowly making its way from the tip to the base, covering my fingers. Missy was stinging with barbwire cuts as the bathwater developed a vivid rose tint. I saw the lump in Mum's throat getting harder to swallow. I tried my best to hold back the tears as I inserted the second, larger dilator. It may as well have been covered in sand paper instead of lubricant for all I knew, the pain was unbearable.

'I can't take this, Mum,' I said, my voice cracking.

'This is just for now, you will get better in time,' she said reassuringly.

I lasted fifteen of the twenty minutes I should have done with the second dilator before I called it quits for the night. My wet skin was beginning to feel the chill of the air, and the water was no longer warming my muscles. I wanted to get out of the tub and into my warm dressing gown, which was exactly what I did. The only positive thing I took from the experience was the weightlessness of being immersed in water. Dilating was terrible, but being in a bathtub full of water felt great, as I didn't have to worry about putting any pressure on Missy. Movement was still difficult for me even though I was at home, but the worst was trying to find a comfortable way to sit down.

For the first few weeks, I couldn't even sit in the living room because as soon as I connected with the sofa cushion, the pressure immediately sent my nerves into a searing blaze. I tried so many ways to find a comfortable position, which normally lasted a couple of minutes before I had to stand up to alleviate the pressure. Soon enough, I found myself having to kneel on the floor with a cushion under my knees and lean on the armrest of the sofa just so I could be in the living room with my family. One day, Mum had an idea of how I could tackle my problem. She knocked on my bedroom door after returning from town.

'Can I come in!' she said from behind the closed door.

'Yeah!'

'How are you feeling?'

'I'm alright. Just finished dilating.'

'I've bought you something!' Mum handed me a white, creased carrier bag. I looked inside and found a deflated, child-sized swimming ring.

'Why have you bought me a swimming ring?' I asked. 'To sit on! Now you don't have to sit on your nu-nu! You can put that on the sofa and sit on it,' she said happily.

'Are you serious?'

'Well, why not? You'll be able to sit properly instead of bloody kneeling on the floor!'

She had a point there!

'I suppose I could give it a try!'

I inflated the ring and took it into the living room. I placed the ring on the sofa and gently lowered myself on it. To my delight, I was sitting comfortably, albeit a little high up. Mum started laughing when she saw how I was sitting.

'You look like the Queen of Sheba sitting high up on your throne!'

'Never mind bloody Queen of Sheba,' I said. 'I look like a bloody giant baby on a booster seat!'

As with any surgical operation, healing takes time. After being home for almost three months, I wasn't healing as fast as I hoped. Bathing helped with dissolving the stitches, but I developed internal granulation tissue which caused a lot of discomfort. Thankfully, I grew out of wearing those hideous nappy knickers and went on to wear standard sanitary towels. Still, having to wear towels every single day wasn't a nice feeling. Granulation causes sporadic discharge, and the continued healing process meant I was releasing both fresh and old blood. During my post-op consultations at Charing Cross, the granulation was treated with silver nitrate. The process involved using the silver nitrate to burn the internal tissue so healing could continue. I tell you, it's a pretty weird sight to have your legs in stirrups and smoke from sizzled flesh rising from between your legs!

Healing was gradual, but I was finally confident to start back up at work. I was going crazy being cooped up in the house, and I really missed work. I didn't want to stay home and be reminded of all the things I wanted to take my mind off of, so going back to work was a blessing. I walked into work and saw Kerry behind the counter. She looked up and saw me as I approached.

'Yvy!' she yelled with excitement.

'Hiyas!' I said as she made her way to me and gave me a big hug.

'How are you doing? How do you feel? What's been happening?'

'Good, good and a lot!' I said, answering all three questions in one go.

'It's so good having you back! So how do you feel? I mean, do feel different, or, sorry, I don't know how to word what I'm trying to—'

'No, don't worry I get it. To be honest, I was in my room the other day thinking to myself, and I realised that I'm a virgin in every way!'

'What do you mean?' Kerry asked, looking slightly confused.

'Everything is new. My body, the way I live, everything. I feel like I'm starting all over again, only I'm in my twenties. Everything I do from this point is going to be a first.'

'Lucky bitch! Wish I could bloody start over sometimes.'

'I never thought I'd feel this way, it just didn't occur to me until now. I've got so much to learn about myself now, especially about the things I want to enjoy.'

'Speaking of which, guess who's been asking about you? Jason!'

'Really?'

'Yeah! He asks for you every time he comes in.'

Jason was a regular who started coming in a few months before I went for my surgery. He was the kind of guy that was adorably cute but had a filthy side that you wouldn't mind taking for a test drive. He worked with teenagers in social care, taking them on hikes to places like Pendle Hill and Darwen Tower and bike rides around the Lake District. He was in his mid-thirties but didn't look it. The fresh air and exercise definitely did him good. He was always pleasant when he came in to buy his porn and Gun Oil and we'd chat briefly before he left.

The first time I met him, he wasn't very chatty. He came in the shop one Wednesday evening through the downstairs entrance, and when he saw me, he did a discreet double take as he was used to seeing Kerry behind the counter. He was quiet, kept to himself, and went straight to the DVDs. I didn't pay him much attention until I looked up and saw him glancing at me. As soon as I caught his gaze, he quickly turned away.

Once he chose a DVD, he walked towards the counter, trying to catch my gaze again. *Here we go. Another weirdo wanting to ask me something creepy.*

'Hiya,' I said with generic salesgirl enthusiasm.

'Alright.'

I took the DVD title from his hands and searched for the disc under the counter.

'You new?' he asked.

I popped my head back up form under the counter.

'Urrm, not really. I've worked here for a while.'

'No, I meant this place. I've only been here a few times.'

'Ooooh! Sorry! Uhh I think it's been here for a while.'

'Aah, right. I usually go to that XXX place near the Arena.'

'Okay.'

'This place is cool though. Nice to see someone like you serving customers.'

'What do you mean?'

'It's better to be served by someone pretty than another perv.'

'Who says *I'm* not a perv?'

He smiled. He didn't expect me to say that. Even *I* didn't think I'd say that.

'I'm Jason.'

'Yvy. Nice to meet you.'

'I hope I don't offend you, but I you don't seem too bothered being in a place like this?'

'Why should I be? I get paid to be here, you're the one spending money.'

'You got me there!'

'Besides, I enjoy it. I like its honesty.'

'It's fantasy, not honesty,' he said, looking serious all of a sudden.

'That's what you think.'

'In my line of work, I have to keep this side of me secret.'

'And what side is that?'

'My deviant side.'

'Well, maybe out *there* you have to,' I nodded towards the entrance door, 'but in here, you can't hide what you want. In here, you have to be honest to get what you want. You walked in and shared your fantasy with me. I know what you're going to watch tonight. You've given me a glimpse of what gets you off. Yet, you don't even know me,' I leaned on the counter, bringing my face closer to his.

'That's honesty.'

Jason stood there, staring at me. His eyes were studying me, trying to figure me out. He was fascinated.

'Anything else you need,' I asked as I put his porn in a pink and white striped paper bag. 'No, thanks. Do you work most Wednesdays?'

'Yep, every Wednesday evening.'

'I'll see you again, then?'

'I'll be here.'

Jason started visiting every Wednesday. Like clockwork, the rear entrance bell chimed at 7:30 pm, thirty minutes before the shop closed. He told me more and more about himself, about his work, his likes and dislikes, almost as if he felt the need to tell me. I liked Jason, he seemed to be a genuinely nice guy who enjoyed talking to me. He was never forward with me, but I could tell he was drawn to everything I had to say.

One Wednesday evening, just a few weeks before I went for my surgery, Jason came into the shop. The door chimed at 7:30 and in he walked from downstairs. 'How's your day been, Yvy?' he asked as he leant on the counter.

'Not bad, I've done a full day shift today so I've been here since ten.'

'What you up to once you're done?'

'Nothing, really.'

'Fancy going for a drive?' he asked.

'Where to?'

'Anywhere. Just fancy spending time with you.'

I had reservations, but I threw caution to the wind and went with him. We drove around for an hour, through Wilpshire and round the outskirts of Blackburn. We parked up in a gravel car park, near a bunch of cars, surrounded by trees. I had no idea where we were, but it was pretty obvious what was going on.

'Jason, why have you brought me to a dogging spot?'

'No, no, I haven't, I just thought—'

'No, no! I'm not that dense.'

'Seriously, that's not what this is.'

'Okay, well, if there are people in those cars and they give us any signals, we're out of here!'

He gave me a nod to say *I understand.*

'I really like you. I like how you speak your mind.'

'Thanks.'

'You seem like the type that doesn't shock easily. Don't you ever judge the guys you meet when you're working?'

'I don't. I've gone through plenty to know not to judge people harshly.'

'Why, what have you gone through?'

'How long have you got? It's hard to answer that question quickly.'

'I've got all night if you have.'

'You really want to know?' I asked. Jason nodded his head.

'I'm transitioning, and I'm going for surgery soon.'

'You mean you're—'

'Umm-hmm!'

'Wow! I would never have guessed!'

I didn't mind telling Jason about my transition. I mean, I already knew he was cool with it in general so I didn't think he'd react badly. He put his hand on my knee and leaned in. As he grew closer, I leaned in too and gave him a kiss. It only lasted a few seconds, as a beam of light suddenly shined in front of us, quickly blinking in three rapid successions. It came from the car parked across from us, indicating they were up for some action. It was then that I was done talking and ready to leave.

'Time to go, Jay,' I said. 'Start this bitch up!'

I didn't see Jason after that night. Only a couple of weeks later I went to London, and I had no way of contacting him as I didn't have a phone number. He always just turned up at the shop. It was obvious that the reason he didn't give me his number was because he wanted to be in control. He set the rules of when he came to see me and when he wanted to talk. It didn't bother me either way because he wasn't some significant other I was crushing on. Matter of fact, I never gave him much thought when he wasn't around.

When Kerry told me that he'd been asking about me, I began to think if his interest in me was a little deeper than I originally thought. Yes, he told me that he liked me, but there was something about him that always seemed a little standoffish. He never expressed any emotion or feeling when he spoke. Anything he said came across rehearsed, like a catalogue of answers he always had stored in his head, ready to reel off whenever somebody asked him a question about himself. Maybe this was a defence mechanism of some deeper turmoil that forced him to put up a barrier but quite frankly, I didn't care.

'You gonna see him then?' Kerry asked. 'He's pretty cute.'

'I don't know. I mean, it's a bit soon, I think.'

'Yeah fuck 'em. You don't want to be dating people who come in here anyway. Too much hassle! Fancy a cuppa?'

'Now that I'm up for!' I said.

'I'll make a brew and then we'll get started on taking the Christmas tree down.'

Getting back into my usual work routine didn't take long. By the new year, it felt as though I'd never been off work for so long. My routine ran like clockwork, everything about running the shop was done precisely. Kerry always felt confident leaving the shop in my capable hands.

One Wednesday evening, I began the usual ritual of tidying the shop floor and prepared to lock the doors. I vacuumed the carpet and swung the dressing room cubicle door open next to the counter. It was a tiny cubicle that housed a small chair, a coat hanger and a large floor length mirror screwed to the wall facing the door. The door opened and I gave the floor the once-over with the Henry hoover. I was just about done when I glanced up at the mirror and caught a glimpse of myself.

For a second, I didn't recognise the person staring back at me, which shook me to the core. Looking at myself, dressed in my uniform black polo t-shirt, pair of jeans and my long black hair falling gracefully around my face, it suddenly dawned on me that I spent so long fighting and persevering to be the woman I always knew I was, but now that I reached that point, I had to build a connection with myself.

For the first time in my entire life, I was able to be myself, inside and out, but what type of person was I? I finally had the freedom to express myself in any way I chose to, but I was at a loss about where I should start. During my transition, I thought that I knew who I wanted to be, and I expected that connection to automatically fall into place once I got there. But it didn't. It had been three months since my surgery, and it almost felt like I was only three months old, just starting out in life and seeing the world with a new set of eyes. My body had changed, my mentality had changed, and I had to start from scratch building a connection to the core of who I was.

That night, I lit a few candles in my bedroom, turned on the fire and lay down on my bed. The door was locked, leaving me alone with my thoughts. I stared at the ceiling, watching the light from the candles turn the ceiling carvings into shadow puppets, frolicking with every flicker of the flames. I took off my clothes, leaving my underwear on. The room was warm and peaceful. I felt my long hair caress my shoulders and brought my hands up to my chest. I wanted to explore myself. *My body.*

It was the first time I truly realised what I had accomplished through the years. I was finally able to own my body, instead of living in a shell that didn't belong to me. My hands ran down to my breasts. I felt their shape, small and round, still developing. My nipples were so sensitive that I could feel the aching tingle from the lightest touch through my bra. The hairs on my arms stood up as my hands gently cupped them, feeling their form fill my palms. My mind cleared of all thoughts and the soft, crackling sound of the fireplace filled my head. My muscles relaxed and I felt the arch in my back loosen and my spine lay flat on the soft cotton sheets. My hands moved down to my abdomen, and my fingers felt the sudden dip as they crossed my ribs and fell down the slope that led to my stomach. My skin was soft, warm, ticklish. A smile grew on my face as the tickles sent my nerves into a frenzy. My hands moved lower, feeling the line of my panties. Already I felt the tension creeping back, but I tried to calm myself.

What I was doing had nothing to do with sex, or dilating, or anything that I wasn't ready for. This was about connecting with my body, about connecting with me. I was always detached from my body growing up because it felt like a prison I was unable to escape from. When I began my transition, I was excited at the thought of finally breaking free. Once I got to that point, I found myself so consumed by all the medical necessities and dealing with post-surgery routines that I was still mentally detached, even though I was physically free. For months I touched my body, but never really connected with it. Every time I touched myself, it was to dilate, or to check my stitches, or change my sanitary towel on a daily basis. It was such a negative experience that I had no connection with the person I was. I wanted to have an experience with my body that was on my terms and not have it turn into a painful, negative experience.

The flames continued to cast their glowing shadows on the ceiling as I slowly pulled my panties down to my ankles, pushing them off the bed. It soothed me to watch the orange flecks of light dance across the room and the warmth of the fire against my skin.

My hands moved to my thighs and I gently opened my legs. *Don't be nervous, Yvy.* This had nothing to do with being sexual, it was about touching the most intimate of areas and no longer feeling out of my comfort zone. I was unable to connect with my sexuality as an adolescent and found it almost embarrassing when my body reacted if I was turned on or in an intimate situation. I just couldn't bring myself to even acknowledge that part of me, but now, everything was different.

Lying on the bed, I brushed my fingers slowly up the inside of my thighs and soon found them caressing Missy. She felt smooth, soft and swollen. My toes tingled and a sudden chill climbed up my spine. I let my fingers stroke slowly up and down, feeling every part of her, being gentle and kind.

She deserves it.

My smile grew bigger when the sudden moment of clarity filled my head. I felt ready, I wanted to explore inside. My knees parted a little further and I felt the warm air enter me. My breath became shallow and my nerves were working overtime, making me feel uncomfortable.

I can't do this.

No matter how hard I tried, I just wasn't ready. I felt stupid.

What is wrong with you?

My whole life, I craved to be in this moment, but now that I had made it, I felt even more detached than I was before. I didn't understand why I was feeling this way.

The following week, it was yet another routine Wednesday shift, creeping toward closing time. I stood by the counter, tallying up the day's sales when the door entrance chimed. I looked up, but didn't see anybody come through the front door. Suddenly, it dawned on me. *What time is it?* I looked at the time on the till screen. *7:30.* The next thing I knew, Jason came walking up the stairs. He didn't see me at first, looking down at his phone as he walked up, but when he looked up and saw me, his face lit up.

'Hi, Yvy!'

'Hey! How are you?' I asked.

'Not bad, how are you?'

'Okay, thanks, everything went well so I'm getting back into the swing of things.'

'Well, it's great to have you back.'

'Thanks.'

He went quiet, making the moment awkward. I didn't know what to say and to be honest, I wasn't really in the mood for phoney chit-chat so I let the air stay dense.

'So, how do you feel now that you've had your surgery?'

'It feels great,' I didn't want to tell him how I really felt.

'You doing anything tonight? If you fancy we could go for a drive again?'

'What, you mean like last time, parking in a dogging spot?'

'No, not that, but we can just, I don't know, drive around or something?'

'Okay, sure, why not?'

Once I closed up and was done for the evening, Jason drove us towards Great Harwood, passing through areas of trees and fields. I wasn't familiar with where we were exactly, but it felt nice to just be driving around at night. We parked up near a wooded area and Jason turned the ignition off. It was pitch black outside, with no street lamps to assist me in seeing any further. I knew we were surrounded by trees, but that was all I could make out. It was silent outside, but I wasn't afraid. In fact, I felt calm, it was a nice feeling to be somewhere I didn't know.

Jason was looking at me intensely, at least it felt as though he was. His honey coloured eyes had a way of looking right through me, making me feel exposed. He put his hand on mine and gave it a squeeze. He didn't speak, he just looked at me. The moon was full, casting its silver light against the dashboard. Jason turned my head to face him and gave me a kiss. I didn't kiss him back, which he acknowledged straight away.

'Sorry. Should I not have done that?' he asked.

'No, it's me. I'm just feeling a bit down.'

'What's wrong?'

'Nothing, I don't want to bore you with my issues.'

'Trust me, you wouldn't bore me.'

I believed him. Somehow, I knew that I could talk to him about how I was feeling, even though I knew he couldn't really help. But sometimes you don't necessarily need someone to help, you just need them to listen.

'I've worked so hard to get to this point, and now that I'm here, I'm scared.'

Jason didn't say a word. He sat quietly and let me own my feelings.

'I've had to endure so much hurt and struggle, but I always held on to the belief that it would be worth it once I finally got to where I need to be. Now that I'm here, I want to feel a connection to myself, but I'm afraid of what might happen if I don't.'

'Do you regret what you've done?'

'No,' I said immediately. 'I don't regret a single thing, but it's scary to start my life over and not have a clue where to start. I wasn't given a handbook on womanhood to give me all the answers, I mean, no woman does. But I'll never get the chance to learn about myself the way I wish I could. My childhood was spent trying to understand the real me, but I lost the opportunity to connect with who I was.'

I looked over at Jason. His head was down, listening intently. My eyes began to well up and I tried my best not to let my voice crack with emotion.

'There's no point me getting upset about things I can't change, it just sucks to think that I have to cram a process that takes years to develop into a short space of time so I can move forward and feel like myself.'

Jason grabbed my hand again, giving it a reassuring squeeze.

'The other day, I tried touching myself. I thought, if I could do that, it meant I'd feel something other than what I have to do on a daily basis. I wanted to come, to have a release.'

'And did you come?' he asked.

'No, I didn't even try. I didn't want to try and not enjoy it. Maybe I need to just let go and give in a little.'

'Maybe you need to stop putting so much pressure on yourself. You can't force yourself to feel. It'll happen when you least expect it,' I stared into the night, the moon cascading over the trees.

He's right.

I didn't look at him, I didn't want him to see the tear running down my face.

'I know. I'm in a crazy headspace, I guess. I'm feeling really, well—'

'Vulnerable,' he said, finishing my sentence.

I looked at him, wiping away the tear on my face.

'Can you take me home, please?' I asked softly.

'Sure.'

He pulled up outside my house, the amber street lamps illuminating the parked cars around him. I reached for the car door handle when Jason put his hand on my shoulder. I looked over at him and gave him a kiss.

'I want to take you somewhere. You free on Saturday?'

'Where do you want to take me?'

'It's a surprise.'

'Okay then, sure.'

Saturday soon came by, and I was ready to meet Jason. He said to meet him at 9 o'clock in the car park behind work. I made my way there and saw him parked up, his headlights turned off. He flashed them at me, letting me know he was there and I got in. I wasn't sure if he was taking me on a date or something, so I decided to dress up nice. I sat in his car, wearing a long black maxi dress with a warm coat covering me up. My lips were stained with ruby red lipstick and my hair was ironed straight.

'You look good, Yvy,' he said with a mischievous smile.

'Thanks. So where we off to then?'

'You'll see.'

He started the engine and drove for what felt like ages. As we drove on quiet motorways, I noticed the road signs gradually indicate the direction of which way we were heading.

'Burnley. You're taking me to Burnley?'

He didn't respond, just continued to drive with a smile on his face.

'Okay, so what's in Burnley?'

'I didn't say we were going to Burnley'

'So where are we going?'

'Just trust me, you'll enjoy it.'

We eventually pulled up outside a building that looked like a working men's club. It was old looking, like it hadn't been used in years. *What the hell are we doing here?* The windows were covered with heavy curtains and the door had a security gate. I had no clue where we were, or whether or not we were even in Burnley. All I knew was, I was beginning to feel a little scared. Jason grabbed my hand and we walked in.

Once inside, I knew exactly where Jason had taken me. The reception area was filled with people dressed in leather and latex. On the table was an array of condoms and chains. A woman walked by with a man crawling on his hands and knees behind her, chained to a dog collar.

'Why have you brought me to a dungeon, Jason?'

'You said you wanted to let go. Here's your chance.'

'I didn't mean this! This is a bit more than *letting go*!'

'Look, you can do or don't do whatever you want. But in here, you belong to me. Nobody else can have you. You're only for me.'

I couldn't deny it; hearing Jason say that turned me on. He picked up a sticker from the reception table and peeled the back off. I could see that it was small red heart. He placed in on my cheek and pressed down gently.

'There. This tells people that you belong to me.'

We walked through a hallway, peering into spaces occupied by people in their forties engaging in oral sex. A few young men in their twenties were joining in the fun, whilst some of the women were just watching. They were dressed in black, leather harnesses and PVC dresses that left little to the imagination.

'Do you want to watch?' Jason asked, putting his arms around my waist.

'Let's see what else is going on,' I didn't want to settle; I was intrigued to see what pleasures were taking place.

Every area we walked past, people were getting off. Some were having sex, others were watching, but everyone was having fun. The mistresses were keeping their subjects in check, shouting orders at them and making sure they obeyed their commands. I was fascinated by it all. I saw so much of this at work, but I had never seen it first-hand.

'So, is this what you meant when you said your deviant side?'

'Pretty much!' Jason said, his intense eyes looking straight into me.

'Are you a Master, or a slave?'

'I think you know the answer to that one,' he pulled me close and kissed me. *Master, definitely Master.*

He led me around the corner into a room lit with red lightbulbs. In the centre was a large, circular platform with chairs scattered around. A number of couples were already in there, talking and drinking. He escorted me in and stopped me in my tracks as soon as we were near the platform.

'Climb on,' he said, his face drenched with red light.

'What?'

'Climb on.'

'Why?'

'Because I told you to.'

The way he said that made me shiver but not with pleasure. I wasn't sure how to feel or what to do. I looked around and a couple of people were paying attention to us. Jason squeezed my hands, bringing my attention back to his intense gaze.

'You belong to me, Yvy. Get up on that platform,' he whispered.

I stepped up onto the platform, my heel making a click that echoed through everyone's ears, causing them to look at us. Jason stepped up on the platform and positioned himself behind me. I felt a little safer, knowing he was up there with me and I wasn't alone.

What the hell is happening?

'This is honesty,' Jason whispered softly in my ear.

Suddenly, I felt powerless, like he'd taken full control of me. His hands ran down my shoulders and pushed the straps of my dress off. He wrapped his fingers around the straps and pulled my dress down, exposing my underwear and bare breasts. Every pair of eyes in the room were laser focused on me.

'What are you doing?' I said, trying to cover myself. Jason grabbed my wrists and held them tight.

'Just let go, Yvy. Give yourself to me.'

My dress fell down in one swift drop. I held my breath and felt my cheeks flush from everyone's eyes on me, examining my body.

Oh my God! What if they figure me out?

I was petrified that if Jason took my underwear off, they'd take one look at Missy and instantly know the truth. *She's a tranny! Kick her out!* I started to breathe again, taking in shallow breaths of air thick with cigarette smoke. As Jason ran his hands down my body, Missy started waking up. I felt her tingle, a sensation I hadn't felt before. I looked around the room, the seats were beginning to fill up with couples wanting to see what Jason and I were going to do next. He put his hand around my neck and slipped his other hand into my panties. I jumped, not expecting him to go straight for Missy so quickly. He pressed down gently on her, but the tingling sensation soon turned to pain.

'That hurts,' I said in his ear.

'Good.'

'Please stop,' I asked, trying to pull his hand out.

'No. Relax.'

He buried his face into my neck, biting my flesh gently. I looked around at the red room, seeing the eyes of every person studying the contours of my body as Jason played with it like a toy. I pulled his hand out and grabbed my dress that was sitting by my ankles. I lifted it back on and looked at Jason. *This doesn't feel right!*

'I said stop!' I stepped off the platform and pushed my way past the voyeurs.

I peeled the red heart from my cheek and stepped outside, taking in the cold air. Jason followed me out soon after.

'What do you think you're doing, Jason?' I asked harshly.

'I thought you'd like this?'

'Not *this*, I'm talking about you! Why did you bring me here?'

'I like you, that's all. I see how damaged you are, that's what I'm drawn to you.'

'So what, you think you can dominate me? Is that it? I am *not* damaged. You don't know even know me. I'm not a toy for you to play with.'

'Okay, I'm sorry, I didn't mean to upset you. I thought you were into this. I misread the signals. I thought you'd be cool with letting me have you.'

'If this is what you're into, that's fine. I don't have a problem with it. But you can't use my feelings to your advantage. You have no idea what I've gone through, and I don't belong to anyone but me,' the moment the words left my mouth, I truly believed them.

'Take me home, now.'

After that night, I came to the realisation that I was feeling lost because I hadn't given myself the time to reconnect with my being. My body had gone through an intense trauma, and it needed the time to heal so that I could connect the circuitry from mind to body and feel whole. My whole life, I was never able to connect the circuits, so why did I think it would be instantaneous the moment I had my surgery?

Of course, it's going to take time, Yvy!

I had all the time in the world to experience sexual pleasures, but it's not something I needed to rush into. Jason saw my vulnerability as a weakness he could dominate. I knew enough about sadomasochistic behaviour to understand that it was all to do with power, the master dominating the slave. That wasn't for me. I didn't like that he took my transition and made it into something weak. He saw my life as one long struggle that caused me to be a person who saw no choice but to succumb to his will. He saw that I was struggling to connect with myself and tried to sever that connection completely. I wanted to be the master of my own being, not give it away to someone for their own gratification.

The following week, I felt nervous at the thought of him coming to the shop. I didn't know if I wanted to talk to him. In some ways, I wasn't mad at him. I was more mad at myself for thinking I needed to rush into things. Standing on that platform, I was at my most vulnerable, not knowing if the people staring at me were going to take one look at me and reject me for being transgender. But they didn't. They looked at me and saw just that, me. The whole world was seeing me for the first time and I didn't need to be afraid, but before I could focus on others, I needed to work on myself.

I stood behind the counter after a long Wednesday shift and saw that it was almost 7:30. *Is he going to show?* As the clock ticked closer, I waited to hear the door chime and see Jason walk in from downstairs. The clock kept on ticking, 7:31 but he never showed.

In fact, I never saw Jason again.

Chapter Eighteen

Springtime had arrived, and the shop floor was beginning to heat up. Every morning when I opened up the shop for the day, I opened the windows behind the counter to let the cool breeze wash away the heavy air that built up throughout the night. I peered out the window frame and felt the warm rays bake my skin. I've always loved spring, it puts me in a good mood. With a hot cuppa in hand, I sat on the step that led from the office to the shop floor behind the counter. I leant against the silver shelf brackets that held the inventory of porn in alphabetical order and felt the sunshine through the window on my face. The mug was heating the palm of my hands as I brought it to my lips and took a sip, feeling the satisfying run of hot liquid tickle the back of my throat.

The entrance bell chimed and I heard a customer walk through the front door. As I stood up and took a few steps to the counter, I saw a man walking towards me with the big smile on his face. I'd never seen him before, and he was holding a black zip-up document holder. My first thought was that he was about to pitch a sale to me for something the shop almost definitely didn't need. He walked past the lingerie and stopped at the PVC nurse outfits hanging off the wall railings. He grabbed the bottom corner of one of the pink outfits and looked up at me with a cheeky grin.

'Do you think I'd look good in this?' he said playfully.

'I don't think you have the legs for it!' I replied.

It wasn't the first time a guy had walked in and used that line, so I already had a response waiting in my mental rolodex whenever someone used it. The man laughed and gave me a cheeky wink as he proceeded to the counter. There was something about this guy that was interesting. He had a certain charm that only came with salesmen. That overconfidence and in your face comedic timing that always seemed a little grating, but you played along anyway because it's the polite thing to do. He was tall and slender, with dirty blonde hair and brown eyes. I looked past his salesman veneer that he almost certainly used in every shop he went in and was intrigued by what possibly laid beneath it.

'What's a nice girl like you doing in a place like this?' he asked.

'I get paid to be here, what's your reason?'

'Well, I'm here to talk to you about your fire extinguishers,' he unzipped his document folder and laid out sheets of papers about fire safety products. *I hit the nail on the head, a salesman!*

'These products are a must-have for any retail establishment. Our company work hard to—'

'Let me stop you there, hun.'

I couldn't help but laugh inside at the thought that everything he was saying and doing was completely rehearsed. From his fake laughter to the cheeky innuendoes, it was all transparent. 'I'm not the person to speak to about this stuff. I'm not the manager, but she'll be in tomorrow if you want to talk to her.'

'Aww that's a shame, I'm only in town today.'

'Yeah, shame.'

'Can I leave my card with you, then?'

'Yeah, sure,' he handed me a business card with a company logo in the top right-hand corner and his name printed in bold in the middle.

'Benjamin Miller. Nice talking to you, Ben.'

'What's your name?' he asked.

'Yvy.'

'That's a pretty name.'

'Thanks. So which sex shop are you visiting next, Ben?'

'Oh, umm, yeah, no I was just passing with my work mate. He's waiting in the car, figured I'd give this shop a try on my way back to Manchester.'

'Manchester? I love Manchester, I'm hoping to move back soon.'

'I live there too. If you ever need help finding a place, let me know!'

'Is that part of your sales pitch?'

'Oh no, I didn't mean it that way, I—'

'I'm just kidding!'

I noticed a shyness come from him that I found entertaining. It was always the case when guys like him came in the shop, all confident thinking they could make me go all shy and pink cheeked. It was so predictable to a point where I could turn the tables on them so quickly that the oh-so-confident demeanour quickly dissipated and they had absolutely no clue how to behave. I could tell that Ben was the same, but I didn't want to do what I normally did because he seemed like a really nice guy.

'Whereabouts in Manchester did you live, then?' Ben asked.

'Oh, I lived in Chorlton, then Salford for a bit.'

'Oh yeah, I know Chorlton quite well. When are you thinking of moving back?'

'Pretty soon, I hope, I'm saving up first for the move. I hope I'm not keeping you from your colleague. Is he alright waiting in the car?'

'Yeah, he'll be fine. Besides, if he got a chance to chat to a beautiful woman, he'd take ages too.'

I smiled. I could tell he was into me, and I was starting to warm up to him. There was definitely an attraction between us. I hadn't felt an attraction to someone in a very long time. Jason was different, it wasn't necessarily an attraction but more a foolish attempt at making a connection. I really liked Benjamin. He seemed sweet and easy to talk to, and I wasn't quite ready to call it a day. I wanted to know more about him. He'd already told me quite a bit about himself, so why not see where this could lead. Yes, my last interaction with a man didn't turn out to be what I wanted, but that shouldn't deter me from trying again. Besides, Ben had something going for him that Jason didn't; he had no idea about my past. I liked that. Every man I'd ever gotten involved with who knew of my past, always saw me for what I was and not who I was, which I loathed. I hated being treated like an experiment for their carnal pleasure. Ben was different, he saw Yvy, not the labels, which gave me the opportunity to be myself without holding back.

'I'm afraid I need to leave now. I really enjoyed meeting you, Yvy. Is it okay if I give you my number?'

'Sure. Here's my number too,' I scribbled my phone digits on a post-it and handed it to him.

'Maybe you can help me find a flat in Manchester soon?'

'Definitely! See you later.'

The door chimed as he left and I sat back down on the office step, feeling the breeze through the window. I folded and unfolded the piece of paper Ben gave me with his personal number on.

Should I text him? Is it too soon? I really liked him, so why not text him? Before I could make my mind up, my phone buzzed in my pocket.

'I don't waste time! I want to see you again.'

I took Benjamin up on his request and we planned to meet up in Manchester. I wanted to look just right for our first date. We weren't planning on doing anything special, just a casual coffee. Still, this was a big step for me. I'd never been on a real date before and although I felt like I was more myself, I still had so much to learn.

Whatever you do, Yvy, don't fuck him on the first date!

All I ever thought about was sex. My libido was kicking in again and I became obsessed with buying erotic movies from Amazon and watching them alone in my room. I had no interest in porn, that's not what was turning me on, it was the passion, the anticipation, the intimacy of two people. Porn was just about the sex, with weak dialogue to string together reasons why everyone was humping. That held no interest to me. I was interested in the thrill of two people meeting for the first time, their chemistry slowly building until they couldn't take it any longer and gave in to their sexual attraction. From *9 1/2 Weeks* to *The Colour of Night*, all I ever did in the evening was watch erotic thrillers and picture myself getting into all sorts of filthy situations. *Seriously Yvy, don't rush into this!*

I spent years waiting for an opportunity like this to come along, and here it was. I wasn't quite sure if I was ready, but I didn't want to miss this chance. The chance to go on a date and have a good time with someone I felt real chemistry with. I decided to dress casually, with a low cut t-shirt and some jeans, a cute yet sexy look.

I travelled to Manchester on the train and met Ben at Victoria Station. I thought it was so sweet of him to meet me at the station. He took me to a Starbucks near Victoria and I noticed that he was nervous, attempting to mask it under his salesman veneer. It made it tricky to get to know what he was like underneath it all. I ordered a hot chocolate with whipped cream and marshmallows and performed my spoon seduction with the cream which worked like a charm. I felt Ben's eyes burning into me with excitement, which was exactly what I wanted. I looked up at his smiling face as he tasted his iced coffee.

'You know how to work that spoon, don't you!'

'I know my way around one!'

What kind of stupid answer was that, Yvy?

He grinned with delight. A clear indication that his mind had drifted somewhere dirty.

'So have you always lived in Manchester?' I asked, changing the subject.

Calm it down, Yvy!

'No, actually,' he said. 'I'm originally from Morecambe but I'm sharing a flat with my best mate. It's his flat and he got me the job so I moved out here.'

'Do you prefer it here then?'

'Yeah I do, there's fuck all to do in Morecambe. But I don't want to be selling fire extinguishers forever though.'

'You seem to be good at it.'

'I am, but it's tough. Doing hard selling takes it out of you. Doesn't give me much time for anything else.'

'What would be your ideal job?'

He paused, thinking about his answer. I looked at him and saw a glimpse of the real Benjamin. He let down his veneer for a moment and was about to give me an honest answer.

'Scuba diving. I love to scuba dive.'

'Okay, I didn't expect that!'

'I'd love to be a scuba diving instructor somewhere, but I have to gain certification first.'

Our first date was going so well. By the end, I wanted to stay longer, but decided to go at a steady pace and make my way back home. He saw me to the train station and gave me a huge hug. I felt his body pressed up against me as he planted a kiss on my lips. My knees turned to jelly and was thankful he was still holding on to me. I got on the train and saw his face disappear as it pulled out of the station. I sank into my seat and put on my earphones. As Brandy's album *Human* began to play in my ears, all I could think about was Benjamin.

Within seconds of leaving the station, my phone vibrated with a message from him.

'I miss you already.'

On our second date, he asked if I wanted to go round to his flat one afternoon and he'd cook me dinner. I was so ready to go to his place, as it had been about a week since I'd seen him and I was really beginning to miss his face. He asked if I was free one Friday so I made sure I had the day off work and went over to Manchester again on the train. So much had changed in my life, and I finally had the freedom to be myself.

By the time I reached Manchester, I was consumed with thoughts of starting a new adventure. I felt free to be myself without worrying about having to explain myself. I didn't want to tell Ben about my past because this was my opportunity to start building my future. *The future of Yvy.*

Ben met me at the station and we picked up some ingredients before making our way back to his flat. His roommate wasn't going to be in, so we had the flat to ourselves. I walked in and saw that it was one of those high spec flats with glossy kitchen worktops and a tiny, cube shaped living room that was decorated with a minimalist look. The block of flats was known for being occupied by working professionals and working girls. From the moment I walked in, I could tell instantly that this was a lad's flat. The kitchen led straight into the living room, with a small glass dining table that broke the room up in the middle. I sat on one of the chairs and watched as Ben started preparing dinner.

'Tell me more about you, Yvy,' he asked.

'Well, I'm the youngest of three, my brother and sister live at home too. I guess that's it really! I can't think of anything else interesting about me!'

'That's a lie, isn't it?'

Ben looked up from chopping green peppers. I caught his glance and instantly felt a brick in my stomach. *How does he know? What gave me away?*

'What do you mean?' I said nervously.

'C'mon! You must have plenty of stories to tell from working where you do! I want to hear about your weirdest customers!'

I was so relieved. *Of course he doesn't know, stop being so on edge and relax!*

As Ben diced the chicken and threw it in the heated wok, he hung on every word I was saying. He listened as I told him about the type of customers that I encountered on a daily basis, and I lapped up every moment of attentiveness. He was caring, taking a break every now and then from cooking to come over to me and give me a kiss or stroke my hair.

After dinner, we moved over to the sofa and watched TV. I couldn't believe how comfortable I was around him, considering this was only our second date. We curled into each other, his hands wrapped around my waist. I felt so sexy lying there in my skinny jeans and short top, knowing that his hands would eventually find my soft skin if they wandered far enough. He pulled me closer and I felt his warm breath against my neck. I rolled over and faced him, giving him a little kiss, then he sat himself up, bringing me up with him and I suddenly found myself straddling him.

That progressed quickly!

223

My knees locked on either side of his waist, my breasts inches away from his face. I felt his hands move up my back, slowly twirling my hair between his fingers. I kissed him gently, sweetly.

'You wanna go in the bedroom?'

Hell yes! He led me to a tiny box room that housed a king sized, low platform bed. As I laid down, Ben joined me, kissing me intensely. I realised that this was it, I was about to have sex. All my sexual frustrations were about to come to an end. A mix of anxiety and excitement washed over me, I had no control over my feelings at all. I decided to just go with it and let my emotions take over, letting the moment take its course. Ben took off his shirt, revealing his svelte physique and tattooed arms. On his back, a tattoo of an ex-lover in capital letters stared at me. I took off my blouse and jeans, leaving on my Calvin Klein bra and panties.

'Close your eyes,' he said, as he laid beside me, his hands running gently up and down my skin.

My eyes closed and I felt his lips from my neck, down to my nipples descending slowly to my pelvis. *Oh holy Jesus, here we go!* My body was shaking with nerves as I felt his kisses travel lower. His head was between my legs and went straight in for the taste. I opened my eyes to the ceiling, feeling somewhat confused.

What the hell is he doing?

It was difficult for me to really understand, considering this was my first time, but whatever he was doing down there felt really weird. I had watched plenty of porn in my life to know that his technique needed some *serious* fine-tuning. After a few minutes of uncoordinated tongue darting, he brought his head back up with such a proud expression on his face, waiting for the look of gratitude on mine.

Seriously, what the actual fuck were you doing!

My first time wasn't going too well. I decided not to be discouraged and told myself to just try and get into it. I could tell that Ben was waiting for me to reciprocate, like he did me some sort of favour for all of four minutes and now it was my turn. It was becoming increasingly difficult to get in the mood; nonetheless, I thought to myself that it's only the beginning and who knows what might happen.

After around thirty minutes of fooling around, Ben wanted to fuck me. I felt ready, but this wasn't going the way I'd hoped and my body was so tense. He put on some protection and moved into position to enter me. I was so nervous, the pressure to perform was getting to me. The last time I dilated was hours ago so I wasn't sure if I'd be okay to do this. *Although, this is sort of the same as dilating, right?*

Ben was adequate in size, but he wasn't exactly King Dong so I wasn't worried that he was going to be too much for me. So much was running through my head that I couldn't put my thoughts on pause. All I wanted was to just relax and enjoy myself, but an attempt to force relaxation didn't bring the desired results. He pushed himself inside me, and a surge of pain rushed through every nerve, causing me to flinch uncontrollably. I passed it off for pleasure, but the pain was constant. Missy was incredibly tight and hadn't been prepared for this. I kept thinking to myself that I should've brought some lube with me, but I didn't think I'd have this much trouble.

Maybe Missy will start getting wet.

Ben was struggling to sink any deeper into me, and I was becoming more and more uncomfortable. We lasted for a while, but Missy was struggling badly. Finally, I couldn't take much more and moving into different positions wasn't helping. We went back to foreplay, but this time it was me that was doing all the work. I finished Ben off to his satisfaction, but I was left feeling the exact opposite to how I thought I'd feel post-coital. I thought I'd be relaxed and exhilarated, but instead I was tense and disappointed. Not to mention Missy who was royally pissed.

Then, I began to smile to myself. Here I was, lying naked in the bed of a guy I liked whom I've just had sex with for the first time. This was my first time.

Of course your first time was going to be a disaster.

If I hadn't been born transgender, Missy would've lost her virginity much earlier and probably had the same disappointment with some sexually inexperienced teenage boy. I had no idea how my body was going to respond to my first sexual experience, so how would I know unless I tried?

When I thought of it that way, I didn't think of my first time as a huge failure. Instead, I reminded myself that I was still learning and even though I was starting my life over at the age of 24, I shouldn't be discouraged if things don't go the way I hoped they would. Ben looked over and saw me smiling. He smiled back and held me in his arms. I curled into him and drifted off to sleep feeling a little less tense.

I woke up, checking the time on my phone; I only dozed off for thirty minutes. The front door latch unlocked and I heard squeaking footsteps, followed by the clicking of heels against the wood floor in the corridor. Ben awoke to the sound of the front door closing and sprung out of bed to get dressed.

'That's my roommate, I'll introduce you!'

'Um, okay!' I said, still feeling a little disorientated from waking up.

I quickly covered myself with the bed sheet as he opened the bedroom door and got dressed once he shut it behind him. It didn't take long for him to return to check if I was dressed yet, slightly too eager for me to meet his roommate. I wasn't really in the mood to meet him, but I didn't have much choice in the matter.

Emerging from the bedroom, I headed into the living room and found both of them standing in the kitchen.

'This is Malcolm. Malcolm, this is Yvy.'

In front of me stood a doughy looking man, mid-twenties, wearing an ill-fitted shirt that pulled at the buttons, exposing his hairy stomach. His hair was receding, and his facial features weren't pleasing to the eye. He wasn't ugly, but he had a permanent smug face that you really wanted to bitch slap, hard, wearing heavy rings. Even though he wasn't rude or inhospitable, I caught him staring at me like a bloodhound eyeing up a piece of succulent steak, impulsively licking his thin lips.

When he introduced himself, I gave him a little wave and sat down on one of the table chairs. Usually when I met someone new, I'd give them a peck on the cheek or a friendly hug but on this occasion, I wanted to keep a safe distance. He and Benjamin started bantering back and forth, like a duo act, and I could see where he got his salesman persona from.

'So you two grew up together, did you?'

'Yeah, we went to school together, didn't we, pal?' Malcolm said, throwing his arm around Ben's shoulders. 'Now we're partners in crime!'

'Really?' I said, trying my best to look interested.

'Is Zhen with you?' Ben asked.

'She's in the bedroom, she's getting ready to go out later.'

'Who's Zhen?' I asked.

'She's my girlfriend,' Malcolm replied.

'Oh, right! Have you two been together long?'

'A few months. She lives in Beetham Tower,' he said, trying to sound impressive.

'Beetham Tower? That's fancy.'

'What can I say, eh!' he said, popping the collar on his shirt.

Ugh, cringe!

'Now we've got an Indian and a Chinese in the flat!' Ben said, his salesman veneer back up again.

'We've always wanted an international pimp palace, didn't we, Ben?' they both started falling over each other with laughter.

Wow. This is getting grosser by the second.

'I'm going to check on Zhen. Yvy, it was nice meeting you.'

Malcolm left, leaving Ben and I alone in the living room.

Despite the rocky first time, I really liked Ben. Even though I didn't like how his demeanour changed whenever he was around Malcolm, I loved that he had no idea about my past. Every time I went round to the flat, I felt so far away from my life in Blackburn and I could be a whole new person with him. He had a few traits about him that I wasn't too keen on, but I wasn't the kind of girl that was looking for the perfect, flawless guy. He was fun to be around, especially when it was just the two of us.

As time went by, Malcolm was rarely in the flat when I came over to see Ben, so I got to see the sensitive, sweeter side of his personality that didn't need to put on a show because his friend was around. Ben turned out to be a very sensitive person. I guess I should've seen through the salesman veneer from the start, but it took a while before I realised that the veneer was just a cover for something he was desperate to hide. He was an incredibly insecure person, and the more I spent time with him, the more I was exposed to it.

It was difficult to come up with reasons why I couldn't stay over at his place. I was still having to dilate three times a day and there was no way I was going to be able to do it at the flat. For one, I needed a good hour of complete privacy, and I also needed to feel comfortable. I felt most comfortable at home, in my bedroom with the door locked. I was never disturbed and I could do what I needed to do in familiar surroundings. Being comfortable and relaxed was so important when dilating. When I visited Ben, it was a great feeling to be myself, but I couldn't deny that I was holding something back. Having to wear sanitary towels every day meant having to be incredibly careful every time he touched me in case he started asking questions that I wasn't ready to answer. Having to make excuses why I couldn't stay over began to take its toll on us, and I could see his insecurities coming to the surface. He started getting blunt with me, almost rude. We sat on the sofa together and I tried to have a conversation with him.

'What do you fancy watching?' I asked. I received no response.

'Should we watch a movie?'

Still no response.

'We can listen to some music if you want?'

Silence, total silence.

'Are you okay?' I asked, trying to tilt his face my way with my hand.

He resisted and continued to stare out the window.

'Have I done something to upset you?'

'No.'

'Then what's wrong?'

'Nothing?'

'Is this because I haven't stayed over?'

I didn't like what was happening between us, all because of me. *It's your fault, Yvy, you're doing this.* I leant in on the sofa to give him a kiss, but he remained still, expressionless, completely cut off. I had to think of some way to fix this; I didn't want to cause a wedge between us. The only way I'd be able to do my dilating at his place at night would either be in the bathroom, which would be incredibly uncomfortable and I'd have to explain why I'm in there for an hour, or in bed once he fell asleep.

These are my options? I decided to try doing it in bed first, because the last time I dilated in the bathtub at home was a disaster, and I need to be relaxed. *If he's fast asleep, he won't even know I'm doing it.* I had my dilators with me, so I decided to give it a go.

'Okay, I'll stay over!' Ben turned to me and smiled.

By midnight, we called it a night and headed to bed. Ben wasn't feeling very tired and decided to continue watching television while I laid with him in my underwear. With his back facing me, he watched episode after episode of *Shameless*, feeling the need to call Malcolm on his mobile to tell him that Debbie Gallagher finally got her tits out, as if they'd been waiting so long to see Rebecca Ryan's pink nipples. *Fucking idiots.*

Listening to Ben talk to Malcolm like I wasn't even there turned me completely off. I rolled away from him and wrapped my body in the blanket, securing myself in a cocoon. Ben soon drifted off to sleep, and after just over an hour, I felt safe enough to do my dilating. I unfolded the blanket and slowly reached for my bag, rooting around, searching blindly for what I was looking for. The bedroom walls were lit by the moving images from the television, which gave me just enough light to see what I was doing. I finally found my dilators and lubricant and searched for the small flannel towels I used to place underneath me during the process. I checked and checked but couldn't find them.

Shit! You didn't bring them!

I had no choice but to improvise and used the pack of tissues I had in my wash bag instead, hoping they'd do the trick. I laid a few tissues on the bed just below Missy and another tissue by the side of the bed and placed my dilators on it. Looking over at Ben, he was still sound asleep with his back still facing me. I opened the tube of lubricant and broke the seal with the other side of the cap, then slowly squeezed some onto the first dilator.

Holding the duvet up with my right hand, I manoeuvred the dilator into position, making sure my legs were open enough to ensure Missy was ready and comfortable. The icy sting of the cold lubricant sent shivers through my body as I pushed the dilator in. That first feeling was always the worst, but it soon dissipated and the inevitable aching of the penetrating dilator soon kicked in.

As I held the dilator in position, I began to relax, realising that the plan was working and everything was fine. Yes, I had forgotten the flannel towels, but as I felt a little lubricant run down my skin toward the bedsheets, I knew the tissue would catch it instead. My eyes were fixed on the glowing green digital alarm clock on the other side of the room, counting the minutes until I had to change dilators. There was nothing interesting on television, and with the sound on low and the remote on Ben's side, I wasn't in a position to see if anything better was on to occupy myself. It didn't matter though, I was fine just lying there being able to do my routine without Ben knowing.

I changed dilators and inserted the larger one. I held it in place, opening my legs a little wider and making sure my pelvis was as low as possible to get a comfortable fit. I managed to get in the right position when suddenly, Ben began to stir. The bed bounced under his weight as he turned his whole body towards me. I froze. *SHIT!* Then, his arm came from under the duvet and reached over to me, covering my chest. *SHIT! SHIT! SHIT!* I couldn't move. My right arm was trapped under Ben, and my left was under the covers, still holding the dilator in place. I took it out, feeling Missy's burning sting, and tried my best to get the wet dilator over to the tissue by the side of the bed without it touching the duvet. I managed to do so, barely, but couldn't clean myself off properly. Normally, I use the flannel towel to dry myself off, then nipped into the shower for a quick rinse. Not this time. I had no choice but to try and use the tissue I was lying on to dry myself, only every time I tried to wipe, I felt the tissue break the wetter it got. I felt disgusting.

By the time I managed to get all the ripped tissue off my hand, Ben began to stir again, this time lying on his back and letting out a deafening snore. I used the opportunity to get up and take my dilators to the bathroom to rinse them off and clean myself up properly. I locked the bathroom door and sorted myself out. By the time I was done, I crept back into bed, securing my dilators discreetly into my overnight bag and laid my head on the pillow. As I drifted off to sleep, I could only hear one thing over and over again in my head.

Don't ever try that again!

Regret Me Not

We've all done something we've regretted at one point in our lives. Hell, I've made some questionable decisions in my time, and I've only covered a few with you so far! However, with every defining moment, there's a lesson to be learned.

No matter what I've gone through, or the decisions I've made, I've always tried to learn from it. Oh believe me, that mentality didn't come to pass until I was much older and less gullible, but in doing so I realised that I was carrying so much unnecessary emotional baggage around with me. I'd find myself falling into pits of anxiety and depression, not knowing what was wrong.

It's an awful feeling to feel depressed and not know why you're feeling that way. For me, I was feeling that way because I was holding on to the past and not learning from it. Relationships ended, hearts were broken, but as time went on, I learnt valuable lessons from it and evolved into a stronger person. It's not easy learning from your mistakes, but the key is not to think of them as mistakes. We all make choices that take us in directions we didn't expect, but that's just part of life. If you learn from your experiences, there's no need to live in regret. When you regret nothing, you can begin to look forward.

Chapter Nineteen

Morecambe, 2009

My mind was wide awake, lying next to Benjamin who was fast asleep. It was freezing cold, the harshest winter I'd ever seen. I snuck out of bed and walked gently to the window to look outside. The street lamps lit up the blankets of fresh snow that covered the ground and trees. It had snowed for days, and it didn't look like it was stopping any time soon. The blissful silence ran through my head as I watched snowflakes dance through the air and caress the ground with a kiss.

Looking over at Ben, he began to toss and turn, almost waking up. I froze on the spot, praying he didn't wake up and start another argument with me. We'd argued enough for the day. I crept downstairs and went into the dark living room. I didn't want to turn the lights on, I didn't want to see anything that reminded me of the mistake I made by moving to Morecambe. I turned on the Christmas tree lights and felt the warm white luminescence pierce my eyes. The tree looked beautiful, with its gold baubles and tulle ribbons cheerfully decorating the branches. I curled up on the sofa and wrapped a warm blanket around me, staring out the window at the snowfall. My mind was racing, not giving me a chance to process anything. All I could think about was how awful I felt.

I should never have come here.

I knew from the start that I didn't want to move to Morecambe, and now I knew I couldn't stay. The truth was shining as bright as the Christmas lights, and it was only a matter of time before I had to face it. As the snow continued to fall, I realised that my relationship was over. I lifted myself off the sofa and walked toward the tree, looking into the lights until my eyes blurred.

What are you doing here, Yvy? You don't belong here.

'I love him. I know I do.'

You love him, but you're not in *love. You should never have moved here.*

'We can make it work, I know we can.'

We don't need to do anything. It's Ben *that needs to get his act together.*

'He's under a lot of pressure. Not working, me taking care of both us. It can't be easy on him. Maybe I'm being selfish, I should try and support him more instead of always nagging.'

Bitch! Listen to yourself! Why are you making excuses for him? I don't see you going on porn sites behind his back? What the fuck, Yvy? Do you honestly think he'll stop at that? No, bitch! What did his friends say about him? That he's a dog! Men like that don't change.

'Yes, he can. I have to believe he can. I mean, it's not like I'm being so honest. I'm keeping secrets too.'

Don't you DARE compare yourself to that bastard. Who you are and what you've been through has nothing to do with this. Besides, you didn't do anything wrong! Your past has nothing to do with him, but what he's doing is unacceptable.

'How did I get here?'

Only you can answer that, Yvy.

It's true, only *I* could answer that. In truth, being in a relationship wasn't what I was looking for initially. All I wanted was to live in the real world, not the transgender bubble everybody saw me living in. Every time I spoke to someone who knew about me, I felt an invisible bubble form, forcing me to keep a distance. I wanted so badly to burst the bubble and be treated like any other person but I couldn't.

What I craved the most was to meet someone who didn't know a thing about me. A person who treated me as just another person who happened to cross paths with and wanted to get to know me. When I first met Ben, only a few months after my surgery, he laid a kiss on me and managed to burst the bubble I so desperately wanted to be released from. Because of that, I did anything I could to make him happy.

After only a few weeks of dating, I was beginning to fall for Ben. He was easy to be around, so attentive and was always thrilled to see me every time I made my way from Blackburn to Manchester to see him. When you start falling for someone, all logic and reason go out the window if you're not careful. I was one of those people. Being around Ben meant I was miles away from the life I led in Blackburn. He was my escapism to a world I yearned for so badly. A world where I was Yvy, nothing else.

I never expected to move to Morecambe, but life took an unexpected turn when Malcolm decided just a few weeks into my relationship with Ben that he wanted to rent his flat in Manchester out to somebody else and move in with Zhen at Beetham Tower. Ben was pissed because he had nowhere else in Manchester to live and no savings to get a place of his own to rent. I wanted to help, but I already gave him all the savings I had to make my own move to Manchester again to help him out of a sticky situation with the courts, so I didn't have enough money to put a deposit down on a flat to rent.

In the end, he had no choice but to move back to Morecambe and live with his mother. I was crushed at the thought of losing him. I'd only just found him and things were going so well. I treated him like a king every time I saw him, buying him expensive gifts and doing all I could to make him happy. I knew we had our differences sometimes, but I always wanted to see the good in him and I knew that if I just stuck with it, he'd let the good side come out more. Benjamin told me all about his struggles with his ex-partners that made me want to be there for him.

'Every girl I've been with has left me,' he said to me. 'They've never given me a chance.'

'I'll never treat you like that, I want to be here for you.'

'I don't want to move back home, I fucking hate this!'

'We'll make it work, I'll come and see you there,'

'What, all the way to Morecambe? No you won't.'

I could tell he was frustrated and upset.

'Listen, you,' I put my hands on his face. 'I'm not going anywhere. I'm all yours.'

Even though I meant what I said, he had a valid point. Ben moving to Morecambe meant I wasn't going to be able to come and visit him as often as we'd like. Manchester was easy to get to from Blackburn, just one train ride and I was there. But getting to the area

234

of Morecambe where his mum lived wasn't an easy place to get to, especially if you didn't drive. The day he moved back to Morecambe came too soon and I went to Manchester to see him off. Ben couldn't hold back the tears as he held me tight. Malcolm waited in the van to drive him back, honking his horn for Ben to say his goodbyes to me. I wanted to make sure he was okay once he got there, and knew he'd have to try and find work, so I gave him a couple of hundred quid to get him through the first few weeks.

'What's this?' he asked.

'Just to keep you going for a bit, until you find a job.'

'What would I do without you?'

'You don't need to think about that. I told you, I'm not going anywhere.'

My heart fell to my stomach as I watched him get into the van and drive away.

For the first few weeks, we stayed in touch via text and MSN Messenger, but it wasn't the same as going to see him in person. The more time we spent apart, the more I felt our relationship was weakening. Ben went from being excited to hear from me, to barely changing his tone every time I called. When we got kinky on a video call, he wasn't acknowledging me in the same way he used to. On top of that, I hadn't visited him since he left and I was stuck in Blackburn all the time, with the invisible bubble forming around me again.

I can't lose him, I just can't.

I decided to go to Morecambe for a visit and spend some time with him for a weekend. I'd never met his mum before but knew they didn't always get along. At first, I had reservations about going, especially after speaking to Ben about it over the phone.

'Are you sure your mum's okay with me staying?'

'Don't worry about her, just come down!'

'Well, I do worry. I don't want to piss her off before she's even met me!'

'Fine! Don't come then.'

Ben hung up.

What the actual fuck? I called him back immediately and he picked up after the second try.

'Hello.'

'Why'd you hang up for? What's wrong?' I was no longer being sweet with him. He was beginning to piss me off.

'Well, you don't want to come and see me so—'

'Did I say that, Ben? No, I didn't. I do want to see you but I don't want to come and stay at your mum's if she doesn't want me there.'

'She does want to meet you.'

'I heard her in the background, she didn't sound very—'

'Seriously, she's fine. So you're coming then?'

'Okay, I will.'

'Yes!' His tone went from dull to thrilled in seconds. *My God, he's like a child.*

I took the train to Morecambe and then a taxi to the address he gave me. As I sat in the back seat, I caught a glimpse of the sea as we drove through and thought about how nice it would be to live by the water. I definitely saw the appeal of living here. I knew very little about Morecambe, and driving through the streets seeing rows of houses pass me by, I felt so far away from the hustle and bustle of Manchester where I usually visit Ben.

As I approached my destination, I saw a few mini markets dotted around but other than that it was pretty much semi-detached houses and nursing homes. It almost felt like I needed to keep my voice down in case I was told off for being too loud. Ben wanted me to meet his friends, so he gave me the address of a couple he'd been friends with for years, David and Cheryl. He told me the night before that they were having a little get together with a bunch of people at their house and wanted to meet me.

As the taxi pulled up to their house, I felt quite nervous. The only friend of Ben I'd ever met was Malcolm, and I couldn't stand him. With that said, I didn't want to put the rest of his friends in the same boat as Malcolm, as he had his own special brand of grossness that only he could produce.

I rang the doorbell but got no answer. I heard laughter and conversation not too far away, so I glanced around the corner and could tell it was coming from the back yard. I followed the pavement slabs and saw a group of people sat around a plastic table having drinks. Ben soon spotted me and the biggest smile grew on his face. He introduced me straightaway to his friends who all seemed really nice. We didn't have much in common, but they wanted to know all about me. They were completely shocked to see me because they apparently didn't believe I actually existed.

Ben mentioned to me before coming to see him that a lot of his friends had seen a picture of me but didn't believe him when he told them that I was his girlfriend. He said they couldn't see how someone so beautiful would be interested in him. At first I thought he was joking but after meeting his friends, it became evident as they were completely shocked that I was real. I have to say, I did feel my ego get bigger and milked it for all it was worth.

As the sun began to set, night took over and so did the copious amount of cheap alcohol that was being consumed. I partook in a bit of drinking, but didn't want to get completely shit faced so I made sure to pace myself. The boys were getting more drunk with every beer, to a point where their inane chatter about how many girls they'd all banged was getting incredibly disturbing, especially when Ben felt the need to try and impress me by bragging that he'd slept with nearly 200 girls and never caught an STD.

At that point, I completely checked out and decided to hang out with the girls instead. Cheryl was lovely, and made me feel really welcome in her home. Her next-door neighbour, Moira, came round to the house and the three of us spent most of the evening getting to know each other. As we chatted in the kitchen, Cheryl and Moira gave me glimpses of their experiences with Ben, most of which didn't paint a very nice picture.

'He's no angel, Yvy,' Moira said. 'He's a fuckin' dog with women. You know he's been married before?'

'No, I didn't. Was it to Maria?'

'You know about Maria?' Cheryl asked.

'He has her name tattooed on his back. I never asked who she was.'

'Yeah it was, treated 'er like shit, he did. He 'as a kid with her too, you know. Doesn't fuckin' bother with 'er neither.'

Don't forget, Yvy, everyone has a past.

I tried not to let it get to me because I knew more than anyone what it meant to have a past that you may not necessarily want to share. Plus, I could tell that Cheryl and Moira took pleasure in spilling the tea about Ben, almost relishing it.

Bitter bitches, maybe?

I excused myself and went to find Ben. I made my way to the living room and pushed the door open to find the boys laughing hysterically with one another whilst sitting on brand new faux leather sofas that looked out of place against the tobacco-stained wallpaper. Ben turned to me, trying his best to let me in on the joke but barely putting a sentence together through the laughter.

'What's so funny?' I asked.

'W-w-we, w-we-ee-ee-ah-haha!' Ben couldn't breathe through his laughter. I looked around and saw three of the four boys. *Ben, David, Matt.*

'Where's Dan?' I asked, trying to avoid the joke Ben was apparently incapable of telling me. The room burst into laughter again, making it clear the joke was on Dan somehow.

'What's so fucking funny? Tell me?' I was growing tired of this. Then I noticed Dan coming out of the bathroom and storming out the house.

'When Dan was in the bog we dipped our balls in his beer and he fuckin' drank it!' Ben said, barely keeping his voice from cracking with laughter.

I tried to find the funny but the only thing I could muster was the taste of revulsion at the back of my throat. I went to the bathroom and locked the door behind me. I turned from the door to find a small box room with a peach coloured bathroom suite that needed a real good cleaning. I closed the toilet lid, wiped it down with some tissue and took a seat. I looked around the room, at the stained carpet, the wicker basket in the corner full of laundry, the damp towels piled up next to the tub.

What the hell am I doing here?

I felt the drunken haze kick in as my head became too heavy to hold up. I cradled my face in my hands and closed my eyes.

***

I stared at the Christmas lights, letting my thoughts take over me. I knew I made a mistake by agreeing to move out here. I couldn't deny it any longer, but beneath that mistake was the truth behind why I made the choice to come here. I mean, I knew the day I first came to visit Ben that I didn't like it. The way he was that day around his friends was repulsive, the town was as dead as a corpse and I was completely alone. I knew nobody when I moved to Morecambe, and sitting alone in front of the warming Christmas lights in the dark, I was still alone. But I knew why I moved here. I truly believed that the further away from Blackburn I was, the further away I was from my past.

In Morecambe, I never had to worry about bumping into somebody I knew. I felt confident going to town with Ben, not feeling on edge in case I turned a corner and spotted a cousin I couldn't stand. I believed I could make it work out here, even though a part of me knew that Ben wasn't the right person for me. We'd been together for eight months, and in that time, the sad times definitely outweighed the good. I went from being a happy, energetic woman, to a paranoid, insecure mess, enslaved by domesticity. All I ever did was go to work at a shitty supermarket until 11 o'clock at night, and come home to Ben, sitting on the sofa watching TV.

When I checked his computer, I'd find that his history was full of porn websites, which made me so angry. I considered myself a sexual person, and although Missy sometimes got tight and sore from time to time, I'd still be up for fooling around. Instead, I was reduced to being a substitute for his own hand, without anything in return. Since meeting Ben, I never came once. No matter how hard I tried, I simply couldn't get there.

Maybe it's me, there's something wrong with me.

In a way, I didn't mind him watching porn, especially if I was at work or out the house, but it bothered me when he began doing it when I was in the house. Whenever I had a shower or cooked in the kitchen, he often had the need to sneak one in. It's not like I was a prude, I was very open to my sexual side, but he had no interest in me anymore, except when it was convenient for him. I knew this was wrong, but if I brought up how I was feeling, it sparked another argument.

You know how sensitive he is. Do you really want to upset him?

Best to keep my feelings to myself. I always had to cater to his feelings, because every time I threw a wrench in the works, he had the power to always make me feel like I'd done wrong by not understanding his feelings. I was too tired for that.

Just then, I heard the staircase creak and the living room door swung open.

'What are you doing sitting in the dark, Yvy?' Ben asked.

'Nothing,' I didn't turn to face him. 'I'm not doing anything.'

'Why are the lights off?'

'I fancied sitting in front of the tree with the lights off, that's all.'

'In the middle of the night? What's wrong?' he asked, his tone sounding nonchalant.

'I don't want to talk about it.'

'Fine, whatever.'

He left the room and I heard the stairs creak as he went back up. Before I could go back to my thoughts, my body jumped out of its skin when the bedroom door slammed shut, sending a thundering boom through the house.

Chapter Twenty

Manchester, 2010

Morecambe life just wasn't agreeing with us. With Ben no closer to finding a job, I felt stuck in a mundane routine of working an eight hour shift in a dead end job, then coming home to a man whose sensitive ego had to be pampered to avoid emotional land mines.

All the while, I had to keep my mouth shut...for the most part. If I kept the peace and didn't ripple the waters, I didn't have to deal with his bad moods. A new year was upon us, 2009 was ending, and we were both tired of Morecambe. Nothing was there for us anymore and our relationship was in dire need of a change in circumstance. I was consumed with feelings of anxiety and self-doubt that I needed a fresh start for us. I didn't want to be riddled with so much negativity anymore, and Ben agreed that going back to Manchester was the best step. He too was sick of not working and not being able to contribute to the house. He saw me going to work every day, struggling to keep up with bills and didn't want me to carry on like that.

With that said, I saw no real effort in him finding a job, which put all the responsibility of the house on my shoulders. I felt resentful that he was getting an easy ride whilst I was slaving my guts out to give him a good life. I felt completely unappreciated. I'd come home from work and feel nothing but tension.

For the times that we were getting along, it was only because I buried my true feelings inside and put on a happy face. But after a while, I didn't have the energy to keep doing it, and the same tension reared its ugly head again. Ben eventually found himself a job in Manchester and we planned to move back. When we thought about it, we were happiest when we were in Manchester. I never felt at home in Morecambe, living in a house I couldn't stand and being in a job I couldn't care less about.

By March, we were back in Manchester, living in a flat together and settling in. Ben was working a lot and I was searching for a new job. Ben and I had been together for almost a year, and although we had our ups and downs, I tried my hardest to make the relationship work. Mum always told me that if I was unhappy I should go back home to Blackburn, but I didn't want to. I didn't want to go back to that bubble again. The thought of living in Blackburn, surrounded by the same gossipy people and judgemental haters, made me sick to my stomach.

I was sick of being seen as the "he-she" and I was damned if I was going back to being the freak of Blackburn. Ben may have had his moments, but he always saw me as Yvy. Because of that, I never wanted to tell him about my past. It wasn't easy, given that I still had to dilate, but I managed to do it. For the most part, I did my dilating when he wasn't around, or I'd tell him what I was doing but not explain the reasons why. He didn't seem to care, which was a relief and hurtful at the same time. My dilating reduced from three times a day to just a few times a week, so it wasn't too excessive.

By the time we settled in, I noticed changes in myself. My body began to blossom in ways I didn't expect. I'd been taking my hormones for long while, and my breasts had developed into a nice A cup which I was happy with. But soon they began to hurt, feeling sore to the touch and grew to a B cup. With that also came my sex drive. For months, my libido had been non-existent, which I chalked up to mine and Ben's waning sexcapades.

Much to my surprise, my sex drive was coming back and all I could think about was sex, sex, sex. It didn't help that we weren't having sex much, and Ben's idea of a good time was asking me to finish him off every time he was making a human tent in his pants, without ever giving it a second thought about my sexual needs. He was clocking an increasing amount of porn time on his laptop, and catching him masturbating when I was in the shower or reading in another room was really getting me angry. Although my body was racing with sexual urges, I had no sexual chemistry towards Ben and felt no intimate attraction.

At first, I tried bringing the subject up discreetly, so not to start an argument. 'Can I ask you something?' I said to him one afternoon.

'Does it not bother you that we haven't had sex in a while?'

'Yeah but you know why. I'm always tired after work and—'

'No I understand, but we don't play like we used to. I mean, I try to but you don't seem interested.'

'I am but if I'm honest, it's difficult when you're so tight.'

My face flushed. I didn't think he'd see Missy being tight as a flaw, but I hated that he noticed. Dilating was essential to maintain depth and width, but it still put me at a disadvantage when it came to spontaneous sex because I wouldn't have a chance to prepare myself first. We weren't having much sex, but for the times that we did, feeling Ben enter me still felt like a blunt blade that hurt so fucking much. It's hard to feel horny when you can't get past the pain.

'I understand, I do. But it upsets me when—'

I couldn't bring myself to say it. I knew that if I brought up the porn issue, I'd either get an earful or he'd just shut down and not talk to me. If he knew how insecure and unattractive his behaviour was making me feel, would he even care?

Of course he wouldn't, Yvy!

A few weeks later and still no closer to having a much-needed orgasm, I laid in bed, feeling restless. Ben was in the bathroom brushing his teeth when he soon emerged to join me. I laid on my side and felt him shuffle up behind me, feeling his arm wrap around my waist. It felt so good. He held me tighter and I felt his breath on my neck. I was dying for him to kiss me, something I hadn't felt in a long while.

It was noticeable of late that his kisses were limited to a single peck on the lips, followed by me attempting a second kiss but ending up catching his cheek or neck as he turned away. Ben took his arm off me and rolled onto his back, pulling my arm over in an indication to face him. I did as suggested and wrapped my arm across his chest. He took my hand and pushed it under the covers, placing my hand on his hard penis. I instantly knew what was happening.

Here we go again, it's all about him.

I was in no mood for yet another session where I satisfied his needs and Missy was left feeling neglected. I took my hand away and turned from him again, lying on my side.

'What's wrong?' he asked.

'Nothing. I'm just not in the mood.'

'C'mon, just do it for me. I'm hard.'

'No, I'm not in the mood!' I said, being more forceful.

'Fine, whatever!' he turned away from me.

'Why are you being like this? It's not all about you, you know!' I got up out of bed and stood up. 'Do you think I enjoy being a substitute for your wanking arm when you get tired of watching porn?'

'You know what, I'm fucking sick of you barking at me all the fucking time!' Ben got out of bed too, the both of us standing on opposite sides. 'All you fucking do is nag me to death, I'm sick of it!'

'Just because I say something you don't like doesn't mean I'm nagging. I do everything for you and it's not wrong to want a little appreciation.'

'And that's what you think, is it? I don't fucking appreciate you?'

'You don't! I feel awful all the time.'

'I'm not talking about this,' Ben stormed into the living and slammed the door.

For days, we barely spoke a word to each other. I was getting so tired of the same routine. Every time I disagreed with him, he blew up.

How much more of this can I take?

He went to work the next day, leaving me alone in the house. I knew that checking his laptop wasn't good, but I couldn't help it. I was feeling so insecure that I had to know if he was still visiting porn sites when I was in the house. I logged onto his computer and found something shocking. I clicked onto his internet history and ran through the visited sites. Porn site after porn site after porn site showed up.

Are you really that surprised, Yvy?

But then, I saw a site that didn't look like just a porn site. It was a hook up site.

'*Be Naughty*'! What the fuck is this?

I saw that the member log-in had a user name but no password.

What the actual fuckery?

I was fuming. It was one thing looking at porn but quite another logging into sites designed specifically to meet people for sex. I didn't know what to do.

Fucking confront the bastard!

I couldn't tell him I knew, otherwise he'd know that I was looking at his computer when he wasn't around. No, I had a better idea. I logged onto my own laptop and created a profile on 'Be Naughty' in an attempt to find out what he was up to. It was pretty obvious what he was up to, but I needed to see for myself. A small part of me wanted to believe that what I was accusing him of wasn't true. I mean, I knew we had problems but would he *really* do that to me? He knew better than to actually cross that line and cheat on me.

Doesn't he?

If I confronted him, he'd deny it and shut me out, then I'll never get to the truth. This was the only way to get the truth. I logged on and created a profile. Given that I spent over two years working in a sex shop, I had a pretty good idea of what to write in my profile. I mean, it doesn't take much to please a man, but I didn't want to be a whore. I wanted it to sound believable.

Priya, 27

Hi,

I'm Priya from Manchester. I'm looking for a guy I can have some fun with and get to know more. I'm open to relationships, but I'd rather have a bit of fun before I settle down.

You should never ask a girl what's she's in to, that spoils the surprise! Let's just say I like to be adventurous, and I want to meet someone who can keep up with a girl like me.

If you're interested, get in touch!

I couldn't put on a photo, that would've given me away, so I waited a few days before messaging him. I saw his profile, and he'd written that he was looking for a good time and wanted to meet someone he could have fun with. I sent him a message saying hello and that I was new on the site, then waited to see if he took the bait.

I waited for a few days, logging in to check if he replied. During that time, I received direct messages from men asking to "smell yo cunt" and "finger you till it hurt".

Fuck off!

It was easy to ignore the messages, but I didn't necessarily get offended by their overtly confident advances. They didn't have a chance in hell with me and it was easy to block somebody if they became too much. But then, I received a message from a guy that didn't seem to be like all the others.

'Hi, Priya. My name is Chris. Be lovely to chat with you.'

Considering every other message I received started with how much they wanted to turn me into their slam piece, Chris seemed to be quite different. I messaged him back to see if maybe this was just a front.

'Hi, Chris, thanks for messaging me.'

'You're welcome. I like your profile. You seem different from the women I've met on here.'

'How so?'

'Classy. Some of these profiles are pretty ropey!'

'Fair enough! What are you looking for on here?'

'Not sure, really. I'm just seeing what's out there and hoping to meet a girl I can get on with.
How about you?'

I didn't know what to say in response. I wasn't looking for anybody, and telling Chris the truth about why I was on here would definitely make me sound crazy.

'I'm not sure either. I've had a few crazies message me, so I'm taking my time!'

'Good idea! I've had my fair share too!'

As we chatted some more, he seemed like a really easy-going guy who actually wanted to talk. So far, he hadn't tried to steer the conversation to something filthy, and given the type of site this was, I found that somewhat refreshing.

Just as I was about to reply to him, I saw that I had a new inbox message. It was from Benjamin.

'Hi. Love your profile. Y no pic?'

My heart was beating hard, not from excitement but from anger. He was taking the bait, now I wanted to see how far he'd take it. I explained to him that I didn't want to put a picture on here because I was still in a relationship and didn't want to get caught. I thought that maybe if I said that, he might also say he's in a relationship. He didn't. He tried hard to get me to send him a picture but I resisted. He continued to message, with each one getting dirtier, and I knew that the awful truth was coming out. He soon asked if I wanted to do a video call with him. When I asked why, his answer was pretty explicit.

There you go, you knew the bastard was like this!

I didn't want to believe it, but the evidence couldn't be denied. I couldn't pretend I didn't know, but I didn't know how to handle the situation. All I could think was what did I do to drive him to this. Was it me?

Am I that shit a girlfriend that he'd rather wank off to porn and meet women online than be with me?

I'd never felt so little of myself in my life. All I wanted to do was disappear. I was about to log off the site when another inbox message came through.

'I hope I'm not being too forward, but I'd love to meet you for a drink. No strings. Be nice to get to know you more.'

Chris seemed like an okay guy, and Ben clearly didn't give a shit, so what's the harm? If Ben could act this way behind my back, he had no room to say anything to me. For all I knew, he'd already met up with girls on here and done God knows what with them. Why shouldn't I get to have some fun?

Fuck it, Yvy! Go for it!

'Sure. Meet at Canal Street this weekend?'

We agreed to meet at Mantos, a club right in the heart of the Village. I thought it best to meet somewhere public and busy, just in case Chris turned out to be a weirdo and I needed to exit-stage-left with haste.

As I made my way into town on the tram, I wondered if I was going too far. Yes, what Ben was doing was very wrong, but am I any better meeting up with a guy I barely knew? I knew I wasn't going to sleep with Chris, but is it still right?

Even though I was absolutely furious with Ben, I still couldn't shut off my feelings. I loved Ben in my heart, but my mind was pulling me in the opposite direction. I didn't know what to follow, my heart or my head. My head told me to go on this date. I tried not to think of it as a date but it clearly was. I walked towards Mantos and text Chris to see if he was already there. He text back, telling me he was waiting for me on the balcony.

I approached the bar and looked up discreetly to see a man sitting alone at a table. *Oh shit! No turning back now!* I made my way upstairs and without hesitation, he knew that it was me. 'Hi Priya!' he said, pleasantly happy to see me.

Chris was so handsome in a rugged yet sweet kind of way. He was around 5ft 7, short dark hair and a slim build. His smile was adorable, and his eyes were inviting swirls of chocolate brown. He was dressed smartly in a pair of jeans and crisp shirt, with a trimmed beard that gave him a rough edge. Definitely a face I could picture myself sitting on.

'Hi! Nice to meet you!' I said as I took a seat.

Straightaway, he offered to get me a drink. When he returned with my vodka lemonade, we got to know each other. He was so easy to talk to, and I found myself really enjoying his company. He wasn't coming across as arrogant or trying to put on a front in any way, which made me think of how Ben was when we first met. When I cast my mind back to the day he walked in at my work, it felt so fake with his plastic smile and cheesy, off putting one-liners.

Why didn't I see it at the time!

Sitting with Chris, I felt like I was in the company of a genuinely nice guy who was completely honest with me.

'You are beautiful, Priya,' Chris said. 'What is a girl like you doing on 'Be Naughty'? You look like you could get your pick of any guy!'

Just be honest, Yvy, don't string him along. He's too nice to be strung along.

'If I'm honest, my name isn't Priya. It's Yvy.'

I waited for his face to change, but he just carried on listening. 'I joined because I actually have a boyfriend and I saw that he was on 'Be Naughty' and I wanted to catch him out.'

'Really? Wow, okay. Well, your boyfriend sounds like a dick, if you don't mind me saying.'

247

I laughed. I was so surprised at his reaction. I honestly thought he'd bolt after hearing I was there under false pretences.

'Things are really rocky between us,' I said, beginning to open up. 'We've not had sex for so long and when we do it's never good. I feel so sexual and he's not seeing that. I try to get him in the mood to please me but it ends with me always pleasing him. It's such a turn off.'

'Well, he's definitely a dick for not wanting to sleep with you! But seriously, you're a great girl, you shouldn't waste time with someone who doesn't appreciate you.'

'I know, it's just hard to walk away for some reason. We're in a really shitty place, but I don't want to be like him. I met up with you because I wanted to feel, well, oh, forget it.'

'Feel what?'

'No, it's stupid, really!'

'Tell me!'

'To feel wanted. Desired. I don't feel very wanted these days.'

'Trust me. If I had my way, you'd be coming home with me. But I get what you're saying and I totally respect that. But if things don't work out with the other guy, don't forget me!'

'I promise!'

***

The most difficult thing to hold on to in life is yourself. It's easy to give your heart to another, feel it break and still feel compelled to continue loving the person that hurt you the most. It never makes sense but we do it, sometimes over and over again in an endless pattern of bad judgement. But hearts can heal. We can learn from our mistakes but only when we accept them first. But all that goes out the window if we don't hold on to who we are. It took over two decades to become the person I knew I was, and I gave it away before I got a chance to truly love myself.

It's not easy loving yourself, and if you're foolish enough to give yourself away, loving who you are becomes almost impossible.

Ben and I continued our relationship, despite the fact that I knew what he was up to. My self-esteem was so low, that not even Chris could pull me out of it. After meeting him, I didn't keep in contact because I felt incredibly guilty. Ben and I fought furiously for months, constantly breaking up and getting back together but for some reason I just couldn't let go. I poured so much of myself into the relationship that I didn't realise I was pouring everything away.

What was left was an empty void that I could only fill with the negative bullshit in our relationship. My life suddenly became bleak, with no bright future in sight. Ben continued to be a ticking time bomb of emotions, blowing up every time something didn't go his way.

I became a vacant space, walking on eggshells around him and trying my best to make a bad situation bearable. Sex between us was getting worse, and I felt like it was all my fault.

You deserve this, Yvy.

By the time Christmas had come around, I was totally checked out of the relationship. Every other day, Ben and I fought about something petty. It seemed as though I couldn't do anything without pissing him off and being around him was the last thing I wanted to do.

So why didn't I leave, you ask? The answer to that one is simple. *Stupidity.* I had no money to move away. Over the course of our relationship, I'd given him so much money and bought him expensive gifts but got nothing in return. I had no savings to speak of, and the household debts were piling up. I was stuck.

As we saw in another New Year, I knew that our relationship was over. No matter how many times we tried to resuscitate what we had, I had to accept that it just simply needed to die. Once I broke it off with Ben, I had to try my best to live with him until I had enough money to move out. Ben became toxic to be around, always trying to make me jealous of women he was speaking to online and then telling me he wanted to be with me again. My mind was scattered with contradictory thoughts, and all I wanted was to escape the hell of living with someone who was ripping me apart. We slept in separate rooms and tried to stay out of each other's way, but the ugly truth was staring at me whenever I looked in the mirror. I gave so much of myself to him that I didn't recognise myself anymore.

I stood in front of the mirror, looking at a face I didn't register was me. I was alone in my room, feeling vacant.

Look at you. You're pathetic!

'I don't know what to do. I hate that he sees other girls.'

He blames you! You did this! You're the one fucking everything up!

'No I'm not! I'm doing the right thing.'

Are you? I mean, look how weak you are without him! You're PATHETIC! You don't even know who you are without him!

'That's not true! I'm Yvy. I'm not going to give myself to him again.'

Too late! You already did! Now look at you! You're nothing!

Knock! Knock! Knock! I snapped out of my haze to the banging on my bedroom door. I opened it to find Ben standing with a plump young woman.

'Yvy, this is Melissa,' Ben said. 'I told you about her, didn't I?'

I was stunned. I didn't know what to say. I couldn't believe he brought a girl he'd been seeing to my bedroom door. She was short, with messy, wiry hair in thorough need of a conditioning and a fringe.

'Melissa, this is Yvy.'

'Hi, Yvy. I've heard so much about you,' she said in a cheerful yet snide tone.

I was so shook, all I wanted to do in that moment was scratch both of their eyes out like a berserk carnival monkey. I pushed my feelings inside and did what I did best, I put on a happy face.

'Hi, Melissa, nice to meet you! So what do think of our Ben?'

'Awww, Yvy, stop!' Ben said, feeling somewhat awkward.

'Urrm I don't know, I guess!' Melissa said, not knowing what to say through the built up tension.

'Well, we're going in my room so I'll see you later,' Ben said.

'Okay! Have fun!' I said as I closed the door.

I thought I was going to be devastated to see him with another girl. Ever since we broke up, all I did was obsess about what he was doing and who he was seeing, being consumed with insecure thoughts of him sleeping with other women. But when I came face to face with the situation, I suddenly realised, I didn't care. Any feelings I had for Ben disappeared, and I saw him for what he was. A pathetic, insecure being that needed validation from others to make himself feel better. He projected his own feelings about himself onto me and somehow convinced me that that was how I felt about myself.

How could I have been so fucking stupid?

My phone began to buzz on the bedside table and saw that it was a message from Chris.

'Hi, Yvy! Long time, no speak? How are you?'

I felt compelled to see him again. Hell, if Ben was fucking around with other bitches, why can't I have some fun? I had such a blast with Chris and I was no longer in a relationship. I had no reason to feel guilty! I told him that I wasn't with Ben anymore and he immediately asked to meet up.

'Do you fancy meeting up next Saturday?'
'Aww I'd love to come to yours... It'll be nice to have a change of scene from here.'

I arrived at his place and spent the evening with him and his roommates. At first I thought Chris and I had an attraction going on, but his roommate Sarah seemed more into me than he was. I enjoyed the mild flirtation, and reciprocated which got Sarah even more drawn to me. It was a first to be around a woman that I thought was attractive, and I enjoyed being free to express those feelings. But I could tell that Chris was feeling a little left out. Sarah and I knew it was harmless, and she soon went to bed leaving Chris and I alone to watch movies.

By the end of the evening, I wasn't getting any vibes from Chris that told me he was interested. *Maybe he's having second thoughts!* It was getting late and we decided to call it a night, making our way up to the attic. I walked into his room, looking at the double bed, thinking about where I was going to sleep. Chris mentioned he had an inflatable mattress, but it definitely hadn't been inflated. I turned around to ask him where it was and suddenly felt his kiss. I kissed him softly, and as he pulled away and looked into my eyes, I suddenly became incredibly shy.

'Why are you laughing?' Chris asked me as I started to giggle.

'I don't know! I'm just surprised! I thought you weren't interested?'

'Are you fucking kidding? I thought I was going to have to fight Sarah to have you to myself!'

He kissed me again, pulling me close and gripping me in his arms. We fell onto the bed, and we peeled out of each other's clothes. I laid on the bed, feeling the nerves of past experiences wash over me. My body tensed up, concerned that once again I was about to have a terrible sexual experience. Chris embraced me, kissing every inch of body. I felt his skin against mine as he worked his way between my legs. As he went in for the taste, I jumped as I felt it tickle, letting out an uncontrollable giggle. Chris tasted deeper, and my body began to melt with pleasure. I never felt such sensation before. Chris continued until my body couldn't take it. I felt my muscles turn to jelly as he pressured his tongue deeper. It was an overwhelming pressure building inside me, turning my stomach inside out. My heart was slamming against my chest and my skin was on fire. I couldn't keep still, bringing my hands up to my breasts as my back arched, letting Chris sink further.

As I tilted my pelvis, I suddenly felt a shock wave of energy course through me as Chris tasted my clitoris. I couldn't think straight, all I could do was lose myself in a moment of unbridled ecstasy, growing to an inevitably beautiful crescendo. *La Vie En Rose* began to play, filling the room with its romantic melody.

Where the hell is that music coming from?

As my screams got louder, I bit the corners of the pillows to try and control them. His rhythm quickened, as did the sensations, while Edith Piaf's serenade filled my head. I saw myself, standing on a glossy black stage with an orchestra. Dressed in a flowing black gown, they played the music as I stood centre stage, facing front, my hair pinned beautifully with pearls, ready to sing.

Quand il me prend dans ses bras
Il me parle tout bas
Je vois la vie en rose

Il me dit des mots d'amour
Des mots de tous les jours
Et ça me fait quelque chose.

The pleasure of Chris' touch built and built to an unbearable level. Every cell in my body woke up, responding to his touch with welcoming pleasure. I was getting closer, and closer, feeling the nerves in my fingers and toes going numb.

It's happening!
I couldn't believe it!

Il est entré dans mon cœur
Une part de bonheur
Dont je connais la cause.

Before I could string a thought together, I came. I came so hard that my body shuddered uncontrollably. A burst of energy blasted out of me and suddenly, I ascended from the stage. Floating above the band playing their sweet music, the silk of my gown faded to ivory as pink rose petals swirled around in a frantic dance. I reached higher and higher, my hands caressing the soft petals. My face was alive with desire, letting pleasure take over as I sang the final words to the heavens…

And when you speak, angels sing from above
Everyday words seem to turn into love songs

Give your heart and soul to me
And life will always be
La vie en rose!

Chris watched as his efforts caused me to explode with every cell in my quivering body. I opened my eyes and heard the audience cheer and whistle in my head. I smiled, laying on a bed of fresh rose petals.

La, la la, la la, la la…

We had sex all night, until we couldn't go on any longer. Chris opened me up in so many ways. He taught me more about my body than I could ever comprehend. Ever since my surgery, I worried that I wouldn't find a connection. I didn't know if I'd be able to be the sexual being I always dreamed of becoming.

Being with Ben, I didn't realise at the time that my body was telling me he was not the one for me. My body shut down to him, and I had to settle with what I could offer. Chris made me realise that what I was doing was all wrong. What my body needed wasn't sex, it was passion. A woman needs to be comfortable, and most importantly, feel passion.

Without passion, Missy was as dry as the Sahara desert. She wasn't interested in being second to a dick. *Hell no!* Missy needed to be treated with the love and attention that she damn well deserved! Missy doesn't come second, she always comes first! Chris gave me the sexual awakening I'd been screaming out for, and in return I chose to reward him in abundance.

By that I mean sex. Lots and lots of sex.

Just So You Know...

So it's pretty obvious if you've got to this point that yes, transgender people have sex! We have crazy, filthy, almost dislocated a hip type sex and also the love-making sex that's sweet, gentle and involves a lot of obnoxiously loved up Facebook relationship statuses post-coital.

Either way, we have sex. Further to this, our bodies do work in ways you may not expect. For years, I didn't know if I could get wet during sex, given that nobody really explained whether I was able to do so. Plus, it wasn't exactly a question I wanted to ask my consultant before I was knocked out for surgery.

However, I was pleasantly surprised that Missy was capable of this if stimulated in the perfect way (thanks for that, Chris!). Another baffling thing that I thought would never happen to me was period pains.

Yes, that's right!

After the first few months of my surgery, my body was no longer producing natural hormones and my hormone replacement medication was the only hormones surging through my body. As a result, I began to experience stomach cramps once a month that felt like my intestines were about to explode. I had no idea what was going on. When I went to Charing Cross and brought it up with my consultant, I was told that they were in fact period pains.

Who'd have thought it!

So there you go people, every body works in mysterious ways, so embrace it!

Chapter Twenty-One

Manchester, 2011

I was packed and ready to leave. My belongings were boxed up and the removal van was outside, raring to go. After two years, I had finally had enough. I couldn't take another second being around Ben, not just because of him but mostly because of what I had become. I couldn't stand looking in the mirror and not recognising myself. I had to get myself back, and getting away from him was the first step. Feroza helped me move, along with my friend Debbie and her partner, Giles. I knew Debbie from work, and we bonded the moment we first met. She soon became my closest friend, always looking out for me and making me smile. I'd only known her a couple of months before I moved out of the flat at the end of April, but she was right there with me, helping me through it all. She knew what was going on with Ben, but she never had the displeasure of actually meeting him.

Living with Ben after I made the decision to not take him back was excruciating. It was only for a few months, but they may as well have been years. Avoiding him at all costs was best, so I camped out in my bedroom and pretty much stayed to myself. Every day, I went to work and when I came home I went straight upstairs in our duplex flat and stayed in my room watching TV. I wanted little to no contact with Ben until I left.

However, that wasn't always possible. Ben wanted to get back together, but I had to stay strong and stick to my guns. His way of making me want him was to start bringing women back to the flat, which included the little Hobbit woman, Melissa. It made being away from him easier, I guess, because I knew he was only bringing women back to our home because he was hurting and he wanted to hurt me more. I did hurt, but in a different way. I wasn't suffering from a broken heart, I was angry at his total lack of respect after everything we'd been through.

But as moving day arrived, I wanted to start looking forward. 'If I bloody met him he'd get a right slap!' Debbie said as she helped bring boxes down to the van.

'Thankfully, you never will! I'm just glad to be getting out of here.'

'Where is he anyway?'

'He's at work, so he won't be around for a while.'

'Does he know you're leaving today?' Feroza asked.

'Yeah, I just didn't want to do it with him around. I can't handle another fight with him.'

'Good point, c'mon, let's get these boxes in the van.'

I joined Debbie on the tail lift that brought us into the van to shift the boxes in. 'It's good you're getting away from him, he was never bloody good enough for you,' Feroza said as she took another drag of her cigarette.

'Too right!' Debbie said.

'You going down then, Yvy?' she asked as she reached for the tail lift button to lower us to the ground.

'I do like seeing two women going down!' Giles said with a grin. Debbie and I couldn't help but laugh.

I didn't have to go very far to my new home; in fact, it was on the same stretch of road I was already living on, just a few blocks over in the same building I used to live in when I moved from Chorlton years ago. Still, Ben didn't know where I was moving to, but he was also planning on moving someplace else so I didn't care. When I found the flat online, it didn't have any pictures, just a description for a spacious two bedroom. It was in my price range and I was desperate so I arranged a viewing with the landlord. Thankfully, it turned out to be just what I needed. Once I had all my belongings in the flat, I looked around and saw boxes towering everywhere and black bin liners stuffed with clothes.

'Don't bother with it tonight, Yvy,' Debbie said. 'You're staying over at ours.'

'No, don't be silly. I'll stay here!'

'It'll all still be here in the morning! It's getting late now so stay at ours and relax. In the morning, we'll bring you back and you can get cracking on all this!'

Debbie had a point. I really couldn't be bothered with unpacking everything. I had no food in the house, barely any furniture, not even any internet connection.

Fuck it, deal with it tomorrow!

I took Debbie up on her offer and stayed over at her place with Giles.

I laid in bed, listening to the ticking clock on the wall in Debbie's spare room, thinking about what I was going to do moving forward. I spent a lot of time on my relationship with Ben and had nothing to show for it. Now that it was over, I felt so lost within myself. I'd gone so long not telling anybody I was transgender, that I never debated whether to bring it up when I met new people, even with Debbie, whose friendship I valued the most.

Being with Ben, I kept that part of my life locked away because I felt that in doing so, I was being honest. You're probably scratching your head right now thinking *what the hell is she going on about?* The truth is, I always felt like my life before my transition was a lie. For years, I lived inside the body of a person who wasn't me. I tried to convince the world that that person was me, until I discovered a way of living my truth. Keeping my past to myself never felt like a lie, but I had to tell lies to keep my secret. Whenever Ben and I spoke about past relationships, having children, even my issues with Missy, I had to lie. They were never too elaborate that I had to try and remember every detail, but I made sure that they were the type that didn't need an explanation. The simpler the lie meant never having to bring it up again, but a part of me still felt guilty.

Don't get me wrong, I never felt guilty about keeping my past from Ben. At the end of the day, it was none of his business, but I felt like I was depriving myself of exploring who I was. I'd gone through my entire transition without ever meeting another trans person. I didn't have any trans friends, or had any advice from someone who'd gone through what I'd gone through. I never reached out to the transgender community because I had no idea how to do it. I learnt to protect myself to a point where I didn't want to reach out in case it ended badly.

As a result, I did everything by myself. But I didn't see that as a bad thing. Doing it alone meant I had nobody talking in my ear, telling me how to live my life. I never looked outward for how to act as a trans woman or how to speak as a trans woman, because I didn't see myself as a trans woman. I saw myself as Yvy. For years I lived that way, not worrying about outside influences, that it became confusing when I began to let relationships into my Yvyworld. The moment I began interacting with people and letting people in, my comfortable solitary way of living suddenly changed. It was hard to grasp the concept of sharing my life with another person, that I went about it all wrong. Instead of sharing my life, I gave it all away, except for my past, as a way of compensating for what I was holding back.

When I met Benjamin, I wanted to keep my past a secret, so I compensated by giving him every other part of me, without thinking about the consequences. By the time we moved from Morecambe and I was back in Manchester, I was empty. I didn't recognise myself because there wasn't anything left in me to recognise. The only part of me that I still held on to was my past, but I couldn't talk to Ben, so I decided that it was finally time to reach out to my community.

As the ticking of the clock continued to tap at my ears, I recalled the time I visited a transgender forum for the first time. I hadn't long been back in Manchester, and Ben and I were getting along, mostly because I felt it was better to keep the peace and was tired of constantly being at each other's throats. I searched online and found a transgender forum in Chorlton, right around the corner from where I used to live in my little attic. I took the 86 bus to Chorlton from Piccadilly Gardens and pressed the stop button as it approached the four banks.

As I made the rest of the way on foot, I wondered if I should even bother going. I mean, I'd come so far without reaching out, why do it now? I stood in front of the big wooden doors of the Wilbraham St Ninian's United Reformed Church, thinking about whether I should push them open.

Why are you here, Yvy? What do you think you'll find?

Ben knew I was going to a group therapy meeting but didn't know much else. It was early evening, around 7:30 pm, and the sun had long gone down by the time I reached the church. I thought it was strange somehow to hold a transgender meeting in a church, but when I opened the doors and walked in, I saw that it looked less like a church and more like a community hall.

'Hello!' a woman said as she walked up to me.

She was much older than I was, with dark hair and a smile that went from ear to ear.

'Hi,' I said.

I looked at the group of women seating themselves in the large circle of chairs.

'I'm Mary Bridgeford.'

'Hi Mary, I'm Yvy.'

I made my way over to the refreshment table and poured myself a cuppa before taking a seat in the circle. I looked around at all the faces. Some looked confident and were outspoken, and others were more reserved and kept to themselves. I was one of the reserved ones.

As the meeting began, Mary spoke on topics about hate crime and what we can do to stay safe. The group began sharing experiences of violence and discrimination that were pretty hard to hear. To think these beautiful people were subjected to physical violence just for being who they were was heart breaking. As I sat with my warm cup in my hands, I remembered when I was assaulted at the bank a few years ago, a memory I had since buried in the back of my mind.

'We'll take a ten minute break now so you can get yourselves a cup of tea and chat to one another,' Mary said as she played a Lisa Stansfield video on YouTube to cut the silence in the room.

It was then that I realised that my tea had gone cold and I hadn't taken so much as a sip of it. I stood up to make another when one of the women came up to me at the refreshment table. She was tall, slender and dressed in a black velvet dress. The choker around her neck and purple lipstick was giving a '90s' vibe that I quite liked.

'I've not seen you here before,' she said.

'It's my first time. I used to live round here so I thought I'd come by.'

'Yeah? I'm from Didsbury, so it's easy to get here. I'm Annette by the way.'

'Yvy.'

'You from Manchester?'

'I'm originally from Blackburn, but I live in Salford now.'

'Cool. So do you do support for trans people, or—'

'What do you mean?'

'I saw you talking with Mary when you came in. She runs this group. Thought you already knew her.'

'Oh no, I don't know her, she was just saying hello. But no, I've never done any support work, I just wanted to check it out and meet some new people.'

'Oh, right. Come to *check* us out, are you?'

I wasn't quite sure where she was going with this. Her face looked stern as she attempted to size me up. The prolonged silence continued as the water for the tea continued to boil, then it suddenly dawned why she was being a little stand-offish. She had no idea that I was trans. She thought I was an outsider, trying to take a sneak peek into a community without being invited.

'Do you do much support work?' I asked, trying to ease the growing tension.

'Yes, actually, I do. I volunteer my time a lot to the Forum.'

'That's great. I wish I knew about stuff like this when I went through my transition,' I said, making a blunt statement of my status. Annette looked up from her tea, stunned.

'You're trans? I would never have guessed!' she said, quickly going from stunned to amazed.

'Well, I guess you shouldn't be so quick to judge!' I picked up my tea and went back to my seat.

The second half of the meeting was an open discussion about any topic we wanted to discuss. I wasn't ready to speak, so I listened to what the women had to say. Every person had a story to tell, and soon the spotlight was on me.

'So, Yvy,' Mary said, 'do you have anything you'd like to share?'

I looked around the room and saw all eyes were on me. I didn't know what to say. My thoughts were so scattered and unfocused.

Don't think, Yvy, just start talking and let the words come out.

'I started my transition back in 2005, and I did it alone. In many ways I feel that kept me from being a part of the trans community, but in other ways, I'm glad it did. I had no choice but to be strong and protect myself. I knew that only I mattered and nothing else came before me. But once I started letting people into my life, I didn't know how to function. I didn't know how to put myself first when I had to make room for other people. It made me lose balance. It made me lose me. Now I'm finding it hard to get that special part of me back again. I'm scared that if I don't get it back, I'll lose it forever, and I won't be myself anymore.'

The room was silent, listening to every word that came out of my mouth. The echo of my voice hit every wall, finding its way back to my ears, creating a soft repetition.

'Who would you be then?' one of the women asked.

'Nobody.'

Nobody. That's exactly how I felt as the ticking of the wall clock got louder, cutting through the deafening silence that filled the void in my head. I was so unrecognisable to myself that I felt like I wasn't alive, like a slip in time that was forever lost.

I hated feeling like an empty vessel, with absolutely no clue how to regain the person I wanted to be. I never went back to the church for another meeting again after that, but admitting how I truly felt to those ladies stuck with me. From the moment those words left my mouth, I knew that being with Ben was never going to last. Still, I stuck with him for almost a year after that before I finally moved out. I tried to think of rational reasons as to why I chose to stay so long, but I was coming up empty. All I could hear was the voice in my head, telling me truths I didn't want to hear.

You know why you stayed with him! You know why!

'No, I don't.'

Yes, you do! You stayed because you were weak!

'No, I wasn't. I'm not weak.'

You didn't start off that way, but you let that bastard in and now look at you. You've fucked up everything you worked for and now you've got fuck all to show for it! You're a mess!

'I'll turn my life around. I know I can do it.'

TURN YOUR LIFE AROUND? DON'T MAKE ME FUCKING LAUGH!

'I will turn my life around. I already am.'

WHAT? You think moving into a flat will magically solve your problems? NO! You still have to live with yourself and if you don't sort yourself out, all the bullshit you do won't mean anything.

'You're wrong. As soon as I settle in my flat I'll be—'

YOU'RE NOT LISTENING! Start with settling into yourself, not your fucking flat! You're the one who let yourself go. You're the one who allowed yourself to be hollowed out! It's all on YOU! So fucking FIX IT!

I was sick and tired of hearing the words swirl around in my head. I didn't want to hear it because I knew deep down that it was true. I refused to acknowledge the truth and attempted to press it down as much as I could, but that voice of reason found a way to claw back into my ear, telling me what I didn't want to hear. I had enough.

***

Living alone again felt so good. I settled into my flat and had been there for almost a month, doing my usual routine of work and home. I had the freedom again to do whatever I wanted, without worrying about anybody else. I saw Chris every so often for some amazing sex, both at my place and at his. There were no strings attached so we had the freedom to satisfy each other physically and not worry about either of us becoming needy or possessive. We were together when we wanted to be and apart when we wanted to be. It was the perfect arrangement. It definitely helped that Chris was incredibly easy to get on with. He always made me laugh, and I loved spending time with him. We'd meet up for sex, of course, but the time before and after always felt like two best buddies spending some time together. He was uncomplicated and I liked that, my escapism. Every time he made me come hard, I felt a surging release that took me away from everything I was feeling. All the confusion and sadness dissipated in that one moment and I found solace.

But as soon as it was over, I found myself back to where I started, feeling empty. Sex was a drug. I wanted it all the time because I wanted to constantly escape the reality of my truth. I didn't want to face the truth and admit my failings. It felt easier to run away from my feelings than deal with them. If I had my way, I'd have had sex every single day, but given how intense my sessions with Chris usually got, I had a feeling it would kill him to have to satisfy my hunger on a daily basis. Besides, it was the climax I was hungry for. It was the euphoric moment of vibration when I felt myself lift away from all my troubles that I needed. Like any craving, it evolves and grows into something bigger and bigger until it's too late to realise that your addiction has consumed you. Sex was amazing, but I needed a harder fix. I started with smoking weed, but all it did was mellow me out when I wanted to be stimulated. A friend from work hooked me up with weed when I needed it, but it wasn't really getting the job done. I dialled his number and asked for a favour.

'Hey, Liam,' I said as he answered his phone.

'Y' alright gorgeous?' he said to me.

'You free after work?'

'Yeah, I am. You want some gear?'

'Yeah, I do. You got anything different though?'

'I'll bring somethin' round for ya.'

Liam rang the intercom after his shift and I let him in. Liam wasn't my type, which made it easier to hang out with him because I didn't have any attraction towards him. The last thing I wanted to do when I got high was start being all weird with Liam because I had feelings for him.

Definite buzz kill.

I knew Liam liked me, as he made it very evident every time he tried to make out with me when he was stoned, but I never took his advances to heart. Liam walked into the flat with his workbag and a smile on his face.

'Y' alright?'

'Yeah, I'm good, how's you?'

'Can't complain. You by yourself tonight?

'Yeah, planning on chilling at home.'

'Not out with Debs, are ya? You two are always out doing somethin'.'

'Nah, we're taking a Friday off. Did you bring something round for me then?'

'Course I did, babes,' Liam pulled out a clear plastic re-sealable bag full of weed and a smaller bag with three pink, diamond shaped pills.

'What are those?' I asked.

'These are for you,' he handed me the bag and I looked at the pills through the plastic. *Ecstasy.*

'Don't take a full one, Yvy. Half it first and see if you like it. If you feel up to it you can take a whole one, but they're proper strong.'

'Shall I take one now?'

'Nah, save these! This is good shit! It's better to have these on a night out, or when you're having sex! So if you want to try it now, I can help you out!'

'Nice try, I'll save 'em instead! Now roll up and let's smoke!'

It was so much easier to run away from my feelings than deal with them, because dealing with them meant admitting that I had failed myself. I couldn't bear the thought of admitting that. Smoking weed was a good way to relax my mind, but I hated the actual act of smoking it. I never even smoked so much as a cigarette in my life, so I hated having to inhale smoke and blow it back out just to get a buzz. Plus, I didn't like smoking in my flat, filling the air with an ashy fog that remained long after I finished a joint.

Ecstasy was so much easier. By summer time, I was a party animal, going out almost every weekend and getting fucked up. I'd get dressed up, meet with friends from work and find every possible way to escape my own thoughts. Most of the time, I hated the clubs and bars we went to. They were never my scene, but I didn't care so long as it got me out of the house. Clubs that played music like

Kasabian and The Virginmarys weren't my thing, but being a '90s' R&B girl, I had to go with the majority as hardly any of my work friends were into my kind of music. I took a little pink treasure with me and tried half like Liam told me too. For a while it was fun, getting a buzz off of it but after a while it wasn't enough. The voice in my head was getting louder and it was hard to shut it off.

One Friday night, I stood in the corner of Club 42s when the work gang decided to go for a few drinks after we finished our shifts. It started off as a chilled gathering which escalated from a few quick ones to taking the tram into town and we ending up in the smoky nightclub. Everybody was having a good time, laughing and drinking. Debbie was there too, having a great time as usual, but I wasn't getting into it all like I normally did. I felt reality creeping in. The music was blasting in my ears, but the voice in my head was clear as ever.

I swallowed a half pill and tried to ignore what was going on in my head.

Pathetic bitch! So this is what you left Ben for? To be in a club, popping pills? Look at what you're becoming. Is this really what you want to be doing?

'Shut up, I don't want to hear it.'

The half pill was working its way through me, but I couldn't feel it. I searched in my bag for the rest of my pills and decided to take a whole one to give me an extra buzz. I took a big sip of my double vodka lemonade and closed my eyes as I leant against the wall. My eyes stayed closed for what felt like a few seconds before I noticed the voice in my head right in front me. I opened my eyes and saw Sal standing before me.

Look at you! You're a disgrace to both of us.

'You're not here, Sal.'

I never left, I'm always here. But you, you're barely here anymore. Is this what you want to become? Nothing!

'What the fuck do you know? You lived your whole life being nothing!'

I'm the one who survived so you could be the person you are, and you have the nerve to throw it all away? You make me sick!

'FUCK YOU!'

FUCK YOU!! FUCK THIS!! FUCK EVERYTHING!! IS THAT THE ANSWER TO YOUR PROBLEMS!

'You don't know what I'm feel—'

Bitch, don't you fucking dare tell me that I don't know what you're feeling. I know you better than you know yourself. Why are you so afraid to build yourself back up? Don't live in the dark. You don't belong there.

Suddenly, I felt a pair of hands grab my shoulders. I opened my eyes and saw a guy from work I was out with, Matthew. He was tall, light-skinned and easy on the eyes. I never thought too much about him except for the fact that most of the gay guys I knew at work fancied the pants off of him. Matt was smiling at me, but I couldn't hear a word he was saying over the blaring music. I felt my little pink treasures tingling my nerves deliciously, making the tips of my fingers go numb. My vision was blurring, turning the coloured lights streaming across the room into dancing stars in a black sky. Matt grabbed my arm as I felt my knees get weak and I lost my balance, falling onto him.

'You okay, Yvy?' he asked me, screaming it into my ear.

'Huhh?'

'Are you okay? Do you need some fresh air?'

'Yeah, why not!'

Matt took me outside into the street. For summertime, it was still pretty cold, but the cool air didn't bother me as I was too high to notice. Matt took me to the side of the club, making sure I didn't fall on the hard concrete. It wasn't until I was propped up against the brick wall that I noticed that Matt was pretty drunk too. 'Why are we outside? Are we leaving?' I asked, feeling the high take over.

'I thought you wanted to come outside!' Matt said jokingly.

'No, not really! What shall we do now then?'

'Uhh, I don't know! What do you want to do?'

I knew what was going through my mind.

Take him home, Yvy, and fuck his brains out!

I wanted to, but I knew that if I did, I'd regret it.

265

'I'm gonna head home now. Tell Debbie I left, okay?'

I jumped in a taxi and went back home. When I climbed into bed, I felt it spinning beneath me, like I was slowly ascending into space. The voice in my head was quiet, but I knew it was because my high had reached its peak and I enjoyed riding the wave until I gradually fell asleep.

I woke up the next morning feeling rough. My insides were attempting to crawl out of my body and the thought of eating anything knocked me sick. I remembered everything that happened the night before, which I hated. I didn't want to remember how I was feeling, I didn't want to think about having to deal with my real feelings. The answer was pretty obvious.

Do more drugs, Yvy.

A couple weeks later, we were only a few days from August when I got a message from Liam asking if I needed anything. I ran out of weed, ecstasy and speed so told him to come around mine. The drugs I was taking just weren't doing it for me anymore, so I asked if he had anything stronger. Liam pulled out a small bag filled with white powder.

After the first couple of lines, I thought to myself that cocaine was pretty horrible. The chalky taste of the drip at the back of my throat after sniffing the line up through a ten-pound note tasted nasty. But once the cocaine kicked into my bloodstream, the sensation was wonderful. I felt so charged, like my nerves were jolted with watts of electricity. All I wanted to do was fuck. The only thing on my mind was having some good, hard sex with Chris.

That weekend, Chris and I had already arranged to meet up for a night out. We hadn't gone on a night out together before, as we usually went to the cinema and then back to his place, or he'd come round the flat and we'd spend a few hours together. This time was different. Even though I knew the end result was us having a lot of sex, it was nice to change it up and have a night on the town.

I stood on the balcony at G-A-Y, waiting patiently for Chris. From the balcony, I had the perfect view of Canal Street and eventually saw Chris approaching the club. As he reached the entrance, he looked up and saw me smiling at him. The evening started off as expected, catching up over drinks, but the more alcohol we consumed, the more we wanted to turn it up a notch. We headed to Baa Bar and set up shop in one of the booths near the bar.

'C'mon, Yvy, let's do some shots!' Chris eagerly proposed.

'Fuck yeah!' I said. 'I'm just nipping to the ladies, I'll be back.'

'I'll be here.'

I went downstairs and pushed past the crowded bar until I was at the back of the club in front of the restrooms. I locked myself in a cubicle and searched in my bag for some coke. At first, I tipped a little on the back of my hand and took it all in but soon made a couple of lines on the metallic toilet roll box and snorted it up with a bank note.

After checking that my face was presentable, I unlocked the cubicle door and went back to join Chris. When I got back to the booth upstairs, Chris was already waiting for me with a line of tequila shots. As I sat down, I noticed a growing smile on his face.

'What's that all about?' I asked as I pointed at his face.

He put his hands on the table, both of them clenched shut.

'Pick one,' he said.

I tapped his left hand and saw when he opened it that he was holding a tiny pill-shaped Rizla. Chris opened the other hand and had the same thing in it.

'What are these?' I asked.

'Something we'll enjoy. Open your mouth, Yvy.'

I did what he said without hesitation. I was thrilled at the thought of trying something new. He placed the pill on my tongue and I swallowed it immediately. I chased it with a couple of tequila shots, as did Chris. From that point onward, everything went black.

I suddenly found myself outside on Canal Street hours later, standing by a bar I'd never been to before. Chris was beside me, looking equally as confused.

'What the fuck are we doing here?' I asked him.

'I have no fucking clue!'

The last thing I remembered was being in Baa Bar, so how did I end up outside?

What the fuck, Yvy?

I unzipped my bag to check what time it was on my phone.

'FUCK!' I shouted, making Chris jump out of his skin.

'What?'

'All my stuff is gone!'

'What are you talking about?'

'My purse, my house keys, my iPod, it's all gone! Oh my god!'

'What? Fuckin' hell!'

I searched my bag and had nothing but my debit card, sixty pounds cash that I didn't have on me at the start of the night, and my mobile phone with the battery missing.

'What the fuck? What fucking happened?' I asked Chris.

'Fuck knows. We need to figure out where we've been. Think, Yvy!' I looked down at my wrist and saw a smeared club stamp.

As my eyes travelled upward, I saw bruises on my wrists, continuing upward and covering both my arms. *Seriously, what the fuck is happening, Yvy?* I panicked, trying my best to recollect the evening in the hopes to understand the situation. I looked at Chris's hand which had the same stamp, only clearer. I recognised the symbol from a club around the corner.

'When did we go to fucking Coyotes?' I asked Chris.

'I have no fucking clue, Yvy. I can't remember shit!'

'Fuck it, let's just go there and see if I can find my damn keys.'

We made our way to Chorlton Street and saw a bouncer standing outside the club. Chris and I approached him to show our stamps to get back in, when he spotted us first and began to approach us instead.

'FUCK NO! WE'RE NOT LETTING YOU TWO BACK IN HERE!'

I was stunned by his advance, I couldn't believe he was talking to us.

'No wait, I just want to check if my—'

'NO! You're not coming back in here!'

'What did we do?' Chris asked but got no response.

'I just want to check if my keys are in there,' I said. 'Please, can you at least check?'

At that point, Chris indicated to me that judging from the bouncer's stern look, he wasn't going to budge, no matter how nicely I asked. We walked away, and I felt even more panicked. I couldn't for the life of me think of what I could do that would be so terrible. I mean, did I start snorting cocaine on the dancefloor or something? I literally couldn't remember a thing. It didn't help that Chris's memory was just as blank as mine. Given that I had no house keys, I wasn't able to get home. The flat required fob entry and without it, I couldn't even reach my front door.

For the first time in a long time, I was frightened. All this time I wanted a fix that gave me the opportunity to leave myself, but now that it happened, it scared me to death. Having a black hole in my memory shook me awake, making me panic at the thought of what could have happened if the situation was worse than it was. I was so disappointed with my behaviour, ashamed even. I stayed over at Chris's house and made my way back to my flat in the morning.

Luckily, my phone still had my SIM card in it so I used Chris's phone to call my landlord for a favour. I waited outside my block of flats, still dressed in my going out gear, covered with one of Chris's black band t-shirts. As I stood on the street in the morning light, looking like a worn out prostitute after a long night of hooking, I saw my landlord pull up by the gated entrance. Tommy was a good landlord, but this was definitely going above and beyond. He let me in to my flat and could clearly see by how I looked that something went down.

'What happened to you, chick? Looks like you've had a right scrap with someone!'

'Don't ask. I had a rough night. I'm so sorry to have to call you out for this. I feel really stupid, losing all my shit.'

'Don't worry about it chick. You gotta take better care of yourself though. Don't wanna be putting yourself in bad situations.'

I knew he was just being polite, but it was as if he was the voice in my head, telling me what I needed to hear. I felt vulnerable, hating the fact that Tommy was seeing me this way. He had no idea what was going on with me, but he was witnessing a moment I hoped nobody would see.

After he gave me his spare set of keys and left, I ran a bath and watched as the water filled the tub. Sitting in the bathroom, my head felt dense on my shoulders. I was holding on to so much baggage that my soul felt too heavy in my chest. I had to let out what I was feeling, but when I tried, nothing happened. I thought that if I let myself feel what I was trying to avoid, I'd cry uncontrollably, but nothing came out. I was so confused. As I undressed and lowered myself into the hot water, I slowly let my body sink deeper, until my entire body was submersed. I opened my eyes and watched the water rippling above me.

Stop running, Yvy. You haven't lost anything you can't get back.

I brought my head back up and let my muscles relax in the water for a while. After drying myself off, I sat in my bedroom, my hands cupping my head, forcing my eyes shut.

It's okay, Yvy. It's okay to have made decisions that weren't right. But what you're doing now, this isn't you.

'I know it isn't me! But I don't know if I can get past it.'

Of course you fucking can. All this bullshit you're doing, drink, drugs, it isn't you.

'I feel so empty. I'm completely hollow. I hate that I let this happen. Why did I give so much of myself away?'

Because you're human. You make mistakes. I don't understand why you're being so hard on yourself!

'I'm like this because of Ben!'

No, you're like this because of you, that's the whole damn point! Ben may be an arsehole, but you stuck around and took it! The moment you realised what was happening to you, you should have left, but you didn't. That's life. You can't keep punishing yourself.

'It's not just that. I don't know how to be anybody else but the person I was with Ben because that's all I've ever been since I had my surgery. I never gave myself the opportunity to just be me.'

Oh, for fuck's sake! You know what, I'm not listening to this. You need to fucking get over this bullshit and pick yourself up! You know who you are because you've fought your whole life to be that person. Just because you had one bad relationship, it doesn't mean it has to define you. Fucking pick yourself up and leave that shit behind!

All this time, I was running away from my feelings, when all they were trying to do was remind me of how strong I was.

Why didn't I realise that before?

I wasted so much energy finding ways to leave my body, but what I forgot to remember was that I fought so fucking hard to have the body I was trying so desperately to leave. I looked at myself in the mirror, my towel dried hair looking messy against my face. I untied my dressing gown and let it drop to the floor, exposing my brown skin. I looked at my reflection, starting at my feet and let my eyes examine every inch. My legs were long, firm and could do with a once over with a Mach 3. My eyes reached Missy, looking smooth and plump. I'd gone through every emotion my entire being could comprehend to achieve her. To feel complete in my mind, body and soul meant everything to me, yet somehow, I forgot that. My eyes reached my stomach, with its slight flabby bump below my navel that I just couldn't shift, despite countless stomach crunches. Still, that bump was a part of me, a beautiful part of me.

I could see the stretch marks on my hips, running down to my thighs. A playful artistry that proved I lived in truth. I reached my breasts and saw how they developed into what Blanche Devereux once described her own as "perfectly champagne-glass-sized orbs of dancing loveliness". I giggled at the thought, making my orbs jiggle. My eyes reached my face, and as I stared at myself in the mirror, I began to well up. It suddenly dawned on me.

Yvy, you're beautiful.

I had just the one life, but that didn't mean I couldn't be reborn over and over. We all go through life being a certain type of person, and it usually involves being around family, friends and partners. As we grow, so do our souls. After a while, you reach a crossroad in your life where you need to leave the person you were behind, and start being the person you need to be moving forward.

I already proved to myself that I was capable of leaving a version of me behind just by standing in front of my reflection, staring at the beauty that was my potential. I didn't need to hold on to a version of Yvy that I didn't need to be anymore, I needed to leave her behind and reach forward. I began a chapter of my life the moment I had my surgery, but instead of finishing it, I jumped to another chapter that I wasn't ready for. I wasn't ready to be with Ben. I wasn't ready to give myself to somebody else, because I hadn't finished learning about myself. I was going about everything all wrong and then tried to run away from the lessons I needed to learn from the mistakes I made.

A moment of clarity hit me like a tonne of bricks, and I realised that I had two choices. I could either face my actions and learn from them or run away and lead a path of self-destruction. It was time to get back to where I started and continue my intended journey. It was time to pick up where I left off and learn from my mistakes. If I learnt from my mistakes, I didn't need to live in regret. It was time to discover the real me!

The question now is, who do you want to be, Yvy?

Chapter Twenty-Two

Six Years Later

It was a sweltering Sunday afternoon in July as I waited in the stuffy garden marquee in Sackville Gardens to go on stage for the Miss Sparkle pageant. I'd never considered myself a pageant queen, but I thought it would be fun considering I'd been to Sparkle every year since 2011. The annual Sparkle weekend turned the Village into a celebration for the transgender community. It gave us the opportunity to celebrate in ways I never saw at the Village throughout the rest of the year. Canal Street gave the LGBTQ community a place to be themselves, but I always noticed how little transgender representation there was when it came to the Village scene.

After leaving Benjamin and moving into my flat, I spent so much time at the Village with new friends I made from work. Even though nobody at work knew that I was transgender, it was still nice to hang out with LGBTQ people and enjoy queer nightlife. With that said, I never came across many trans spaces that truly celebrated us. It saddened me to think that the transgender community weren't as inclusive and outspoken as we should be, but then again, I was still living with my past secretly put away so I wasn't really helping to change things.

I'd go to Sparkle weekend every year with my two best friends, Adam and Lee. Lee was a darling that had a heart of gold and a love for a good glass of wine. Adam could only be described as a larger than life soul in a body that couldn't be bothered. Adam and I first met at work when I was planning on moving out and away from Ben. We instantly hit it off when we met, bonding over a mutual love for Alanis Morissette and To Wong Foo, and I thought he'd make an amazing roommate. We planned to move in together, but it didn't turn out that way in the end, but we ended up with a tight friendship based on mutual love, conveyed by savagely reading each other every chance we'd get, followed by having a laugh and referencing Buffy the Vampire Slayer and Sex and the City in almost every conversation.

The three of us together called ourselves The Golden Girls. Lee was Rose, Adam was Dorothy, and I was Blanche. *Slut!* We assumed Sophia was still at Shady Pines. The three of us would go to Sparkle and have an amazing time. The main area of Sparkle was at Sackville Gardens, just off Canal Street. The Gardens would be packed with marquees, selling wigs, breast forms, clothing and much more. Some marquees were dedicated to trans issues and trans awareness projects that gave both the community and allies information on how they can get involved in supporting the trans community.

The statue of Alan Turing that sat in the centre of the garden was always cloaked with a trans pride flag and the Sparkle stage was set up at the back, with musicians and trans acts performing all weekend. The Golden Girls and I spent the day in the sunshine, drinking and stuffing ourselves with nachos with melted cheese, whilst watching the festivities unfold, having a great day.

As the years went by, I saw Sparkle in a different light. Unbeknownst to my friends, I started to feel as though I was missing out on celebrating with my trans family. I call them family because, in a way, they were. We as trans people share an experience that's hard to describe. The experience of transition differs for each person, but the feeling is the same. The feeling of being incomplete and wanting to live an authentic life. I knew that feeling intimately, and I realised that Sparkle wasn't just a reason to go out and party, it was a celebration that honoured people like me. The only thing was, nobody knew that I was a part of it expect for me. I knew my friends wouldn't ever judge me for who I was, but I had kept that part of myself locked away for so long, that I didn't know how to even bring it up. I didn't know where to start or how to go about telling people, if at all. It was easier to just not say anything, and that worked fine for a long time, but as I evolved and pulled myself out of a darkness that almost consumed me, the more I began to connect with myself and realised that I wanted to embrace a part of myself that literally defined me.

I eventually came out in 2015 to my Manchester friends, which gave me an unexpected feeling of release. I felt a huge weight lifted off of me, not because I told them, but because I no longer held back a part of me that I was so incredibly proud of. It took so many years to build up the confidence I had, and now I wasn't afraid to let people know why I was so confident. The moment I told my friends,

I prepared for the best and worst reactions. I had a feeling of who would embrace me with unconditional love. Debbie was definitely one of them.

Debbie and I had become such close companions that it transcended any friendship I ever had. She was more than a friend, a sister, a lover, everything. When we got together, it was always magic, like we'd known each other for decades. I knew for a fact that if I told her I was trans, it wouldn't change her view of me, and I was right. I already experienced hate from people in the past, but this time around I was more prepared. Thankfully, I didn't have any negative reactions after telling people this time around.

I waited patiently backstage in the marquee, feeling so nervous. *Why did you think this was a good idea, Yvy?* It was my second year volunteering at Sparkle, but I thought it would be fun to put my name down and see if I got picked to compete for the title of Miss Sparkle 2017. I didn't care for pageants, and the only knowledge of pageants I had was from watching Sandra Bullock in *Miss Congeniality* countless times.

Still, the thought of going up on the stage and having all eyes on me was too sweet to pass up. I submitted my application a couple of months before Sparkle and hoped for the best. I didn't think I'd get picked, but it wasn't long before the Sparkle committee told me I was chosen to compete and it became all too real. As the days and weeks grew closer, I was beginning to question whether or not I should do it. I mean, do I really want to stand on stage and prance around like I was on show? And what if I don't win? Will I have to stand there on stage and watch the winner do her Queen's wave and pretend to be happy? Even though I didn't care for pageants, the chance to compete and win was incredibly inviting. Plus, I didn't want to admit to myself that doing this was a big deal for me. Regardless of whether I won or not, I'd be stood on that stage in all my Yvy-liciousness, celebrating the person I worked so hard to be. I didn't need a crown to know that, but it would be the perfect finishing touch.

'Okay, ladies!' the announcer said as she came into the marquee from the main stage. 'You'll be going on stage in number order in about five minutes, so I'll need you to line up!'

I looked around the marquee at all the other contestants. There were around twelve of them, all dressed up in long ball gowns and sparkling jewellery. One girl wore a trans pride mini dress that she hand made from scratch. Another was an older lady that didn't want us to see what she was wearing and braved the growing heat in a tan overcoat. I could see the sweat beads forming on her forehead, but it didn't seem to bother her as much as the thought of giving away her gown before going on stage. I contemplated wearing a gown too, as it's the expected thing to do in a pageant but decided to go back to my Indian roots and wore a rich purple Anarkali suit, embellished with sparkling white gems. My hair was tied up in a high ponytail, and my face was beat for the Gods, with deep purple eyeshadow and matching lipstick. Safe to say, I looked real good! I was just about to join the girls in line and find my place when my phone vibrated in my hand as I put it in my bag. I looked at the screen and saw that it was a message from Jack, my husband.

'Good luck, Yvy! Win this! I love you x.'

Jack and I knew each other from work but didn't officially get together until mid-2011. I'd only been single for a few months before getting together with Jack so I was a little apprehensive to jump into another relationship so soon. He understood that I wanted to take it slow, but by the end of the year, we decided to stop being casual and start officially dating. Dating quickly turned into a relationship and by 2013 we were madly in love, and he popped the question, asking me to marry him. Like with Ben, I didn't tell Jack I was transgender, but once he proposed to me and we began to plan the wedding, I found myself feeling heavy-hearted. I wasn't feeling excited about the wedding, which I chalked up to the fact that I never gave marriage a thought in the first place.

Jack was very vocal about never wanting to get married since the beginning of our relationship, which was fine by me because I wasn't the type of woman who needed to get married to validate anything. I was happiest with him, and having a piece of paper with our names on it wouldn't change a thing. It came as a total shock to me when he proposed, that my initial response was 'WHAT!'. But once the shock dissipated and I said yes to his question, something inside shook me to the bone.

Deep down, I knew what was troubling me. I knew that when the time came, and I stood in front of him on our wedding day, I wouldn't be able to recite vows about giving my all to him until death do us part, knowing that I was holding back a part of myself he had no knowledge of. I knew that before we got married, I'd have to tell him about my past. For months, I tried to find the right time to tell him but never found one. It's not like there's really a perfect time to tell someone something so major, but I didn't want to just blurt it out. We planned the wedding for months and by early 2014, we decided to set a date for spring 2015. I had just over a year until I walked down the aisle, and I knew that the clock was ticking to tell Jack. So many questions were hammering away in my head.

What if he hates me? What if he can't handle it? Am I really ready to tell him?

Six months before the wedding, on a dark November evening, I found the right time to tell him. It was a typical Thursday night, and we'd both been at work all day. Every penny we were making went toward paying for the wedding so we spent most evenings at home instead of going out. We were working hard and planning the wedding was going smoothly, but I didn't have an ounce of excitement within me. I wasn't even interested in buying a dress. Too much was playing on my mind and I couldn't get past it until I spoke to Jack. Being a heavy metal lover, Jack and I didn't have anything in common, except for each other. We adored each other for who we were and never tried to change a thing.

But this was different, I had my fair share of encounters with people who said they were open minded, and changed their story as soon as what they deemed acceptable came too close for comfort. In my mind, I prayed that Jack wasn't one of those people. Jack had always been vocal about his stance on equality and his distaste for people who discriminated against sexuality, gender and race. I had a hunch he'd be okay with what I was about to tell him, but you just never know how a person can react.

'What do you fancy watching tonight, Yvy?'

'I don't know, what mood are you in?'

'Something I haven't seen before.'

I paused for a moment, scanning the hundreds of DVDs we'd accumulated and arranged alphabetically on shelves that covered an entire wall in our living room.

'How about *Paris Is Burning*?'

'What's it about?'

'It's a documentary about the New York Drag Ball scene in the '80s.'

As the movie played, we watched the likes of Pepper LaBeija, Dorian Corey and Willy Ninja tell stories of life as an LGBTQ person in New York. Jack was fascinated by it, as he'd heard of the Ball scene but didn't know much about it. We watched queens strut their stuff at a Ball, winning trophies for each category and talked behind the scenes about the struggle and heartbreak that was the price of daring to be who they were.

A particular story that made my decision to tell Jack that night was the story of Venus Xtravaganza. Venus was a young trans woman who wanted nothing but to be a beautiful woman. She was part of the House of Xtravaganza, walking Balls and snatching trophies, but outside of the Ball scene, she was a sex worker and hoped that someday, she could meet a man who'd treat her right and give her the "rich white woman" lifestyle she so desperately coveted. Venus' dream was cut short when she was found in a New York hotel room, strangled to death. Although every person's story was fascinating, I related the most to Venus. All she wanted was to live an authentic life. I watched *Paris Is Burning* a few times before, but that night sitting with Jack, Venus' story cut through me and I knew the moment the movie ended that I found my moment to talk to Jack.

'That was really good,' Jack said.

'Yeah it's one my favourites. It's just terrible what some people have to go through to be themselves.'

'Yeah. Nobody should be treated that way. Really powerful, the way that movie depicted their lives. It makes me so angry to think that people still discriminate to this day.'

I felt a wave of fear wash over me, causing my skin to chill and the hairs on my arm to stand up. *Just tell him, Yvy. This is your moment.*

'I can relate so much with this movie,' I said, trying to prepare myself for what was about to unfold. 'My whole life, I've been told that who I am was wrong. That I didn't belong. It's shit being treated like an outsider.'

I waited for Jack to respond but he didn't. Instead, he was listening intently, his beautiful brown eyes looking at me.

'Because of what I've gone through, I keep a lot inside. I get scared to tell people about who I am and what I've been through, including you.'

'Well, I know whatever it is you've gone through is your business and you don't have to tell me, but one thing I want you to know is that you never have to be scared about how I'd react. I love you.'

A hard lump in my throat began to form, forcing me to take shallow breaths, 'I know you do, but I'm scared to open myself up so much. I want to share my life with you, but it's not easy.'

'I fell in love with you, so whatever happened in the past doesn't matter. It won't change how I see you now.'

My eyes welled and I tried to compose myself, but a tear soon started to fall down my cheek. I looked at Jack and saw a mix of affection and concern. I could tell that it hurt him to see me so upset. The pressure of the moment was unbearable, as if my heart was about to crack my chest open and reveal all my secrets. I never felt so overwhelmed with worry, like a pressure cooker that was ready to explode.

'If I tell you, I just want you to know that if you don't want to marry me or you decide to leave, I'll understand.'

Jack soon went from concern to worry. His eyes were fixated on me, but I could tell his worry had nothing to do with whether or not he would leave me. His eyes told me that he was worried about my wellbeing, knowing that he had no way of comforting me, given that he had no idea what was happening. I was choked up, barely capable to get the words out, but I eventually calmed myself as I felt Jack put his hand on my knee.

'My whole life, I knew I was female. But I didn't come into this world presenting as a woman. It took a lot of time and soul searching, but I soon realised that I was transgender.'

I told him. I really told him. I looked at Jack and saw the expression on his face. No judgement, no hatred, he simply looked at me and listened to every word.

'I transitioned in my early twenties and had my surgery when I was 23. I didn't want to tell anybody because I want to be treated as Yvy, nothing else. I'm sorry I didn't tell you sooner, but I've always told you that whatever happened in our pasts is exactly that, ours. I was never bothered about your past because it doesn't matter to me what your life was before I knew you. I love you for you, and that's all that matters to me. I know this is a lot to take in, but I'll understand if it's too much.'

Jack looked down, not speaking. For a moment, I thought he was disgusted with me, taking his hand off my knee and not making eye contact. *Say something. Please, Jack, say something.* He looked up, and I saw the emotion in his eyes. I'd never seen him that way before. I felt my heart swell, waiting to be shattered.

'I feel so bad that you felt you had to keep that a secret from me all this time…'

His words cut through me. If I could hear my heart, it would've sounded like the sharp, shrieking splinters of a mirror as it begins to crack.

278

'…because I didn't think it was possible to love you more than I already did. I'm so honoured that you finally told me. You're the most beautiful person I've ever known.'

I looked up at his face and saw him smiling back at me. The pressure left my body in one huge blast, like a balloon that burst from too much air. He leaned in to kiss me, and I met him in the middle.

Before he pressed his lips to mine, he told me again how he felt. 'I love you so much.'

***

'Right, girls! Time to get in place for the main stage!'

I didn't have time to reply to Jack's message so I quickly took my place in line. I wished he'd been able to come and see me, but he'd been so ill all weekend and I didn't want to make him any worse. I was seventh in line to go on stage and stood between two contestants. The girl behind me who wore the trans pride dress had competed in previous years and was hoping to win this year.

'So what does the main stage stuff actually entail?' I asked, not actually knowing what to expect when I went on that stage. For all I knew I was supposed to perform or have a talent ready.

'Oh nothing much,' she said, 'just go on stage, introduce yourself and then walk to the front so everyone can see you.'

'That's it?'

'Yeah but it's pretty nerve wracking. Everyone is watching you, and the judges are right at the front of the stage. A bit of advice, try and make eye contact with them.'

'Thanks, I'll remember that!'

The dance music started to blare out of the speakers outside and the MC began to talk to the entire park, gearing up for us to go on stage one by one. As my turn got closer and closer, I watched as contestants went up, introducing themselves and doing their little walk across the stage. They seemed comfortable on stage, and their outfits were gorgeous, but I wasn't seeing much entertainment in their execution. We were told that we had three minutes to walk the stage and make the most of it, but the girls were simply doing a couple rounds and then walking off.

Show them how it's done, Yvy!

I stood at the metal steps that led to the stage, as I was up next. I grabbed the metal railing and suddenly had a thought. *Give them a*

279

show, Yvy! Serve it like you're snatching trophies at a Ball in New York City, henny!

I took the purple chiffon scarf that was sitting elegantly on my shoulders and straightened the fabric out. The girls around me weren't sure what I was doing but then watched as I placed the scarf over my face like a veil and let the rest hang off the back of my ponytail. The chiffon was transparent enough to see through as I walked up onto the stage and saw the crowd cheering. I strutted like a supermodel toward the MC, watching her look at me with puzzlement. Once I stood beside her, I lifted the veil with dramatic pause, giving the audience a taste of Yvycake.

'Isn't she beautiful!' the MC said. 'And where are you from?' She put the microphone to my face for a response.

'I'm from the enchantment of…Blackburrrn!'

The crowd laughed through the pounding music and I saw that all eyes were on me. I felt like a star on that stage, commanding their attention. I Naomi Campbell'd my way to the front of the stage, hitting the beat of the music with every step. I lifted the scarf off my ponytail once I got to the front and paused for the audience. The crowd was ecstatic, loving the attitude I was bringing. In the distance I saw the volunteers from the LGBT Foundation I'd been working with all weekend going wild and screaming my name. I knew my time on stage was almost up, but I wanted to give the judges something unexpected.

As I turned to walk off, I spun around as fast as I could, causing my dress to lift up in a beautiful flourish that twinkled in everybody's eyes. It felt as though I was spinning in slow motion, watching my dress lift and the gems catch the sun in a beautiful sequence of flashing lights. I felt like I was floating on air.

Oh, don't get too carried away! You might fall!

I gave the judges a quick wink and walked off the stage, waving at the crowd as I made my way down the metal steps.

After a ninety-minute deliberation, the judges had come to a decision. I spent the wait time walking around the Gardens, enjoying the sunshine and pretending not to care about winning. I mean, I knew that putting my name down was just for a laugh at first but being up on that stage made me feel wonderful. It felt amazing to know I was being celebrated for being me, which was something I worked my whole life to achieve. I made my way back to the backstage marquee and waited for the MC to call us back on stage. The girls and I lined up again in the same order and walked up the metal steps, forming a line across the stage.

'Here are the finalists for Miss Sparkle 2017! Give them a round of applause, everybody!'

The crowd began to applaud and whistle. I smiled and held my composure, trying not to feel nervous. You'd think I was competing for Miss Universe by the way I was positioning my body from head to toe, poised and regal. I noticed a couple of the contestants throwing a shady look my way, but it only boosted my confidence as my smile grew bigger. *Touch this! Touch all of this skin, honey!*

'The judges have made their decision, and I can now confirm that the winner of Miss Sparkle 2017 is…'

The crowd went silent, waiting in anticipation for the MC to reveal who was going to win the title.

'…YVY DELUCA!'

The crowd burst into celebratory cheer as I stepped forward to receive my crown. Well, it turned out to be a tiara and a sash, but I was over the moon to have won.

'Congratulations, Yvy!' the MC said. 'Have you anything you'd like to say?'

'Thank you so much! I promise to reign as Miss Sparkle with class, sass and a whole lotta…personality!'

The tiara was placed on my head and I strutted to the front of the stage opening my arms to the crowd. The smiles on their faces were a beautiful sight to see. I turned to walk off but gave them a model pose before I did, looking over my shoulder and blowing them a kiss.

Once the contest was over and I made my way through the Village, I was stopped by people wanting to take photos and selfies with me. It felt so surreal, listening to them tell me how inspiring it was to be so confident and funny on stage. One woman in particular told me that I had an incredible presence and to never stop being me. I was so overwhelmed by her words, because I didn't think I had that kind of influence. Being on that stage, I never thought it would give someone so much inspiration to move forward in their own lives positively. It was then that I realised that I had the opportunity to share my energy with others and seeing it make a real difference to another person meant so much to me. After she gave me a hug, I walked down Canal Street, towards Piccadilly Gardens and caught the bus home to see Jack.

***

Being as fabulous as I am didn't come easy, but I wouldn't change anything I've gone through because my experiences shaped me to be who I am today. The same can be said about anybody, and we shouldn't regret decisions in our lives that helped us live through good times and survive through the bad ones. Not a single person on this planet can say they've made zero mistakes in the past, and if they do, they're fucking lying! Making mistakes give us the opportunity to learn something new and grow from it. It seldom happens instantly, but as time goes on you realise that those experiences gave you a new perspective on life that you can take forward with you. The catch is, before you can learn from your mistakes, you first have to admit to making them. Now this only applies to choices that life presents to us and whether we choose what's good for us or not.

However, there are things in life we don't get to choose, like how we come into this world. Society can often fear the unknown, and as such find ways to distance themselves from people they don't understand. We shouldn't be punishing people because of who they are and the choices they make, especially when it doesn't affect other people in any real way. I stared at the hundreds of photographs collected over the last thirty-three years, studying every expression on my face. I saw Sal, during his early years, grow and evolve from a care-free infant, to an adolescent riddled with confusion and anxiety. The memory of those emotions were still raw. The pain of isolation still constant. I saw him slowly fall into a safe place as I began to surface. I took his pain and channelled it into my own journey, which gave me the strength to begin my transition and walk this world with renewed potential. As I sifted through photographs on my computer, I saw early Yvy grow from a confident, yet slightly naive young woman who wasn't afraid to take a chance, to a well-rounded woman who learnt from her experiences to become stronger in herself to live positively.

I thought about the future, of what might be in store for me, and it suddenly dawned on me that I was never really "transitioning"; I was evolving. My transition didn't define me, it was simply a process of which I had to go through so that I could evolve into the person I knew I was. We never stop evolving, and for a period in my life, my transition was the physical evolution I needed so that I could continue forward with a spiritual evolution, strengthening my authentic self to reach new potentials. I took out a piece of paper and began to write. My emotions were heightened and I knew that I had to release how I was feeling. I knew that there was one mistake

I was yet to admit to. An apology that was way past due. As I sat at the living room desk, I heard the front door open.

'Oh, hi, Jack. How was work?'

'Hey! Yeah, it was okay, same old, same old. What are you doing?'

'Nothing, just writing a letter.'

'To who?'

'Just someone I haven't spoken to in a while.'

Beneath every single name and label I've ever been called was the true me. When it comes to labels, I see that I am transgender, I see that I'm a woman, I see that I am Indian. I accept all of these labels, because I don't see any of them as a negative thing. A lot people say that they don't wish to be labelled, but I've never seen it that way. Gender, race and orientation all live on a spectrum and it's those labels that help shape and define us in our own image. Nobody can tell you who you are, and when they try to, it's easy to let the opinions of others seep in and cause you to think negatively. I've been a victim of this many times, but I eventually understood that only I had the power to decide my own fate. Once I understood and embraced that, I expelled those negative feelings and became the woman I always knew I was.

The things that make our lives happier, love, friendship, marriage, they all pale in comparison to embracing who we are. I never believed that I needed best friends and a husband to make my life complete. All I needed was me. Being who I am gives me an incredible insight to life that a lot of people won't ever get the chance to experience. I see the power of tainted beauty. I see beneath the flaws that society deem unnatural and find the beauty in not giving a fuck about the opinions of others. The moral of this story is simple. *Be yourself!*

We all have to face adversities in life, but we have the power in ourselves to not inflict hatred on others and use that power to enrich not just our own lives but the lives of others. It all starts with acceptance. Accept the beauty in others, even if you may not understand it yourself, because others may not understand the beauty in you. Or to put it another way, don't be an arsehole! A life filled with negativity will get you nowhere. Let's change how we see the world, starting with ourselves.

Epilogue

Dear Sal,

It feels strange writing this, considering I'm pretty much writing this letter to myself, but a part of me feels you can hear what I have to say.

I know you more than anybody else, and I know what you had to endure for so many years. But I want you to know that you are the strongest person I have ever known. You gave me security to grow at a time when I wasn't ready to face the world. I didn't know how I could be myself and you had no choice but to take everything society threw at you, which almost broke you.

Throughout my life, I've made many mistakes, gone down roads I shouldn't have and made my way back to a place where I found solace. I've not regretted the choices I made because I learnt from them, but there is one mistake that still sits heavy on my heart. I don't know why I haven't faced this mistake until now, but I can't carry it any longer.

I'm so sorry for trying to erase you from my past. After I completed my transition, I wanted nothing to do with my past, especially you. I thought that if I acknowledged my past, I'd never be able to escape it. So I buried your memory away as if you didn't exist. That wasn't right. I had no right to do that. I know that we are the same person, but I didn't want to admit that. I hated the thought of having you as a part of my past. For some reason, I treated you as a past life. I shouldn't have done that.

You gave me the opportunity to be who I am. We didn't choose to come into this world the way we did, and we did the best we could to survive, but the one thing you didn't do was deny me. Even when I was locked away inside and we didn't know why we felt the way we did, you never gave up on me. When society told you that you were broken, you didn't accept it. You fought through and held on to the hope of one day living an authentic life.

Well, now I do live authentically, and I owe it all to you. Now I'm proud to say that Saleem was a part of my life and he was fabulous even when he didn't know it. I am a part of you and you will forever be a part of me. I love you deeply and will forever keep you safe in my heart as you did for me.

Rest now, Sal, you fucking deserve it.

All my love, your sister,

Yvy x

PS – Missy says hi.